A GIFT BEFORE DYING

RAH RAH'S COACH'S CREED

Pardon me, but may I talk to your child
about the powers of God? May I teach
him self control? May I teach him the
importance of life? May I stress the
importance of an education? May I teach
him to never be selfish, to help somebody?
May I comfort him when needed? May I
demand that he surround himself with
good people? May I influence him to be a
good person? May I be a father figure for
him? May I talk to him about my
"Game of Life" and lastly, may I teach him
the game of game of basketball?

MRS. CYNTHIA CLARK SCOTT

A Gift Before Dying

The Legacy of Robert Scott's Final Season for the Crimson Tide

Stephen Warren Thompson

NewSouth Books

Montgomery

NewSouth Books
P.O. Box 1588
Montgomery, AL 36104

Design by Randall Williams
Printed in the United States of America

To the Memory

of

COACH ROBERT SCOTT

I hope you knew how much we loved you.

Contents

Foreword

BY MARK GOTTFRIED

UNIVERSITY OF ALABAMA HEAD BASKETBALL COACH

When I first met Robert Scott I knew that if I ever became the basketball coach at the University of Alabama he would be the one person I would have to hire. Robert loved Alabama and had all the qualities I look for in a coach. He was knowledgeable about basketball, understood the game, and had noble convictions that I also believed in. He strongly believed in discipline in a tough love sort of way. He never cheated a young player out of learning from every situation the difference between right and wrong. Robert saw the big picture. He coached because he loved kids and he loved to see them develop as players and as people. One of the first things I noticed about Robert was his willingness to work. He loved to work. He was not afraid to stay up all night recruiting kids or driving wherever he needed to go to be ready to recruit the next day.

His children were (and still are) extremely well-behaved. This, to me, tells a story of a man and what he is all about. If a man is disciplined at home, it is real. Robert and his wife Cynthia have done an outstanding job as parents. Their three children understand discipline, respect, and authority. They are humble, patient, kind, and loving. And, just like their father, they are fierce competitors in the best sense. They reflect a strong presence like Robert when the cameras aren't rolling. This I loved.

I remember clearly the exact moment I heard the news. It was a beautiful fall afternoon in Hammond, Louisiana, and Tom Kelsey and I were eating a hamburger with a high school basketball coach on a recruiting visit. My cell phone rang and I stepped outside to get better reception. My heart began to sink as I was told that my friend and assistant coach was diagnosed with cancer and that the cancer was inoperable. I was told that there was little hope; the cancer was terminal and in its later stages. I found it difficult to breathe as I began to wonder what to do. Questions raged through my mind. How were Cynthia and the kids? Could I make it through a recruiting presentation in less than half an hour? And what about the team? What was I to do? What would I tell them? I didn't want them to hear it from someone else and the information be inaccurate. What was I to do? I was despondent.

I talked to Robert shortly thereafter and as I expected he was a pillar of strength. He acted as though nothing had changed.

Robert and I had many discussions about life during his last year. His faith was put into practice as he neared the end. His desire to read the Bible grew and his faith in God became even more evident as he began the biggest challenge of his life. He faced his death with dignity and grace, sturdy in his faith and determined to share his source of strength with others.

MY FIRST response to the proposal for a book about that season was that it was not the year for it. Our team was still a few years away from where we wanted to be and the foundation was (and still is) being laid. Since becoming the head basketball coach here at Alabama I am extremely proud of where we are heading. The character of the young men in this program, and depicted in this book, is astounding. I love our players. I love what we have become and what we are capable of becoming.

But this book is not about a season standing by itself. This book is about a young team that went through an experience unlike any other. Robert's hardships pulled the rest of us together, even as the season came apart. We struggled through the year with many different challenges.

Yet, we grew together. We experienced maturity. As a family growing through pain often bonds together, so would we. We were about to embark on an odyssey that I knew beforehand would be painful and unpleasant. Our maturation centered around the toughest thing I'll ever have to do as a coach. I had to absorb and watch others absorb the lessons surrounding my friend and assistant coach as he slowly died.

We developed a bond few teams ever experience. I was part of a national championship at UCLA in 1995 and the bond there was unbelievable. The players for that team came together as soulmates. The experience of winning the NCAA tournament was unlike anything else I had been a part of and what we shared as a team cannot be broken, by anything. But however remarkable this experience was, it was profoundly different from what I was to witness in the months after that phone call about Robert's illness. As a young coach, I never dreamed that on a fall afternoon, in the same locker room that I had used when I was a player at Alabama 13 years earlier, I would have to deliver the toughest message ever to a group of young men.

I gathered the team in the locker room the day after hearing about Robert's cancer and rehearsed in my mind a million times what I was going to say. How much was I supposed to tell them? How was I supposed to say it? I felt it was very important to be honest yet not try to paint a picture of despair. I knew Robert would fight as valiantly as anyone regardless of his chances. I also knew I would break down and cry if I thought about his pain too much while trying to talk to the players. I wanted to get through that as quickly as possible. It was the hardest message I've ever delivered to a team. Robert was very much respected in that room and very much loved by the players and coaches. It is a day I will never forget.

The season that followed was difficult for many reasons, but none was greater than trying to coach a team while trying to assist a friend in a battle for his life. I cried a lot that year. I remember driving alone in October to a high school in north Alabama and simply breaking down and crying alongside I-65 by myself as cars passed me by. I cried during practice that year as I watched a formerly strong, healthy athlete come into the gym at 3 o'clock every day looking thinner and thinner. Those times were tough but, as in everything, God has a way of teaching you. I've read many times of the letdowns the season had, but in this book you'll discover the many lessons we learned and the blessings we received from the difficult experiences we encountered because of Coach Robert Scott. You see, it was a positive experience in the midst of a trying time that bonded this group of people together. This book (and the lessons learned in it) was born out of frustration and despair. Yet, as I said before, the end result was togetherness.

Robert taught a real life lesson in courage. He taught a group of people about love and about selflessness. Robert taught us to compete and never to quit. Robert Scott defined determination to our young men.

I'll never forget those special moments Robert and I shared while on recruiting trips. Trips to New York, Las Vegas, and all over the South. Robert had a way with people. He could make them laugh. It was a gift he possessed. He was always able to make me laugh. He was an attractor and people felt comfortable with him. I learned very quickly that people in Birmingham had great respect for his character and his genuine care for young people. Parents felt comfortable with Robert disciplining their children. They trusted him and I appreciated that about him. Again, Robert saw the big picture and he understood the role he could play in the lives of others. We are blessed in so many ways to have shared in this story; it is my hope that you will share also. This book was born by accident. The young law student who authored it began to write about a young team and the trials that would accompany it throughout the year. Little did he know the events that would take place and the real story he was about to witness.

This year's Alabama team has not been guaranteed more wins or successes because of the trials we underwent last season. But the maturity, and the unity, it reaped because of the despair we faced has propelled these young players and coaches into a deeper appreciation of life. And that, above all else, is a gift worth receiving. Robert Scott gave us that gift, and I will never forget it or him.

Preface

A *Season on the Brink* is my favorite book. I love John Feinstein's inside perspective of the 1986 Indiana University basketball season. Indiana Head Coach Bob Knight's fiery and charismatic personality drives that story. When I approached Alabama Head Basketball Coach Mark Gottfried about spending a season with his team to write a similar book about his 1999–2000 campaign, I wanted to explore the inside story of a major college basketball season with a coach who contrasted sharply with Knight. It seemed to me that the intimate study of a season could also be compelling with a warm and charismatic personality driving the story. However, the extraordinary circumstances associated with Alabama assistant coach Robert "Rah Rah" Scott's diagnosis with stomach cancer in early Autumn changed everything.

I carried around a microcassette recorder from mid-October until March in an attempt to capture the essence of the team's journey and Scott's last months. Taping hours upon hours of conversations, pregame talks, and training sessions, I tried to document every moment of the players' and coaches' lives. I sought to capture the complex interrelations between the players and coaches, and the ups and downs of a regular college basketball season. However, thanks to Scott's heroics, I learned so much more than I expected.

While people often belittle sporting events by saying they are "just games," some games are a celebration of life. Robert Scott loved games.

He loved what sporting competition demands of a person. Throughout his final campaign, he taught us so much about sacrificing for one's team. So this story belongs to a man I was proud to call friend—Robert Scott.

THE MAN who hired Scott obviously remains a central character. Mark Gottfried was an assistant coach at UCLA when I first I met him at his annual summer basketball camp in Northport, Alabama, just across the river from Tuscaloosa. Gottfried made that annual return to the home of his alma mater, the University of Alabama, to visit old friends and conduct a camp with a spiritual message at the Northport Baptist Church. We connected immediately. I have learned that connecting with people is Mark's best talent. He has the magical gift of being able to make people feel special. I cannot remember our first conversation. The magic was not in his comments—his is a warm energy and a concern for the everyday struggles of people. His eyes expose a soft heart, often full of joy. His smile is incredibly sincere. Mark glows.

Those who have read *A Season on the Brink* and now read this book will realize that when Bob Knight allowed Feinstein to witness and report the inside story of an Indiana basketball season, Knight obviously did not get the benefit of a writer biased toward his subject as I am. I will not attempt to make an objective evaluation of Gottfried's program. Mark has fed me too many times. I swam with his daughter when she had chicken pox. We are too close. Instead, I can only promise an informed perspective on the everyday struggles of a major college basketball program during a year that turned out to be more momentous than any of us could have imagined going into it.

My insider's view was heightened by my own background in basketball. I was an assistant basketball coach at Milford Acadamy, an athletically geared Connecticut preparatory school. My most intimate knowledge of this business comes from riding around New England in a packed van with a bunch of players chasing the dream of big time college basketball. I supplied the humor after wins. We frequented McDonald's. I vividly remember the long trip home from the last game of a season when our 6-foot-10 center (signed by Syracuse), dove across the bus to swing his right fist at our shooting guard (signed by Dayton). I ducked. The punch fortunately missed both of us. The contrast between the packed vans and fast-food dinners of Milford and the plane rides and sit-down meals of Alabama is not lost on me. The dream of our Milford players was to enjoy the fruits of major college basketball. While a season experiencing the bright lights and chartered flights of the big time was spectacular, I also look back fondly at dreams shared over McDonald's french fries.

I researched this project during my third year of law school at Alabama. Out of respect to my wonderful professors, I would like to add that I maintained great attendance thanks to careful scheduling.

So here is the story of Alabama's 1999–2000 men's varsity basketball team. After spending more than six months with the team, and after transcribing more than fifty hours of tape, I have a deep affinity for all the players involved. I have written this book with the hope that, after reading their story, others will also. I am confident that everyone will agree that it was quite a season.

A GIFT BEFORE DYING

I

The Coaching Staff and a
Very Brief History of UA Basketball

Mark Gottfried won an NCAA championship ring in 1995 as an assistant coach under Jim Harrick at UCLA. A widely publicized photo from that victory depicted Gottfried hugging Coach Harrick after the Bruins captured their record eleventh NCAA title over defending national champion Arkansas. Ed O'Bannon scored 30 points and grabbed 17 rebounds as the Bruins overcame the disabling injury of the most outstanding player in the tournament, point guard Tyus Edney, to win the title game. ("It was like the 49'ers making it to the Super Bowl and not being able to play with Joe Montana," Gottfried would later say.) Gottfried wears the ring only occasionally. He keeps his ring finger free because he wants to earn another. As head coach. For Alabama.

Gottfried is 6 feet, 3 inches tall with straight dark hair. He loves basketball. It is more than just a job. He grew up in the lobbies of the Final Four because his father was a college coach who regularly attended the annual coaches' convention. Gottfried was a very effective shooting guard at Alabama in the mid-1980s, so effective that he was drafted by the Eastern Conference Champion Detroit Pistons in '87. He nearly made that team—a team that went on to win the NBA championship two years in a row. He began coaching soon afterward. His overwhelming love and understanding of the game is infectious.

While in Los Angeles, Gottfried was introduced by Jim Harrick to the most successful college coach of all time, former Bruin Head Coach

John Wooden (10 NCAA titles). Wooden became one of Gottfried's main models for coaching. Gottfried would later say:

"[John Wooden] is so giving. He shares his time. It was phenomenal. He rubs off on you. His philosophy is one that is easy to buy into. My nature and personality shift toward him. He shaped my coaching philosophy—how important praise is and courage is. He's very wise. He has the whole package—the content and the teaching ability. I can remember hustling to my car to look for a pen to write down something he just said."

Gottfried left UCLA to become head coach at Murray State in Kentucky. He led the Murray State Racers to the NCAA tournament in two of his three years there. In his second season, the Racers lost in the tournament by only three points to perennial powerhouse Duke. His final Racer team tallied a 29-4 record with an appearance in the top 25 and a blowout win over Arkansas. He had a good record at Murray State and was much loved by the players and fans.

Although he enjoyed Murray State, Gottfried eagerly returned to his alma mater in 1998. His obvious loyalty to the program in which he had played was perhaps the most important. The higher profile and better pay didn't hurt.

He brought most of his Murray State staff with him—assistant coaches Philip Pearson, Tom Kelsey, and Darron Boatright. He also wisely hired fellow Alabama graduate Robert "Rah Rah" Scott away from UAB. Gottfried and those four assistants formed the nucleus of a rebuilding Alabama basketball program.

Scott had appeared to be very healthy. He was 42 years young, and had a strong background and history with the sport as both player and coach. He was (and still is) a high school coaching legend in Alabama. He rescued the West End High School basketball program in a ten-year stint that climaxed in a state championship. He made the leap to a major college assistant in 1996 at Alabama-Birmingham. Respected and loved by his peers and players as a genuine and caring disciplinarian, Scott found recruiting high school players to be a natural extension of a blossoming career. When Gottfried called about the job at Alabama,

Scott gladly accepted the invitation to come home.

"It's special to return where I played after all these years," Scott said in a press conference at the time. "It's great to be back."

Scott primarily recruited and helped develop the guards. He also kept the staff and players laughing with his wit, humor, and unique way of looking at the world.

Tom Kelsey, a blond 6-foot-7 tower of strength, had been the head coach at NAIA Faulkner University in Montgomery, Alabama, where he had led the school to its first NAIA tournament appearance. Kelsey is known for his organizational skills and ability to coordinate the recruitment of hundreds of players across the nation. Kelsey primarily recruited and helped develop the forwards. He is a jovial giant, friendly and knowledgeable.

Philip Pearson, a 6-foot-3 man with a narrow frame and dark hair, is another Alabama grad. He served his former coach Wimp Sanderson at Arkansas-Little Rock before joining Gottfried at Murray State. Pearson handled the scheduling and summer basketball camps, but team defense was his specialty and his passion. (Pearson later took over the recruiting when health complications kept Scott at home.) Pearson can be easily recognized as someone working tirelessly everyday to become a head coach. He is determined, professional, and driven.

Another relatively tall man with dark hair is Gottfried's close friend, Darron Boatright. Gottfried recognized Boatright's talent when he showed up as a 19-year-old middle school coach bringing his team to a Murray State camp. Since their connection, Boatright has been the consummate friend and confidant, solving a myriad of everyday problems so Gottfried could focus on more important decisions. Boatright is now the Director of Basketball Operations at Alabama. He still ties up all the loose ends for his boss—and there are always loose ends.

These coaches were a close-knit group. They spent much of their free time together. Their warm fellowship was often balanced by the gentle jibing common to great friends who are comfortable with each other. The inevitable conflicts that arose out of constant close proximity never developed further than a few harsh, then quickly forgotten, words.

A trainer, a conditioning coach, and two student managers rounded out the staff.

John Morr is the certified athletic trainer for the basketball team. Morr, a patient and friendly man, has the responsibility of the many medical needs of the team that do not involve the team doctor. At the beginning of the 1999–2000 season, he had no idea what he was in for. He spent countless hours improving the health of the players, and he did what he could to minimize Robert Scott's pain.

Steve Martin, a tall mountain of muscle, is the strength and conditioning coach. With the mentality of a kindly drill sergeant and a humorous enjoyment of pain, Martin drives the players to work extremely hard. He is their conscience and their punishment. He is great at what he does.

Partly because three members of the group played for the Crimson Tide, the coaching staff has a healthy respect for the history of the program. Alabama basketball is a program full of pride. Over the past quarter-century, it has sent 35 players to the NBA and won eight SEC Championships (second only to mighty Kentucky). However, the Tide has not won the big one, the all-important NCAA tournament. All of the coaches are constantly aware that the Final 16 of that tournament has been anything but sweet for the Tide. Alabama has failed seven times to advance past that cursed round.

Over the years, national prestige has narrowly escaped the grasp of several Tide teams. Coach Hank Crisp's 1930 team beat Duke for the old Southern Conference Championship to finish a perfect 20-0, but there was no national tournament at that time. Johnny Dee's '56 team finished 14-0 in the SEC, but all of the key players on the team were declared ineligible for the NCAA tourney. C. M. Newton's '76 team beat North Carolina in the first round, but then had to face Bobby Knight's indestructible Hoosiers—the last team to go undefeated in the modern era. The Tide fell dramatically, 74-69, though Knight was impressed enough to declare the Tide the best team Indiana had played.

The eighties were the era of Wimp Sanderson, longtime Tide assistant coach who gained the head coaching job and then put his unique stamp on it as few others have. Sanderson's teams repeatedly flirted with greatness. His '82 team beat St. John's only to face another of the great teams of all time—North Carolina with James Worthy, Michael Jordan, and Sam Perkins. Playing in hostile Raleigh, North Carolina, the Tide fell by that same eerie score, 74-69. The '87 team (including Gottfried as the shooting guard) raced to a 28-4 record and SEC tournament and regular season titles before a monumental disappointment in the Final 16 against Rick Pitino's Providence Friars. Alabama narrowly missed the Final Eight in '90 with a 62-60 loss, blowing a late lead against an emotional Loyola Marymount club which was on a crusade for deceased team leader Hank Gathers. The Tide's 1991 team included Latrell Sprewell, Robert Horry, and James Robinson and encountered a handicapping illness before being embarrassed by Arkansas in the Final 16.

To use a nautical metaphor, if winning an NCAA title or getting to the Final Four can be considered reaching port, then skipper Sanderson was suddenly pushed off his ship in 1992, leaving his crew adrift in a storm. His 32 years of service to Alabama were hastily dismissed when a female secretary claimed Sanderson had struck her. Sanderson opted against a viable self-defense justification to protect his family from the intense scrutiny of litigation. The situation was exacerbated because Sanderson had become unpopular with many university officials because of personality conflicts and widespread envy of Sanderson's extreme popularity among fans. He was the sad victim of zero presumption of innocence.

Sanderson dominated the SEC as a head coach with five league championships. He guided the Tide to 10 of 11 NCAA tournaments, stealing many headlines from the Kentucky Wildcats who were trapped throughout Sanderson's tenure in a drought that would eventually last 18 years without a national title. Meanwhile, Sanderson's players were enormously talented. NBA playoff veterans Horry, Sprewell, and Derrick McKey were only three of 12 Sanderson players drafted by NBA teams. Before Sanderson was washed overboard, Alabama was slowly pushing toward greatness in the manner that Arizona and Connecticut progressed before making history with NCAA titles in the '90's. His were big shoes to fill.

When David Hobbs replaced Sanderson as head coach in '93, he was overwhelmed by the same expectations that he had helped to build as a Sanderson assistant. Hobbs watched the wheels fly off the wagon in his first year, failing to reach the NCAA tourney for only the second time in 12 years, and suffering a catastrophic loss to Alabama-Birmingham in the NIT. With the Tide led by Antonio McDyess, Hobbs recovered for two good seasons before a period of deep despair. Once-proud Alabama was defeated by non-scholarship Bucknell in the consolation game of the 1996 Cessna Classic, signaling the beginning of the end for Hobbs. He closed out his tenure with three consecutive NCAA misses and a final losing season. The 1997-'98 Tide was beaten by a Division II school and by Florida International. The decision to fire Hobbs was finally made during a stretch of ten losses in 12 games.

Then came Mark Gottfried. He and his staff inherited a program that had lost 30 of 52 games and the proud Alabama was at low tide. It would be up to Gottfried and company, including Robert Scott, to pick up the pieces.

2

The Team

S tanding before a packed room of media to accept the head coaching position at Alabama on March 25, 1998, Gottfried confronted the demons in the Tide's closet.

"I don't think there's any reason why the goals of this basketball program are anything short of putting a national championship ring on your finger," he boldly stated.

He easily could have hidden behind the team having dropped 30 of 52 games and missed three straight tournaments. He could have begged the public for patience and job security. Instead, he began to feverishly improve the talent level. The Tide signed four quality high school seniors in the early signing period of '98. Erwin Dudley (Uniontown), Terrance Meade (Scottsboro), Kenny Walker (Jacksonville, Fla.), and Rod Grizzard (Birmingham) were the first building blocks in the foundation of the Gottfried era. Robert Scott had also begun immediately an intense pursuit of the most highly publicized recruit in Alabama history, Gerald Wallace. Ranked by many publications as the number one high school prospect in America, Wallace was hailed as the chosen savior of the Tide program.

Scholarship limitations allowed only one addition for the '98-'99 team. Gottfried chose Travis Stinnett, a 5-foot-11 shooting guard from Maryville, Tennessee. In addition to his basketball skills, Stinnett, who loved to hunt and fish, would have added an interesting personality to

the team, filling the role of rugged outdoorsman. He even enjoyed
enough facial hair to complement the rugged look. Stinnett would have
supplied a desperately needed perimeter threat but was finally advised to
take a medical redshirt season due to an inflammation of the pelvis joint.

The '98-'99 campaign was relatively successful. A 17-14 regular
season returned the Tide to post-season play for the first time in three
years. The Tide claimed an emotional win over ruling tyrant Kentucky
for the first time in eight years! Alabama also reached a first by sweeping
Arkansas. Attendence and enthusiasm improved drmatically under
Gottfried. Despite these tremendous successes, the Tide lost two critical
home games to begin the SEC season versus Georgia and Mississippi
State that kept the Tide out of the NCAA tournament. Auburn pounded
the Tide three times in an unprecedented and unforgettable embarrassment. The Tide finished 17-15 with a road loss in the NIT.

The outlook for the '99-'00 campaign was positive. Several maga-
zines picked the Tide to reach the NCAA tournament. The 6-foot-11,
250-pound senior Jeremy Hays was predicted to carry a young team.
Serving as the spiritual and physical center of the club, Hays was a
polished scorer and an excellent rebounder. He was expected to fill the
gaps for the newcomers. The Boaz native was also expected to serve as
glue for the team off the floor because he is kind and likable.

Schea Cotton, a 6-foot-6, 220-pound sophomore transfer from Long
Beach City College, was once an intensely desired recruit. He signed with
UCLA before he encountered eligibility difficulties associated with the
legitimacy of his SAT score. Although he was eventually exonerated, the
NCAA investigation disrupted his college education. Structured like a
Greek god, Cotton was a cocky slasher whose speed and size made him
almost impossible to defend when his first step off the dribble was not
deemed a traveling violation. He was plagued by injuries through his
prep career, and rumors circulated about his inability to play through
pain. Rumors also abounded about his cockiness. His best play was
initiated by beating guys off the dribble and forcing them to slam into his
near-steel physique. Cotton, though notorious for his extensive history
of injuries, thrived on absorbing contact and smashing into defenders at

full pace. The irony of this was not lost on the coaching staff. Cotton had supreme confidence on and off the floor. Some would say to a fault.

Rod Grizzard, the 6-foot-8, 186-pound freshman, was probably the most offensively gifted guard in Alabama basketball history. His dribbling ability, quickness, and shooting stroke make him a phenomenon at his height. However, he desperately needed to gain weight when he appeared on campus. Critics had bombarded Grizzard about his alleged lack of mental toughness. Questions had been raised about Grizzard merely being able to maintain an offensive and defensive stance with his knees bent—which was sure to be a nightmare for the coaching king of the fundamental stance, Mr. Mark Gottfried. Generally, Grizzard was simply a relaxed person.

Terrance Meade, a 6-foot-2, 225-pound freshman guard seemingly built of bricks, was recruited to play the point guard position. Through voluntary workouts and the conditioning program, Meade had established himself as a great athlete. Whether a freshman could run the team at point guard remained an ominous question. Meade was mild-mannered away from the floor, and he was well-liked by his teammates.

Erwin Dudley, the 6-foot-8, 225-pound freshman power forward, was expected to help Hays with the rebounding duties. Dudley has the smile and demeanor of an angel. The coaches hoped his play would be more like a barbarian.

Local product Terrance "Doc" Martin, a 6-foot-3, 195-pound junior guard, had developed into a very solid defender in the SEC with his long wing-span. Martin was yet another guy who could contend for a congeniality contest on a team of nice guys.

Kenny Walker, the 6-foot-9, 214-pound freshman, was expected to score immediately with his polished post moves. Walker has a smile like a seven-year-old who just got his first bike. His sense of wonder makes him almost impossible to dislike.

Sam Haginas, the 6-foot-8, 235-pound sophomore power forward with a great physique, started ten games in the '98-'99 season. Haginas was expected to be a versatile defender. He distanced himself from the team when he chose to live off campus. The buzz around "Hag" was that he did no longer enjoyed basketball.

Tarik London, the 6-foot-1, 190-junior point guard, was a very tough competitor. He was expected to battle Meade for the starting role that the younger player would inevitably win. London served as a critical team leader because he was a passionate player and an outspoken floor general.

Alfred Moss, the 6-foot-8, 210-pound senior, was expected to increase his playing time after success in voluntary workouts. Moss was adored by most of his teammates because he was extremely genuine and always ready for a battle.

D. J. Towns, the 6-foot-2, 185-pound freshman guard, was expected to be an occasionally used perimeter threat. Towns probably had the toughest personality on the team. With weights in his room, he did arm curls for fun.

Soloman Davis, a 6-foot-6, 210-pound sophomore walk-on, probably set the all-time single season record for shot attempts in practice at Alabama last season. Thus, Davis was a man after Gottfried's heart. He came to campus on an academic scholarship. Davis was expected to serve as the team comedian.

Jim Bakken, the 6-foot-6 junior walk-on guard, was a newcomer who earned his spot in a try-out. He had impressed the team by making open perimeter shots in voluntary workouts. Bakken's personality remained a mystery before the season.

Meanwhile, Travis Stinnett's injury was feared to be career-ending. Without him, the Tide had no real perimeter threat at the beginning of the season. The coaches hoped to push one of their other players in that direction.

The outlook of the coaching staff was very tentative in the months leading up to the season. They were extremely excited about the future, but they knew that had too many freshmen to be thrilled about the upcoming campaign. Gottfried summed up his concerns in a casual staff meeting in response to many positive reports from voluntary workouts where the newcomers were apparently excelling.

"We've got a bunch of guys who don't know what it's gonna be like when we start going for real. Rod Grizzard is a pick-up game all-star. He has no idea what's about to happen to him. We'll be lucky to get him in a stance . . . Dudley and Walker are not strong enough yet . . . I'm tempted to throw Meade into the fire early—we'd have a true freshman running our team. We've got our work cut out for us, fellas."

With Gottfried's blessing, I came on board around this time to begin my documentation of the year to come. The coaches and team were anxious as the season loomed closer. I immediately got caught up in the growing excitement.

This excitement was not to last for long. As the days progressed toward the anticipated first practice on October 16, basketball slowly became a secondary issue for the staff. We had been worried about Scott for months because he had appeared to be perpetually tired. He knew that his body was not functioning normally. After every trip to several different doctors, Scott returned in a state of frustrated helplessness.

"I don't know why these doctors can't find what's wrong with me," he would say while pondering his complete lack of energy.

Scott finally found his answer in early September. Gottfried and Kelsey were eating in a small hamburger joint in Hammond, Louisiana, on a recruiting trip. Gottfried's cell phone rang. It was Bruce Sokol, one of Scott's long-time friends. Sokol had the results from Scott's latest tests at the Kirklin Clinic in Birmingham. "I've got bad news," Sokol said.

Sokol reported that Scott was suffering from stomach cancer and only had months remaining in his life. He was likely to die in three to six months. Gottfried felt like someone had called him to report that a loved one had died in a tragic accident. From that moment, Kelsey and Gottfried were already in mourning for their friend and colleague. We were all devastated. Scott had a strong relationship with the entire staff.

I was desperately anxious when I was told that Scott had been diagnosed with stomach cancer. Nobody was revealing to me the poor odds of his survival and I now think that everyone was protecting me from the news—it was no secret that I adored the colorful Scott. I asked Scott's friends with medical connections, Sokol and David McCloud. I was crushed when they reported that he needed a miracle. Rapidly spreading cancer cells had probably doomed his fate even before he had begun his string of doctor visits several months ago.

Former administrative assistant Howard Pride liked to tease me about getting excited when I watched Scott coach. Robert had a sense of urgency in his voice that I loved. He also entertained me with one-liners while watching Sports Center together.

On the day that Gottfried gathered the players to give them the news, he turned the corner and nearly broke my nose by accidentally hitting me in the hallway after that wrenching team meeting. He was jolted by the experience. He looked pained as he relayed to me what happened.

"It was the hardest thing I've ever done," he told me. "I broke down."

The players seemed completely bewildered by the news. It was not a good way to start a season.

3

October Hope

"Great competitors really love a hard battle," Gottfried began his first message as his players gathered closely around him and a board covered with the outline of his short speech in the corner of Coleman Coliseum at 10:00 A.M. It was Saturday, October 16, 1999, before the beginning of the first practice. "Be at your best when you best is needed . . . Listening is a skill just like shooting. This is a chance for you to learn, fellas. Be a great listener . . . Finish everything. In all the drills that we do, finish it. Get the ball and put it back in. Finish everything you do . . . You may recognize this guy's name here. Terry Coner. In four years here, Terry Coner probably lost no more than five pick-up games. Competitive greatness, guys. His teams never lost. He always made sure that they won. All the time. Let's get in here," Gottfried continued as his players begin clapping and moving even closer together by raising their arms and forming a commonly used team sport show of unity by hands touching hands. "Let's go, fellas. We have a chance to be a great team. We can be a great team. A great team. Let's be unselfish. Cheer for one another. Encourage each other. Nobody cares, fellas, who the star is. We're a team. We're all a team. We're all fighting together as a team. Let's have a great year."

A veteran player is customarily allowed to choose a chant.

"Hard work on three, baby," senior Alfred Moss said.

"One. Two. Three. Hard work!" the team exclaimed in a ritual that will be performed hundreds of times through a long season. This chant kicked off the first practice of the season.

And thus, the journey of blood, sweat, and tears began. The October renewal of hope for a college basketball team springs eternal. Over 300 Division I teams can still dream about seeing the name of their school on the NCAA tournament board when CBS reveals the field in March. They can dare to hope for a conversation with CBS announcer Billy Packer on the subsequent Monday night in April when their team could be crowned king. Every team is undefeated. Every team feels invincible in October.

Scott slowly walked into the coliseum moments later. Nobody seemed surprised. With cancer cells having invaded his intestines and chemotherapy destroying his energy, Scott's suffering often prevented him from working. He had declined Gottfried's offer to take a lengthy vacation. He chose to remain, pledging to do everything in his limited power to help the team. And on the first day of practice, he found the strength. (I am reminded of his asserting time and time again that he would not play in a Legends Game in August created by Gottfried as a reunion for the Alabama basketball family. Already missing over 20 pounds, he did not have the strength to participate. He decided on the day of the game to play. The people involved meant too much to him. He played hard under the circumstances. We both complained repeatedly that Gottfried and his former Tide teammate and roommate Jim Farmer had unfairly stacked their team coached by Wimp Sanderson. Scott hated the idea of disappointing his former coach and Legends Game coach C.M. Newton even though the game was just a warm and fuzzy exhibition for the fans. Scott was angry when his team lost.)

Two chairs were placed on the sideline beside half-court. Gottfried instructed Schea Cotton to sit next to Scott and listen. John Morr, the trainer, informed Gottfried during the annual pre-practice Coaches versus Players softball game that Cotton had a cyst on his chest that would need to be surgically removed, resulting in the player missing the beginning days of practice. (By the way, I played for the Coaches team and helped motivate our team to a stirring 12-11 win while the players angrily complained that they were cheated.) Cotton's attempt to learn the offense in the first few days without practicing was important.

Practice began with five offensive players executing the high-post offense against no defenders. Two drills introduced the first variations of the offense. Variation after variation is added throughout a season. The signature characteristic of the offense that Wooden made famous is the repeated usage of a player standing with his back facing the basket in the area around the free-throw line which is 15 feet from the goal. This player is the high-post. The commonly used low-post is an offensive player positioned much closer to the goal with his back also facing the basket. The high-post player is typically a big man—a forward. Thus Wooden's offense takes pressure off the guards but requires a forward who can operate far away from the basket—catch a pass, maneuver, and pass effectively.

One of those two initial offensive drills required the players to run the length of the floor before beginning a patterned motion. Gottfried's newcomers are generally exhausted in the first days of practice because he forces his team to run. He talked early in practice about being a "fast break team" and "the best conditioned team in the country." He constantly pushed the tempo, yelling "game speed."

"This is not a Sunday jog, fellas. This needs to be the Indianapolis 500," Gottfried said.

Gottfried's other recurring practice theme is playing above the rim. At one point, Walker failed to score.

"Dunk that! Jump up there high. The game at this level is played above the rim . . . Get down and ready to jump!"

(A Gottfried practice is almost always upbeat. The positive atmosphere of his practice is the all-important fact underlying almost every practice situation. He will praise his players early and often. However, I will tend to emphasize his colorful criticism. Please remember this editorial decision. I am refraining from reporting much of his endless barrage of praise.)

Scott could hardly speak. He was in noticeable pain when he tried to do so. He continued to coach anyway, keeping his yelling to a minimum.

He began using me as a means to convey messages to the players.

That first day, he asked me to get Grizzard's attention. Grizzard, his lanky, muscled frame breathing heavy from the workout, walked over to his chair. Scott told him to get lower in his defensive stance. Scott's West End High School teams were extremely well drilled. They defended with fundamentals and passion. It had become something of a Robert Scott trademark. This young team desperately needed Scott's animated and urgent instruction. Instead, Scott scratched and clawed to whisper words of wisdom.

Gottfried typically enjoys a controlled scrimmage at the end of practice where statistics and scoring are recorded. Managers Clay Pruitt and Scott Hewitt, who were working in their first season, operated new machines that conveniently organized the statistics. The typed copies of the practice schedule listed a red team that would play a white team. Assistants Kelsey and Pearson coached the teams while Gottfried coached everybody.

Erwin Dudley controlled the first scrimmage, leading his team with 14 points. Dudley was relentless near the basket in his rebounding and low-post scoring. Tarik London gave the red team great energy. Playing with great intensity, London seemed determined to be a coach on the floor. Gottfried had been disappointed with his lack of leadership the season before. London seemed determined to re-establish himself. Sam Haginas shook off a nightmarish summer trip to Japan with the SEC All-Star team, shooting five for eight from the field. (Haginas had received very little respect or playing time from All-Stars Head Coach John Brady of LSU. The whole experience affected him negatively.)

Gottfried checked the statistics after the scrimmage while the players finished practice with their customary 30 free throws. For every free throw a player misses above four misses, he runs the length of the floor twice within 11 seconds. More than a few players had to end practice sprinting up and down the hard gym floor.

NCAA rules mandate a day free from practice during every week. Gottfried is relatively generous about additional rest days. He has to be because his practices are so vigorous. Thus, he will sporadically grant a rest day that is not mandatory. His practices typically last two to three hours. Practices will be shorter later in the season to keep the players' legs fresh. The most strenuous practices are conducted from the first day until the opening game.

"Let's practice and play with poise, fellas . . . Don't allow yourself to lose your composure. Be confident but not cocky . . . We're not gonna fear anyone," Gottfried said in the same position as the day before, but this time it was 7 A.M. A few of the players looked sleepy as they listened.

Gottfried chose to practice his young team without extended morning rest after a rigorous first practice. Morr explained that Kenny Walker was so fatigued after practice that he could not move his arms to bathe in the shower. Cotton sat in a chair on the sideline appearing to deeply regret his departure from bed. I could relate. Most of the team arrived by 5:30 A.M. to prepare. Morr spent his early morning treating injuries and taping ankles. But this was not the extent of his responsibilities. He had to deal with all manner of illnesses and injuries. Diarrhea, dehydration, and the flu to name a few. (These were a more common problem than one would think. The total immersion of the athletes into a sweaty world of exhaustive, seemingly endless exercise, and the inability of some of the players to eat properly due to that exhaustion, added to the massive amounts of fluids that they must ingest, lends itself to these uncomfortable conditions. Many athletes deal with this type of thing regularly.)

At about 7:30, Gottfried dove on the floor to demonstrate the kind of intensity that he wanted when his players go after a loose ball. This display kicked off the next part of practice.

Rod Grizzard struggled in the war rebounding drill. This drill often climaxes the energy of a Gottfried practice. Its name is revealing. A coach throws a ball toward the goal. The players bend their knees and wait to crash into each other when the ball is released from the coach's hand.

The men battled for position with reckless abandon until someone grabs the rebound. Oftentimes the more determined player wins. Grizzard's slight frame and gentle demeanor handicapped his efforts. His spirit appeared to be crushed. War rebounding is a test of wills. No fouls called here. Pearson scolded Walker for allowing Jim Bakken, a shorter walk-on player, to grab a rebound. Walker appeared bewildered.

In a later drill, the team divided into forwards and guards on either end of the floor. Pearson coached the guards. Scott would have normally been working extremely hard on that end, but he had not arrived for practice. The forwards were coached by Kelsey and Boatright. Boatright coached when Scott was absent. Gottfried roamed from one end to the other.

One of the players left a drill due to sickness early on. Morr had known about it, but had decided not to worry Gottfried with unimportant details.

When an uninformed Gottfried became frustrated with the player's absence, he asked me why he was out of the gym. Gottfried's face revealed anger after my explanation.

(Dealing with a head coach can be very difficult for a trainer. In one sense, Morr is an independent actor, and the head coach wants him to handle his area. But everything overlaps between the trainer and the coach. The coach quickly grows tired of hearing about the minor bumps and bruises. So Morr chooses not to inform him about every little thing. When that little thing impacts the team, faces become grim.)

Gottfried became visibly frustrated with Walker when the player's legs appeared to be hurt. Walker's reputation for dropping out of summer conditioning had preceded him.

"Go see John, Kenny. Go over there with John," Gottfried said sarcastically.

Walker's shin splints were bothering him. Kelsey sent one of the managers, Clay Pruitt, to Morr for an update.

"He is ready to go," Morr snapped in frustration.

After a few typically mild explosions by Gottfried in successive drills, he finally reached a boiling point when Meade casually launched an ill-advised shot.

"[Imitating Meade with an exaggerated casual motion] Don't jack around out here! Terrance Meade gets a rebound and throws it up like this! Play the game right! Play it right! If you wanna jack around, do it in someone else's gym!"

A few minutes later, Gottfried gave a brief speech about loose balls. On the following play, three guys wildly collided while diving out of bounds for a loose ball. I caught Pearson and Boatright smiling.

A group of us watched the practices sitting from the sidelines, including Kobie Baker, the new administrative assistant, managers Minor and Pruitt, and myself. The players were tired from the relentless practicing. Meade especially.

"A sniper seems to have Meade in his crosshairs," Baker said. (A common team joke was to blame a sniper when a player fell due to fatigue, clumsiness, or injury when no one else was near him.) Meade did indeed look as though he was about to fall.

I followed up on Baker's joke by asking Minor and Pruitt if they had combed the top of the coliseum for a gunman.

Meade turned the joke on us by canning three consecutive perimeter jumpers. He showed us why he had such a strong reputation for toughness. Not long after, Hays failed to communicate to Meade that a screen was coming, sending Meade full speed into Moss. Meade crashed to the floor from the impact. He jumped up and furiously yelled at Hays. A sympathetic Pearson criticized Hays a moment later.

Gottfried closed practice by referring any injured players to Morr for a 6:30 P.M. session. The players limped gingerly out of the gym. A trainer's work is never done.

Cotton, who was visiting the doctor at the beginning of practice three, had an "hour-to-hour" status according to Morr.

"He's really having a tough time . . . He doesn't have anybody here," Morr said.

The newcomer was far from his California home. I asked Morr about his recovery status.

"It's sore. He shot yesterday without jumping. When he started elevating, it was killing him . . . This is a skin surgery—nothing involved with the muscle. It's uncomfortable. I don't know when he'll be back. I do know that deep down in my heart of hearts—with my medical knowledge—that he can practice."

The next practice began by emphasizing defense. Video coordinator

Patrick McDonald was filming every practice. When Scott inevitably missed practices, Boatright normally drove the tapes to his home. The films revealed many defensive deficiencies. Grizzard, Walker, Dudley, and Cotton were all advanced offensively, but they all needed to defend dramatically better. All four of them defended poorly in those early practices. Boatright relayed to me later how tired Scott looked when he dropped off the tapes.

The coaches began zeroing in on the problems the team faced. The forwards were not tough enough. The guards, save for London, were lacking in experience. Some of the players fluctuated with their intensity and speed of play. And most importantly, the team defense was terrible.

Kelsey spent much of his time with the two forwards, Walker and Dudley. I watched him at his instructional best with these two big men. He was so locked in on these two forwards that they seemed overwhelmed by his insistence that they improve. He spent the majority of his time molding them into better, craftier players.

Pearson reached a similar level of intensity with Grizzard. The player needed a mental toughness overhaul, which was coincidentally Pearson's specialty area.

"Push up, Rod. Push up," Pearson said, insisting that Grizzard pressure the ball-handler.

"Push up, Rod. Get down, Rod. Come on, Rod."

Grizzard was beaten by a dribbler on a play.

"Where are you, Rod? Let's go, Rod," Pearson said in controlled frustration and sarcasm.

"You've got to get down and guard somebody, Rod," Gottfried added.

"Get down, Rod," Pearson followed immediately.

"Let's go, Rod," London said. The encouragement from the older player was good to hear.

While Grizzard struggled, Cotton returned from a doctor's visit. He began peddling a stationary bike set up for his conditioning. He pumped his legs methodically while the team ran through a series of drills. He looked neither bored nor excited.

While peddling, Cotton spoke to me in reference to the doctor's opinion. "Coming back too soon would keep me out for months."

Cotton's missing those critical early practice days after a minor surgery intensified the tension surrounding him and his teammates. He had sporadically missed summer conditioning sessions and voluntary workouts. His constant problems with various injuries created speculation about his pain threshold. The situation was exacerbated by Cotton's insistence for privacy on the issue. He kept his own counsel about his injuries. Kobie Baker once asked him about his condition called jumper's knee, and Cotton declined to answer because he only discussed his injuries with a "certified athletic trainer."

Jim Bakken was humbled in the first two practices. Having recently joined the team, Bakken was the darling of voluntaries because he made bunches of open jumpers. He did not adapt well to the fast pace and the tough physicality of practice in the SEC. By the middle of the second practice, the youngster was unable to hit the broad side of a barn with a shotgun. His bad experiences climaxed when he had a three-point shot blocked.

"Shoot that at the rec. league," Gottfried said.

As the scrimmage started, Scott slowly walked into the Coliseum. He appeared especially weak. Scott sat and shook his head as Kenny Walker made play after play.

Gottfried joined Scott after practice. Gottfried bubbled with excitement.

"What Walker doesn't have right now is strength in his lower body. He's like a flimsy tree in the yard. When he gets stronger, he'll have the total package . . . He had a day! Wow!"

Scott's unexpected presence brought cheer to Gottfried's face. He anxiously discussed his team with his aching friend.

"In three days, London has done everything that we wanted him to give last year. He's giving us leadership and direction," Gottfried said.

"Competition will help us this year. That's what we didn't have last year," Scott responded in reference to a young but talented roster.

"Fred Moss is just getting blown away," Gottfried said.

"Fred always fouls. He doesn't want to play position defense. He just mugs people in there. I've told him that. Erwin is at least learning how," Scott responded.

Coaches have to know their teams to excel. An art of coaching is the constant reflection on players—the continual discussion of a staff about what different people can give the team. Gottfried, Scott, Pearson, Kelsey, and Boatright are no exception. Their conversations are dominated by different characteristics of their players, their strengths, their weaknesses. Scott was blessed with an especially keen eye for developing players. He was still practicing his skills, and that must have encouraged him in his battle for life.

THE FOURTH practice on Tuesday, October 19, was proceeded by a relatively short message from Gottfried.

"Don't let a day go by without making it a masterpiece . . . Make it your best day . . . Team spirit is the willingness to sacrifice personal glory for the welfare of the team. The most talented team is not always the best team . . . It's the team that's willing to sacrifice . . . The team comes first, fellas. Every time we make a decision it should be what is best for the team. Let's go, fellas. Let's have a great day." The team came together clapping.

Cotton managed to join the first couple of drills. He ran well in the flanker drill which is one dribbler moving the length of the floor with two players flanked on his right and left, ending with a pass from the free throw line to either flanker for a jump-shot from a convenient angle to bounce the ball off the glass. It's a simple drill appreciated by Wooden. And Gottfried loves it. Fundamentals. It's all about the fundamentals in the Wooden school of thought.

Gottfried yelled, "Push yourself."

I immediately wondered whether Cotton felt ready to push himself. I'm sure his teammates wondered the same thing, illustrating how Cotton's circumstances captured the attention of everybody around the team.

Going one-on-one from the wing, Grizzard humiliated a spirited

London with three buckets in a row. Then he dropped six buckets in a row on Martin and Towns. Switching to the defensive role, Grizzard tasted his own medicine. The punishment for allowing three scores in a row is ten push-ups. If Grizzard kept up his defensive mistakes, he would be the strongest guard in the league from the thousands of push-ups he had in store for him.

Soloman Davis, who fired more shots in practice last year than a Vietnam veteran, fired a questionable shot.

"That's a terrible shot," Gottfried responded.

Jeremy Hays was scored upon easily.

"Take your weak defense back to Boaz today if you can't guard anybody," Gottfried said.

Cotton was given the option to play in non-contact drills for the next practice, and he accepted the challenge. Morr explained that he was giving exceptional effort in his training role to make Cotton "feel comfortable." He was scheduled to see a doctor at 2:30 P.M. on Thursday for clearance to play in contact drills.

GOTTFRIED began the next practice with another short speech. "Alertness. Be alert . . . Be observing constantly. Think. Be a smart player. See the game develop. Don't just play hard when the coach is watching. Play hard all the time. I watched the film of practice yesterday. We've gotta get better at guarding the post. The ball is going into the post way too easy. We've got to do a better job of understanding help-side defense . . . Make a decision right now whether you're gonna get better today or not. We can fiddle-fart around and go through it . . . or you can make it a great day. Let's make it a great day. Let's go to work."

Jeremy Hays had a gargantuan blister on his foot today. It looked like a moon crater.

"I'm going anyway," he told me with pride.

Pearson ran one of his favorite drills that requires using a forearm shiver to push a player cutting into the painted area back out of it. Grizzard was hesitant to deliver a blow. He did not want to belt somebody with his forearm.

"Come on, Rod. That's too easy, Rod," Pearson insisted after the weak effort.

Later, Gottfried became unhappy about the negotiation of a screen of a defensive man guarding the ball-handler.

"Many times in life, we pick the path of least resistance. But you can't take the easy way out. You gotta keep fighting! You gotta fight to get over that ball screen. You can't bail out."

An AAU coach entered the Coliseum. AAU summer basketball has evolved into the vital recruiting time. Coaches are allowed to recruit off campus for a large chunk of time in the summer. Most of the great recruits play in the summer. So the AAU coaches have become absolutely critical figures. Robert Scott coincidentally entered the gym at the same time. An uncomfortable silence followed them. These two had known each other for years. The AAU coach, who sat in the front row, intentionally damaged Alabama's chances with an incredible talent the season before. Losing that player was devastating. Scott saw a long friendship damaged. But Scott labored to join the AAU coach and greet him warmly. Watching this develop, I was shocked. Asked about their warm exchange later, Scott explained that they were "old friends" so he would not let one situation "ruin that." Facing the end, he had chosen to focus on the positive memories. I wish that I had a videotape of his explanation. His body language was so graceful.

Kelsey tried to push the right button for Alfred Moss.

"You've gotta be one of our best defenders, Fred—hard to put you on the floor if you're not . . . It's a battle, Fred. It's a battle, Fred. It's a battle. It's a battle." Moss jockeyed for position to prevent a pass to the man he was guarding while Kelsey coached in his ear.

The next drill was the 60-point game which focuses on passing and moving without the ball. The offense cannot dribble after the first pass of their possession. The goal is to complete 60 passes before the opponent does. The defense must force a turnover to get the ball. The action is always wild because the game extends to the entire floor. People are running everywhere. Reserve players are leading the cheers. Elbows are flying. The defensive player is pressuring the ball-handler with his nose near the waist. Coaches are yelling "rip through" to the ball-handler who should sweep his flexed forearms near the upper body of the pressuring defender with the hands holding the ball angled down and away from the defender. A bruising time is had by all.

The following scrimmage featured some especially horrid defense. After "Sollo" Davis effortlessly drove 25-feet to the basket and casually flipped the ball in the basket without challenge, Gottfried moved toward a volcanic eruption. He began by calmly teaching how many principles of help-side defense had been violated, but conceptualizing the play made him angry.

"We're gonna guard somebody around here or we're gonna be on the sidelines running about twenty 17's," he screamed.

(17's are the coaches favorite conditioning exercise involving 17 timed sprints across the width of the floor in roughly a minute. No player likes doing them. They are dreaded.)

After practice, Cynthia Scott, Robert's wife, said that Robert had not enjoyed the carbohydrate drinks that Morr had given him the other day. Everybody around him was trying to find a way to give him some energy. The food that worked best was ice cream. He happily ate vanilla ice cream that Cynthia served with extra vanilla seasoning. It made him feel better.

COTTON returned from his Thursday trip to the doctor with clearance to practice in competitive drills. The staff, especially Kelsey, guessed that Cotton would dramatically increase the energy level of practice.

As was customary, Gottfried started the practice with an inspirational speech. "Let the game come to you . . . Think about that for a minute . . . Sometimes guys want to force the action . . . Sometimes, it's best to let the game come to you. Some days it will come more than others. Be ready when your opportunity comes. If you're ready when your opportunity comes, you'll take advantage of it. Let's have a great practice today, fellas."

In the first drill, Gottfried was hit in the head with an errant pass. Given that this team had shown an early tendency to not value the basketball, many coaches would have exploded.

He never changed his facial expression. He said nothing.

The next drill for the guards was one-on-one starting from half-court. This was Cotton's first contact drill. Anticipation had been high about his joining practice. Baker said earlier that a different NBA scout called the office about him every day. Early on, Grizzard prevented Cotton from scoring. Then London welcomed Cotton to practice by scoring against him. Cotton later established himself by overpowering Martin. Grizzard blew by Cotton again. Cotton finally managed a stop.

In the following drill, Cotton drove with reckless abandon to the basket, colliding with Martin. Both guys hit the ground hard. They lingered on the ground. Martin rose. Morr checked with him first because his knee was somewhat twisted on the play. Cotton landed on his posterior.

"We oughta put you in football pads to play," Morr said jokingly to Cotton.

"Sh—, it would be better," Cotton responded in a tone that was not amused. "Get me some ice, man. My elbow and my ass are killing me."

Morr nursed Cotton back into practice. Cotton blew by Martin at the wing, rushed the paint, and exploded for a thunderous dunk. For a man with an extensive history with injuries, Cotton's explosive movements never appeared tentative.

After being fouled in a two-on-one drill, Cotton walked over to Morr.

"They're out to get me," he said, glaring at his teammates.

"They just love you, man," Morr replied jokingly.

"I've already had my share of injuries," Cotton responded.

Later in a two-on-one break situation, Cotton tried a low percentage pass that was completed to Dudley for a score.

"Save that pass for the summer league," Gottfried said.

"It hit him in the hands," Cotton responded, speaking very quietly so that none of the coaches could hear.

During a water break, Gottfried finally showed genuine frustration with Cotton.

"I'm afraid Schea will be on the ground all year complaining to the referees," he told me.

During the customary end-of-practice scrimmage, Cotton appeared mentally and physically spent.

"I'm tired as hell, and I need a sub," he said to no one in particular.

Gottfried was disappointed with practice for the first time.

"We didn't concentrate very well today. You've got to get your mind right. Get yourself prepared. You can't turn it on and off like a faucet. Tomorrow . . . we're gonna practice for a little bit and then we'll bring it up and go. We've got SEC officials coming in," he said in anticipation of Friday's officiated scrimmage.

THE DAY of the scrimmage, one of the players told me that Cotton was questionable to play because of butt discomfort from his fall the day before. Morr did not comment when I asked about it.

Before Friday's scrimmage, Morr described to me his working relationship with Cotton.

"I think I have his trust enough right now to keep him playing. But that is a day-to-day issue. If I can convince him that he's gonna be fine, I think he'll be all right . . . It's gonna be a challenge [to keep him playing during the season]. There are many things that I can't do in this world. But if I could do this, I can do something that many other people can't do."

The team gathered before the scrimmage.

"I evaluate everything you're doing. Offense. Defense. How you're playing with the team. Everything! I'm gonna switch up the teams four or five times. It's not necessarily the five best, but it's five that play the best together. That's what we're looking for . . . I'm more interested in our defense than anything. I want to see who can get down and guard somebody," the head coach said.

Alfred Moss needed a good scrimmage.

"Moss is getting blown by like he's doing 50 on the German autobahn," Gottfried told us at lunch the day before.

(We typically ate lunch at Paul W. Bryant Hall. The conversation usually drifted toward gentle jibing. The coaching staff enjoyed gently irritating me until I became angry. They did it well. I was not a hard target. I have defended Bobby Knight in more situations than Notre Dame has beaten Navy in football. We seldom discussed the progress of the team during the season. But Alfred's troubles inspired.)

. The scrimmage began with the coaches and staff on the bleachers. Walker offered an excuse after he failed to execute on a play early in the scrimmage.

"I don't want to here any bullcrap excuses, Kenny," Gottfried responded.

Terrance Meade's white team fell behind early. The point guard on every team is expected to be the leader.

"Terrance Meade, run your team," Gottfried exclaimed.

Apart from a few spectacular dunks, Cotton played poorly with ugly shots and uglier turnovers. Cotton finally decided to take himself out of the scrimmage because of butt discomfort.

Jeremy Hays had been outworked by Erwin Dudley and overshadowed by Kenny Walker in the early practices. In the scrimmage however, Hays, a senior and a proven SEC player, taught the youngsters a lesson with 16 for 20 shooting.

Haginas made a bid for a starting role with 38 points on 16 for 21 shooting. His private monster of being unable to consistently score around the basket had disappeared momentarily.

Gottfried loudly asked Morr about Cotton's status during a timeout to apparently challenge the player and the trainer. A frustrated Morr indicated with uncertain body language that he was not holding Cotton out of the scrimmage. So Gottfried turned to Cotton.

"I'm good. I'm done for the day," Cotton asserted.

Gottfried's face revealed his disgust as he walked away.

Gottfried found happiness when Gerald Wallace came into the Coliseum. Wallace was rated first in his class nationally by many recruiting experts. He had committed to Alabama. Wallace began his official visit by talking to Gottfried on the sideline while the scrimmage continued. The recruit is viewed by many as the answer to Gottfried's prayers. The threat of him entering the NBA draft after high school or having his allegiance purchased by a rival left the staff concerned. Gottfried had poured every ounce of his being into recruiting Wallace. Meanwhile, the player's basketball legend was growing like the Wallace of Scotland depicted in the movie *Braveheart*.

"You're gonna love this offense because you'll get open shots all over the floor," Gottfried told Wallace.

Morr was left to cope with Cotton. Morr came over and sat next to the rest of us. The game continued. He stated slowly that Cotton was accusing the training staff of forcing him to play, despite his injuries. Morr did not look happy about it.

"I never said that he had to play. I do say that I want him to play . . . He is a self-fulfilling prophecy. He expects you to have a negative idea about him based on what other people have said about him. So he responds in a way that is defensive . . . and it becomes exactly like everybody said it would," Morr said. I could tell that working with Cotton was beginning to wear on him.

The scrimmage sparked a difficult analysis of the point guard position. Terrance Meade scored 39 points to lead everybody, but a one to seven assist-turnover ratio reflected youthful decisions. London's 11 assists against four turnovers made him viable even without scoring punch. It was a tough choice.

Gottfried introduced Wallace to the team after practice. He desperately wanted the recruit to feel like he was part of the family. Wallace joined the familiar stack of hands.

"One, two, three. Hard work!"

A CROWD of around 4,500 people arrived for the Alabama Fan Jam on October 23. This was an opportunity for the fans to meet the new team. The players just had fun in a few drills.

In the halls of the Coliseum before the team took the floor, an excited team enjoyed the promise of a new season. Scott's presence put a smile on every face. It was like a game without the pressure of competition. Jokes and laughter filled the packed hall. There would be nothing humorous about this team taking the floor again.

A standing ovation greeted the team. Tony Giles, the P.A. announcer, labored to excite the crowd. The bright lights of the Coliseum
and the pictures on the JumboTron alarmed the senses. A good time was
had by all. The coaches seemed a little more relaxed, and the players
seemed to enjoy themselves.

During a team three-point contest grouping players with fans, Kelsey
came over to me and commented on Cotton.

"He's just going crazy to the basket. He's off balance. If he were under
more control, he'd have less injuries."

The informal exhibition ended quickly. The rest of the season would
be work. The day was swiftly coming when every team in America would
no longer be undefeated, and the crowd would not cheer just because the
team arrived to have fun for 40 minutes.

4

A Sniper Struck on Wild Wednesday

O n Monday, October 25, Gottfried began to express his
difficulties with Cotton in a coaches' meeting. While others
had criticized, Gottfried had up to that point been reluctant
to do so. He made the decision to gamble on great talent. I had been a
vocal advocate for patience with Cotton. Awed by his display in voluntaries, I had been pushing for tolerance with any and all borderline injury
situations. Having coached at Milford, a prep school that attracted many
athletes who had not succeeded in the high school setting because of
academic or disciplinary problems, I was extremely familiar with guys
who have not flourished because of their idiosyncrasies. Gottfried had
grown tired of my perspective. He shared his thoughts in the mid-day
staff meeting that I joined.

"You can take him back to Milford with you, Coach. He'd be a
perfect fit there. I'm afraid he's not gonna make it here."

I declined to respond.

Pearson set the tone for practice with the guards. Grizzard had a pass
intercepted and relaxed his body in disappointment, casually uttering
"Oh, sh—."

Pearson stopped the action abruptly.

"Grizzard! I don't want you to throw a bad pass like this and say 'Oh,
sh—' while the other team runs to the other end and dunks!"

The team huddled around the head coach to officially begin the scheduled practice.

"Come with the mind set that you're gonna get better. Don't wait. You can't get today back . . . It's your job to come out here and do the best job you can . . . Throughout your life, you're gonna develop some great, great friends . . . You are not all going to be great friends . . . but respect each other and be devoted to one another . . . As a player, I know that you think about whether Coach Gottfried cares about me. I mean not caring about how well you shoot or dribble, but does the coach care about you as a person. You ask the question about your teammate. 'Tarik is my teammate. Does he care about me?' And y'all should care about one another. Develop within yourself the ability to care about somebody else. 'I'm interested in you, Alfred. You didn't play well today. Coach Gottfried got on you pretty hard.' Who's doing that in the locker room to encourage him? Who's encouraging each other on this team? Pulling for each other all the time. Looking out for each other. 'I'm looking out for you' . . . Today, our points of emphasis are post-defense, ball pressure, and offensive execution . . . Let's go."

Sensing that he might be losing Cotton and refreshed after releasing anger earlier in the staff meeting, Gottfried began teaching Cotton warmly and individually in the first five-on-zero offensive drill. He nearly embraced the player five times while teaching him in the first 45 minutes of practice.

Stopping an offensive drill, Gottfried made a revealing demonstration about his love for the high-post offense.

"The reason I like this offense is because you learn how to come up here [to the free throw line] and be a basketball player—pass, shoot, or dribble," he said.

Gottfried revealed another core belief about basketball in a three-on-four contest-the-shot drill.

"We've got three guys trying to stop four. How are you going to do it? We just have to figure out that problem! Problem solving is the game of basketball."

Cotton dominated in the war rebounding drill. His teammates cheered for him.

Despite widespread bitterness about his low pain threshold, his teammates seemed able to forgive. I cheered with them. Heated action in a one-on-one drill from the wing between Meade and Cotton created more cheering from teammates. They collided repeatedly in short explosive movements.

Moss set a screen that freed a teammate for an open score. Gottried praised him. Cotton followed with three jolting screens.

Kelsey scolded Dudley and quickly became mild-mannered again. He could radically change his demeanor within seconds.

Jim Bakken later locked up Cotton's arm. Cotton once again walked off the court toward Morr. "It's hard to play when they're trying to injure me and sh—."

Morr managed to calm Cotton who successfully completed an entire practice for the first time.

"Every day I can come out and scream, but you've gotta come out here motivated, thinking I'm gonna make myself better today. Don't cheat yourself. Don't be the guy who has to look back and wish that he would've worked harder. If I just worked harder, maybe this or that would have happened . . . Be a self-motivated, self-start guy. All you can do is look in the mirror and ask if you did your best," Gottfried said, concluding the practice.

Sadness filled the coaches' locker room before Tuesday's practice. Reigning U.S. Open golf champion Payne Stewart and former Alabama quarterback Robert Frailey died in an airplane accident. Gottfried addressed his team about the tragedy.

"None of us know, guys, when God is gonna take us. Last night on the news, you guys probably heard that Payne Stewart and Robert Frailey, who was a quarterback here, died . . . I take for granted sometimes that I'm always gonna be around. Just like basketball, fellas, you take for granted the fact that you can come practice every day . . . You can't get it back! You can't rewind the clock . . . You don't get do-overs. You've been given a gift to play. You've all been given size and speed. Take advantage of it. Be the best you can be. Don't have any regrets. When basketball is over or something tragic happens, you should know that you became the best that you could be. Know your strengths and your weaknesses. Everybody's got 'em. Know your game, fellas. Everybody brings something different to this team . . . Some things that I'm not real good at, my assistants do well. I do some things better than they do. It's no different in basketball. Some things you do a lot better than him. He does some things better than you. So figure out your game and what you will bring. That's how you start fitting a great team together . . . Know your role. Know your game. Play to your strengths. Use your strengths . . . I'll tell you this story real quickly. We had a guy out at UCLA that Schea probably remembers. His name was Trevor Wilson . . . He had 38 points and 17 rebounds against Louisville on national television. He was 6-8 and a strong leaper. He could go and get it, fellas. But he couldn't shoot dead. He just couldn't shoot. I liked the guy, but he could not shoot. He went into every NBA camp and shot every time that he got a chance. And he went about two-for-60. Instead of using his strengths—he could rebound and get offensive boards—he tried to prove to the world that he was Mr. Complete Player. Michael Jordan was a complete player, but there are not a lot of guys who are totally complete. So if you've got something that you are good at, do what you're good at. Get better at your weaknesses, but play to your strengths. Let that part of your game shine."

Early on, Cotton complained about hip/butt pain and big toe discomfort to Morr. Morr recounted to me a conversation he had with Hays earlier that day, wherein he tried to dispel any doubts, defending Cotton.

" . . . the guy is in strange land. He's far from his California home. His high school coach probably had to tolerate anything because of Cotton's talent. You know how summer leagues are . . . The guy is in a foreign land." Morr did not tell me Hays's response.

Boatright gave practice a spark with intense coaching of Walker in the flanker drill. He showed signs of comfort with his new coaching role during the occasional Scott absence.

Robert Scott slowly walked into the gym. His hat looked bigger. His body appeared smaller. He was eroding. Within minutes he was instructing Tom to coach Grizzard and Dudley on two different problems. After he sat down, Scott referred to how tough his drive was today.

I offered to pick him up in the future.

"I don't want to trouble anybody," he responded.

Scott and I laughed about the cable in his office finally being repaired. It had not functioned for months, and he repeatedly asked to have it repaired. Scott was a true sports fan. We loved to talk about sports. He watched ESPN's Sports Center daily, and his sense of humor was keen. I will never forget when I was admiring the intensity that the Cincinnati Bearcats play with under Bob Huggins.

"Their mentality is 'nobody likes us, but us,'" Scott commented.

Scott said that he would be attending practice for the next couple of days. He claimed to have more energy. In a voice of concern, Scott said before he left, "I wonder how well this team will respond to pressure."

London, Martin, Dudley, and Hays led their team to a stellar day of scrimmaging.

Winning a half-court drill 11-0 and starting 10-0 in the later scrimmage, the older guys plus Dudley made a statement. Dudley had been a rebounding machine, leading the team every day.

The head coach closed practice, saying "You can't mentally stay at home for a day."

Gottfried joked about point guard London having to stay after practice every day for missing free throws. London did more sprints due to missed free throws than anybody. Only a few other guys ran consistently. The team was generally good from the free throw line.

The buzz around the coaches on Wednesday's practice was the amazingly inconsistent Kenny Walker. His play had been brilliant at times with polished post moves. But at other times he disappeared for stretches and played with low confidence. His game remained a mystery.

Manager Matt Minor complained that we did not use the take-the-charge drill anymore. Minor was used as the offensive player delivering the charge, and seemed to really enjoy it.

"We don't have anybody around here that can hand out a charge," Pearson responded.

(Pearson's sarcasm toward Minor revealed the extreme tension in their relationship. Minor had bailed out on summer basketball camp at a late date the previous summer. Irate, Pearson was left with an understaffed camp. Coordinating an understaffed camp is hectic given that it requires the management of hundreds of young people. Pearson had not forgotten Minor's abandonment. Adam Stevens, a manager who worked the annual camp, made a controversial misjudgment during camp that infuriated the staff. Gottfried subsequently relocated Stevens to another job within the athletic department. Stevens sat far away from the floor in Coleman Coliseum to watch some practices. He missed the program and regrets how he handled several situations. I couldn't help wondering if Minor wouldn't eventually join Stevens in coliseum seating.)

The team huddled.

"Loyalty, guys. You're gonna learn something about that word your whole life and what it means to be loyal to somebody. To have loyalty to your teammates, to your family . . . I need to be loyal to you. I'm not going to go out and dog you out publicly. You could stink it up today. You could have the worst practice ever. But you're never gonna pick up the newspaper and see where Mark Gottfried says that Jeremy Hays was awful today. You're never gonna hear it because that's not what I believe in. Nor should you be that way toward me. One thing that I always ask you guys, no matter what you do, don't ever, ever lie to me. If you make a mistake and do something wrong, I can help you out of trouble if you tell me the truth. I want to help you. We all make mistakes. Don't ever lie to me. If you lie to me, I don't want to help you . . . Let's all be honest with each other. Be loyal to yourself, guys, and those that are dependent upon you. We're all depending on each other. Be positive. Lift each other up. Encourage each other. Don't tear each other down. We're all trying. Everybody is trying out here. We're all gonna make mistakes. And at the end of the day, we should be able to come together and hug and hold on and say 'hey, man, good job' . . . Find a teammate at the end of the day and encourage him. Don't be a discouraging guy. Don't be a locker room lawyer. Don't go into the locker room saying 'Terrance Meade never passes me the ball so I can't stand the guy.' That doesn't help our team.

Be positive with one another . . . That's how you build a team, fellas. That's how you end up with something special. One day when you're old, you'll look back and say that team was special because of the way we treated each other." Gottfried said the words with great sincerity and warmth.

Practice typically consists of a long series of five to ten minute drills. Toward the end of the flanker drill, I noticed Gottfried preparing for the next drill. This type of preparation allows the practices to run smoothly. Without solid organization, valuable time would be wasted. When time is wasted, the practices get too long. And players become mentally drained by long practices.

A later one-on-one length of the court drill revealed the tremendous defensive deficiencies of this team. Grizzard was whipped. His body language seemed to say that he did not care about guarding anybody for any reason. A series of players were blown away by the dribbler. Grizzard must have been struggling mightily to draw attention away from several other guys who also couldn't move their feet to defend. Kelsey later told Grizzard, "You might be sitting the bench because you can't guard."

The coaching staff showed signs of irritation. Kelsey especially.

Shaking his head at Moss in a later drill, he finally said, "It's a tough league, Fred."

London showed some veteran leadership by scolding Moss for dropping a pass. Moss's hands betrayed him too often. At least he wasn't forced to worry about dropping a pass from Davis. Davis never saw a shot that he didn't like. Gottfried criticized a typical perimeter shot from Davis in a drill that was premised on moving the ball to the area around the basket.

(Travis Stinnett walked the sideline those first few weeks. He had not practiced in roughly a year. "This injury is the hardest thing I've ever been through," he later said.

Morr had been pursuing information on a unique procedure for a condition that could be causing his osteitis pubis. Thinking about the surgery brought hope into a situation that had seemed hopeless for months.)

The intensity of a five-on-five half-court drill sparked Gottfried to bring one of the teams together to talk about a play on their final possession. Cotton stole a final pass to preserve a 6-4 win. Clapping and cheering by the winning team accompanied the losing team who were forced to run the floor twice within 11 seconds.

The end-of-the-practice scrimmage began with a series of horrible decisions and ugly turnovers. Gottfried finally stopped the madness.

"We just throw it away. Jeremy throws it when no one is open. Sam throws it out of bounds over there. Terrance Meade throws it away. Tarik throws it away. We're just throwing the thing away. I don't care what we run. We could run a hundred different offenses. If we can't pass and catch with one another, we're in trouble. We are in trouble," Gottfried yelled.

Three more nasty turnovers and a crazy missed dunk attempted by Grizzard, and everybody in the gym waited for Gottfried to explode. He remained patient. Two more turnovers and tension flooded the Coliseum. He still did not react. Another turnover. No reaction. Finally, an exhausted Kenny Walker attempted the wildest pass I have ever seen, a behind-the-back outlet pass which was intercepted, giving the opponent a great scoring chance in his team's paint. Gottfried sounded his whistle.

"I've seen enough. On the sideline."

Lined up on the sideline, the players had to run 17 times across the floor in 65 seconds. This is a traditional end to an early Gottfried practice. (Gottfried's approach is that one player failing to make the time means the team fails. "You're only as strong as your weakest link," he likes to say. This day in particular was the wrong day to finish late.)

Dudley was the weak link, and he finished late by one second.

"We play for 39-and-a-half minutes and can't play for the last 30 seconds. When he loses, we all lose. When the team wins, we all win," the head coach exclaimed.

Soloman Davis began yelling to motivate the group. Uncharacteristically, Davis barked urgently at his exhausted teammates. Gottfried waited to give them a brief rest before they returned to the sideline for another attempt. Battling a cold, Hays did not approach the line.

Gottfried requested that Hays join the team on the line.

"I can't go," Hays responded.

Gottfried dropped his whistle and waved his arm at Hays to dismiss his actions.

"You guys are a bunch of sissies," Gottfried barked angrily.

Without Hays, the team tried again. However, Walker barely finished, missing the time by ten seconds. Like a marathon runner, his body appeared to be on the brink of collapsing. Gottfried began walking out of the gym. His assistants followed.

Davis screamed desperately, "Coach is walking out on us! There go the coaches! They're walking out the door! The coaches are walking out the door!"

London boldly took control of the team in a close huddle.

"They're more disappointed in you than anybody, Hays! You're a senior, Hays! I've been hurt! Everybody gets hurt! I'm hurt every day! You should be able to look at the whole team! Look at the team! That should be good enough to get you going. We've got to win games, man! We're trying to get to the dance, man! We've got to get to the show! We've got an opportunity. When an opportunity comes, we've got to step up! I know you're hurt. I'm hurt too! I feel bad too! Some days, I feel so bad that I don't feel like practicing. But I have to step up. That's why I'm here! I'm a basketball player! I'm a basketball player! Come on, man. We've got to win games. We ain't gonna win any games like this."

John Morr and I shared a moment watching the team bond. Not just with his words but with incredible passion, London had captured the essence of the game.

The team decided to shoot free throws like they would at the end of any practice.

Gottfried came back in alone. He quietly gathered the team.

"We've got to have some mental toughness. We've got to pick ourselves up and finish strong. We can't just roll over and die like a bunch of dogs. It's like—all of a sudden—somebody acting like a kamikaze ran in with a gun up there and just shot us all down on the sideline [Gottfried even references the sniper]. When the going gets tough, fellas, I want to find some guys who I want to jump in a hole with me to fight with me. Sometimes, I find which guys aren't gonna fight with me. You don't want to be one of them . . . I want you guys to put the balls up and go home. Don't shoot free throws. We're finished," Gottfried concluded, ending a very somber message.

Cotton started the ritualistic chant.

"One, two, three. Pride!"

Wild Wednesday, October 27, served as an awakening for a team full of newcomers. They had their first lesson on the seriousness of big-time college basketball. Far from the fun and games of Fan Jam or the isolated rigor of pre-season conditioning, the youngsters touched the tip of the iceberg of expectations—the unwavering notions of a highly successful coach about a winning basketball team—and the consequences of falling short of his goals. Gottfried is a player's coach, but he is a winner first and last.

5

Distractions

I ate lunch with the staff almost every day. They probably would have kicked me out if I hadn't provided some humor. We ate lunch at Bryant Hall alongside various members of the football and basketball teams—this small dining hall was open to all students, but they generally opted for more options at Burke Hall. With Gottfried eating elsewhere, the Thursday discussion between Kelsey, Pearson, Boatright, and I centered on whether the head coach had chosen the best option when he returned to make closing comments after leaving the previous practice. Note that the great thing about not being the decision-maker is the chance to be a genius after the fact. (Unlike many insecure coaches, Gottfried actually encourages his assistants to reflect on how they would cope with situations if they were head coach. He considers this kind of discussion an important training tool on the path to a head coaching job.) The consensus was that he should not have gone back. We all loved the impact of his bolting, but we feared that he lost momentum by returning. The assistants did not, however, hear his closing comments which did not exactly stroke any egos.

Kobie Baker coached for Division I Southeast Louisiana the year before. He shared a story that added spice to lunch about a wild experience during their season. A player's parents threw and hit his head coach with hot dogs during a game because he had taken their son out of play. After the game, the father repeatedly told the coach that he would "kick [the coach's] ass," and the mother echoed those sentiments, telling that coach's wife that "I'm gonna kick your ass too, bitch." The player's father went toward his car to grab a gun, but was arrested before he returned. These types of stories dominated our lunch conversations.

The coaching staff had regular meetings, at irregular times. I was only allowed to attend a few of them. The meetings consisted of Pearson, Kelsey, Gottfried, Boatright, Scott, and Baker. They were private, and Gottfried was jealous of their time and content.

The meetings were professional but friendly. The coaches would joke with one another and talk about their days before the meetings officially began. Gottfried always conducted the meetings, occasionally turning them over to Boatright, Kelsey, Pearson, or Scott for comments and feedback.

I had the luxury to attend one of the early staff meetings prior to the exhibition season. Only about a week's practice had gone by at that point, and the coaches were enthusiastic about their prospects. They sat around a regular-sized business table in comfortable chairs.

Pearson and Kelsey started the interchange.

"Well, I'm so far pleased with the players. I think we have this thing headed in the right direction. Erwin, Rod, Meade—all of 'em. We've got good guys. Just need a little toughness," Pearson said.

"We just need to prepare them for the pressure," Kelsey responded. "They've certainly got all the talent they need."

"And all of these guys will listen to us. We don't have any knucklehead-type guys. But they might struggle to adapt to the intensity."

Kelsey agreed. "Like Kenny. You know it's really hard with him. I love the kid to death. He's a great kid. But he's too nice. I've got to push him every day toward being a little nastier."

"As frustrating as coaching youth can be," Gottfried interjected, "I have to say that I'm thrilled about the character of our kids. I agree that they need to be tougher. But they'll get tougher with experience. You can't play the schedule we have and not get tougher. They just need a year of growth. All in all, we're lucky. You guys know how much worse it can be. You look around the country, fellas. Most coaches deal with headache after headache."

As Scott's condition worsened and he inevitably missed meetings, so did the substance of the meetings turn to worries about Scott and his family. At times it seemed more like a concerned group of friends than a collegiate basketball program. Still, the tone of these gatherings was almost always positive and upbeat.

After the previous day's ending, the Tide players seemed curious about how the next practice would begin. Gottfried gathered the players together and began to tell them a story.

"This morning I was in Birmingham visiting with a 41-year-old guy who fainted in his front yard a year ago. He went to the doctor and found out that he has Lou Gehrig's disease. His body just started to basically shut down. Now, a year later, he's in the bed and can only answer by looking toward one of his wife's hands after she says which hand means yes and the other no. We realize how fortunate we all are. How fortunate to come out here and play basketball every day," Gottfried began. "Ambition, guys. Have some ambition. Do you have any? Goals. Dreams. Where do you want to be? What do you want to do? What do you want to accomplish? Being properly focused every day to prove yourself daily. You got nobody watching you closer than me. Don't kid yourself into thinking that it's gonna be easy to get in a plane and fly over to Georgia, or go down to LSU, or go over to Arkansas, or go to Kentucky—and win. Don't think it's gonna be easy. They're not rolling over for you, fellas." He concluded the speech with a clap.

London led an intense defensive stance drill. The guys formed lines and moved their feet with great intensity. Gottfried's stance drill is a perpetual part of his summer basketball camps.

(The drill served him well at UCLA where it was so emphasized that they made basketball shorts with "stance" written on the back. I gladly accepted his old shorts before he trashed them, but I try not to wear them in public too often because I look strange with "stance" covering my buttocks at the post office or the grocery store.)

Gottfried had been talking about the importance of flu shots. Every player and coach received an injection. Boatright relayed a story just before practice about Gottfried telling a player that "if you don't get your flu shot, don't come crying to me when you get the flu."

Terrance Meade struggled in the war rebounding drill. He finally did the ten push-ups required when a player fails to claim three rebounds after an extended period.

(When a player struggles in this particular drill, a sinking feeling sets in. The player's frustration peaks because he can't grab a ball, and he knows that the coach will finally bang the gong and send him to the side.)

Pearson asked Rod if he could "just get one stop" with the guards going one-on-one from the wing. Kelsey had bodies flying around at the other end with the forwards. Gottfried walked over to monitor the forwards. He coached Haginas to face the basket as much as possible.

(He had privately dismissed the possibility that Haginas could score consistently with his back facing the basket. He had tried to softly dance around Haginas's scoring problems. He feared that if he attacked the problem directly, Haginas would just have a bigger mental block.)

Basketball practice was a minor concern for two guys setting up parallel ropes across the top of Coleman Coliseum. They had an object resembling a large bird resting on one end. The thinking man's guess was that the object was built to travel across the ropes. Boatright approached the guys.

"If this thing starts flying across the coliseum, Coach Gottfried will go crazy."

They left disappointed.

Kelsey continued to push his forwards.

"Fight, knock him down or whatever, but he can't catch it there," Kelsey said to Dudley.

With the forwards and guards together again, Gottfried grimaced when he watched Martin hurting after a play.

"You can't hurt Doc. He's made of kryptonite," Gottfried said somewhat sarcastically.

An early turnover in this five-on-five half-court session brought memories of yesterday flooding back.

"We ain't gonna have that crap again today! Value the ball! Value the possession!" Gottfried responded.

The players seemed determined to avoid the previous day's fate. The team was generally more careful with the basketball.

During a water break, Gottfried approached Scott in his chair. Boatright happened to be standing nearby. Scott inquired about a meeting time. Gottfried uncharacteristically set one for 1:30 P.M.

Boatright laughed. "Hey, we've got a meeting time. Good job, Rah Rah."

(Gottfried had been extremely hesitant to set exact meeting times because his job involved so many unpredictable and urgent phone calls. Recruiting high school players is one of the more mercurial and stressful processes in the business. Any related phone call supplying information could be vital. He freely admitted being frustrated as an assistant for Harrick for the very same reason. Boatright had recently confronted Gottfried about the assistants' difficulty with the policy. Gottfried's willingness to listen to Boatright's joking and complaints about this matter reflected his policy that staff members are always allowed to voice their concerns. This time Gottfried dismissed Boatright's laughter with a casual wave of his hand.)

Cotton made several penetrate-and-pitch plays for assists in the closing sequence of practice. After practice, Scott and Gottfried agreed that Cotton was very unselfish when he was playing.

"On the floor, I love him," Scott said.

The conversation turned to the lineup.

"Chances are that Meade will beat Tarik out at some point. If he does beat Tarik, that first start will be a new experience for him. We probably ought to just go ahead and do it now rather than later. But maybe not. He might go out in the first five minutes of the opener and take a dump," the head coach said.

Scott agreed that Meade's initiation would be difficult whenever it happened. He pulled his cap off momentarily. His head was closely shaved. We expressed surprise.

"I thought I would go ahead because it will fall out eventually," he explained.

At the end of practice, Gottfried firmed up plans to take the players to the Stallings Center where a program called R.I.S.E. enriches the lives of Down's Syndrome children. The building is named after Gene Stallings who coached Alabama to its most recent national title in football. Stallings contributes significantly to R.I.S.E. His son has thrived with Down's Syndrome. Gottfried wanted the team to play with the kids.

OCTOBER 29 was an exciting day because of the second formal scrimmage. The first exhibition game would be next week. The teams played a regulation game today. The increased formality and the continuity of teams added competitive tension unlike any other scrimmage. Before the scrimmage, Gottfried discussed the value of recording the action.

"The eye in the sky won't lie. I'm taking that tape home with me tonight."

Kelsey and Boatright co-coached the white team. Scott and Pearson commanded the red. Scott appeared to be feeling better. He attempted humor in the pre-practice period by commenting that "Rod is moving like a turtle" in a drill.

Morr reported to Pearson that red team member Cotton was feeling some discomfort.

"I don't care," a disgusted Pearson responded.

Gottfried addressed the team before beginning the game.

"Take care of the basketball. If an opportunity is not there, keep it and make the sure pass. The definition of a good pass is a completed pass. If I throw it to Soloman and he drops it, then one way or the other it didn't get done. He and I have to play catch."

The red team consisted of Towns, Davis, Hays, Cotton, Martin, London, and Walker.

The white team fielded Meade, Dudley, Haginas, Grizzard, Moss, and Bakken.

The red team resolved the dispute early, rolling to a 46-21 halftime lead. Tired of hearing about the success of Grizzard, Meade, and Dudley in the casual setting of voluntary summer games, London, Martin, and Hays used their experience and intensity to quiet the youngsters. The older guys put the kids to bed early with defensive pressure. Every red player claimed at least two steals except Davis who had little interest in winning the red badge of courage on the defensive end.

Gottfried interrupted the red huddle at the half.

"Keep the defensive pressure up," the head coach interjected between Pearson's comments.

"That's where we're getting it done. I don't know how many points we've gotten off turnovers, but it's a bunch. Keep it up," Pearson echoed.

The white team managed only one moderate surge, closing the gap to 12 with 8:17 left with a three-pointer by Meade. On the following trip, Haginas retreated from the ball in Martin's hands to guard somebody else, and Martin calmly stroked a three-pointer from the wing to terminate white's hopes. Kelsey exploded in disbelief.

"We work and work to cut the lead to twelve, and you just leave Doc Martin wide open with the ball! What are you doing?"

Meade and Grizzard combined for 50 points in the loss. Moss added 12 points and 11 rebounds for the white team who did not have another player score in double figures. Martin and Cotton led the red with 17 points. Hays added 16 points and eight rebounds. Walker added 15 points and eight rebounds. London may have been the most valuable player with nine assists, one turnover, and seven points. London's defensive assignment, Meade, had seven turnovers.

Gottfried announced that the team would not practice on the weekend.

"I don't want you to break down your conditioning this weekend. You guys have gotten yourself in pretty good shape. We're getting there. And we're not taking two days off so you can stay up until five in the morning running around and lose what you've gained. Get some rest. Mentally and physically, you walk in here on Monday ready to go. You play next Friday. There is a team coming in here Friday. And then another on Monday. And we open on the following Saturday. It's coming."

I'm not exactly sure how the coaches spent their weekend, but I know it involved their usual rain of activities: watching video tapes, scouting high school players, reading pre-season reports on other SEC teams, and other, more personal activities. I don't have any idea how the players spent their free time. The month of October ended with two days off.

BAKKEN began November practice on Monday with a forearm in his face from Towns in a negotiate-the-trap drill. Pearson especially enjoyed this drill because it creates some intensity in the pre-practice period and helps the guys when they're being trapped by two defenders in Fayetteville, Arkansas, with 20,000 people screaming.

Cotton was out with butt discomfort, left nipple discomfort, left knee discomfort from jumper's knee, and a left shin contusion. I asked Morr to identify his worst injury.

"They're all bad. I'm surprised he's alive today," Morr replied.

His sarcasm revealed a constantly growing frustration. Fully aware of Cotton's extensive injury history during the summer, Morr had been supremely confident that he could handle the roller-coaster ride. But he seemed almost overwhelmed at this point. He often joked about not making it through the season. Morr felt the pressure of a disappointed Gottfried staring through him every time he performed his duty and reported that Cotton chose not to practice.

Gottfried opened practice with a long commentary on the scrimmage. He mentioned too many turnovers and insufficient help-side defense. Cotton was criticized along with Haginas for poor defensive rebounding. Cotton was criticized along with Grizzard for poor offensive rebounding.

After a few drills, students entered the gym with large equipment for the second time in three days. They carried a giant slingshot made to toss t-shirts into the crowd for the volleyball team. Gottfried's eyes opened wide in disbelief. He had a habit of doing this whenever he was annoyed. Boatright quickly chased the students out of the Coliseum.

Agitated, Boatright quipped about the incursion. "I'd like to see them try that stunt at football practice. I'd like to see them try and walk into

Nolan Richardson's practices with big experiments every other day."

Practice continued in spite of the interruption. Soloman Davis pulled the trigger quickly on a 22-foot shot, three seconds into a possession.

"Patience, Soloman. Patience. Patience," Gottfried said in a subdued tone.

Two consecutive turnovers.

"Take care of the ball! I'm gonna find five guys that take care of the basketball! I'm gonna find five guys that can!" Gottfried exclaimed angrily.

After another bad turnover, Hays launched an intensely contested jump shot 15 from the basket just five seconds into the possession.

"We're gonna get some good shots, fellas! We better start playing like a team! Handle the ball! Take care of the ball! Get a great shot! You can't jack it up with a guy's elbow down your throat!" Gottfried exploded.

A poor pass by Hays led to another turnover. Gottfried just bowed his head. Two more ugly turnovers. Gottfried sent the team to the baseline. It was time to run sprints. Thankfully for the players, they all finished on time.

Back to action and a voice from a group battling for rebounding position complained about being pushed. Most, if not all, coaches do not sympathize with that kind of complaint.

Gottfried is no exception. "We need to make sure to call Northern Iowa and tell them to not push us in the game, Coach Boatright." Northern Iowa was their first scheduled opponent.

Not uncharacteristically, Davis pushed the envelope with an extremely contested jump hook shot.

"What kind of shot was that?" Gottfried inquired, throwing his hands up in the air.

Davis found his role complicated because he was often asked to imitate the opponent's most trigger-happy player. During the nonconference season, there are inevitably smaller school players who will shoot like they breathe. Davis truly enjoyed imitating them in practice.

With Gottfried attempting to build his team, the last thing that he needed was a guy taking wild shots on every trip. The dreadful result can be a phenomenon that Coach Jim Harrick liked to call "catching the disease." He coined that phrase about playing Paul Westhead's Loyola Marymount teams whose rapid fire exploits were notorious. Westhead's team was always terrible on defense. They could not defend a brief case full of one hundred dollar bills. But they had a sneaky ability to lure their opponent into a high pace game full of short possessions. They played that way all the time so it was almost impossible to beat them at their own game. Harrick thoroughly dominated Westhead by preaching the virtues of not trying the shots that those crazy guys are taking. Do not catch the disease. Gottfried tried to prevent Davis from spreading the disease to the rest of his team.

After Gottfried escaped one November day without cardiac arrest, the next day presented the third major disturbance in four days. Over 50 German exchange students appeared to watch some of practice. We were utilizing the practice gym behind Coleman Coliseum when the exchange students walked in. In the much smaller gym, 50 people looking on was much harder to ignore. Gottfried's eyes opened very wide when they entered, and, given the context of a series of practice disturbances, I had to turn my head to restrain my laughter. Boatright, once again, ushered the students out of the gym with a few quips about protocol and etiquette. I'm not sure the students understood him.

(Gottfried's generosity occasionally leaves him in strange predicaments. A YMCA athletic director called last year to request permission to attend practice before the all-important Auburn game. Gottfried agreed. Practice is generally open anyway, and this visitor had attended practice earlier in the year. The visitor forgot to mention that he was bringing around 75 people. Alabama happened to be practicing in the so-called "back gym" that day as well. Gottfried eyes nearly swallowed his head. He ordered Boatright to ask them politely to leave. Wimp Sanderson would have chuckled at that situation because he was so secretive about preparing for Auburn. Gottfried closed practice on the following day for the first time.)

Gottfried began the pre-practice huddle by criticizing the players for having failed to arrive in time to warm-up before practice.

"When we go on the road in the SEC, I need to know who I can count on. I will play the guys I can count on. Last year when number three Kentucky came in here, I played the guys who I could count on because I know how they will perform. I need somebody I can count on to come in and work hard every day. If I can't count on you, then I'm not playing you."

That introduction seemed to be aimed at Cotton. He even had to signal for Cotton to join the huddle before talking. Cotton appeared to be a million miles away. Gottfried probably could have shoved Cotton down, and it would not have grabbed the player's attention. When practice began, Cotton sat on a chair in the corner with his injured foot. Sitting in the corner of the gym with a look of loneliness, the team's best scorer was completely isolated from his teammates.

John Morr looked like the loser of a prize fight. He had received a phone call from Schea's father, James Cotton, at 11:30 P.M. James monitored his son's injury status closely. The conversations between Morr and Mr. Cotton were cordial. Determined to meet the challenge, Morr had been logging substantial overtime to treat Cotton at the player's convenience. The calls from Cotton's parents were invited by Morr. His face revealed regret. His typical 12-hour work days had stretched even longer. He admitted that he was not getting enough sleep because of stressing about his job.

In a span of ten minutes, four players were sent to Morr because they were bleeding. Hays followed them with a big toe injury.

"For God sakes, they're falling apart," Morr joked. I'm not entirely convinced, however, that he was really joking.

Taking a close look at Hays, Morr made a quick decision to send him for an X-ray immediately.

"I guess I need a new trainer," Gottfried joked as he stopped momentarily to monitor his team's developing medical problems. He laughed heartily at his comment. It was not meant to be taken seriously. Still, Morr was a little disheartened.

"I will lose my job by the end of the week," Morr said to me as he led

Hays out of the gym.

Rod casually jogged down the floor.

"Rod, you've go to go. I want you to run! I want you running! You're not playing for Princeton! This is the Crimson Tide," Gottfried barked.

Gottfried loves the idea of Alabama running the floor in offensive transition. If his college coach, Sanderson, completely sold him on anything, it was that cheap baskets are like gold.

"Rah Rah" Scott stayed relatively active. He periodically left his chair to give instructions. Kelsey asked about his ability to sleep. Scott happily replied that every morning he woke up "feeling rested."

Bakken fell out of a drill in pain.

"I took a knee to the dick," Bakken said while gritting his teeth. Doubled over, he limped off the court. Nobody stopped to check on him. Practice continued around him. I had learned early on that if there wasn't blood or a substantial injury, it was not serious and practice would not stop.

As practice neared a conclusion, the managerial staff noticed a visitor who looked like Barry Switzer, legendary former football coach of the Oklahoma Sooners and the Dallas Cowboys. Gottfried noticed Switzer, and they exchanged warm greetings. Because of his close relationship with his uncle Mike (ESPN college football color commentator), Gottfried can always talk about a mutual acquaintance with football coaches. Switzer, who was traveling with a friend, agreed to speak to the team. Switzer won three national titles at Oklahoma (more than any active coach and equal to Bobby Bowden and Steve Spurrier combined) and thoroughly dominated Tom Osborne at Nebraska before leaving for the NFL's Dallas Cowboys, where he won a Super Bowl Championship over the Cowboys' nemesis, the Pittsburgh Steelers. He is one of only two men to win a Super Bowl and a college championship and is quite simply the most accomplished college football coach over the last 25 years.

Gottfried introduced him and asked him to show the players his Super Bowl ring. It is gigantic—beyond gaudy like most professional championship rings.

"Six-and-a-half carrots," Switzer said as the team laughed. "Your coach and I were visiting and he asked me whether I liked pro or college better. Obviously to me, it was the collegiate game because of the people you're dealing with. You're dealing with 18-, 19-, 21-year-old men. Coaching to a lot of people, whether it's basketball or football—and I'll relate it to football—people think it's winning a whole bunch of football games every Saturday in the fall. Many of the alumni and fans think that's all that coaching is. Coaching is dealing for 365 days a year with those 18-, 19-, 21-year-old men, trying to prepare them for the next 30 to 50 years of living. That's what college coaching is all about. I know that's how I felt when I dealt with my players because we cared. We really do care about you. We want you to be successful. That's why we give you all the resources to be successful in the college atmosphere. Hell yes, we want to win. You want to win. We all work together to make that happen. You know what it takes to win ball games. But coaches care.

"The professional game is entirely different. You're dealing with older men. Some of them are 34 years old. They've got millions of dollars. It's a business for them. They dictate and control the game. Coaches don't anymore. But the college game—you're so fortunate, you're so damn lucky to be here. Take advantage of your opportunities. I don't know how many of you will ever make it to the professional ranks. I hope you do. But take advantage of these resources. I want to relate something that Coach Bryant always said when he walked into meetings. He would say 'have you called you called or written your momma today?' and a few guys would raise their hands. And he would say 'I wish I could.' I think the message is take advantage of your opportunities. Take care of your family. Be a good person. Be a good citizen. That's what it's all about anyway. Have a smile on your face. Say yes sir, no sir, yes ma'am, and no ma'am. Sh—, that will carry you a long way in life—a hell of a lot more than you'll ever get out of any f—ing books. I know what I'm talking about. Be a good person. Take care of yourself."

Switzer was a momentary distraction from nagging injuries. Cotton's foot was hurting. It was the latest in what was becoming a grocery list of injuries. According to Cotton, he had more aches and pains than some guys who were at Valley Forge. The good news was that Hays came back with a negative X-ray report on his big toe from the doctor. Gottfried decided to take Wednesday off to heal some wounds and let the players recuperate.

College coaches have a hectic life. I had no idea how hectic until I tasted a slice of Gottfried's life on a Tuesday night, joining him on the University of Alabama plane for a booster function. The job of a big-time college coach is never done. Leaving the room to answer nature's call during the question-and-answer session, I noticed a woman beginning a question. When I returned, the same woman was still asking questions. Gottfried is a predictably talented public speaker, but he often grows tired of the constant barrage of demands for his services. Although important, events such as this one tear him away from his home. The traveling keeps him away from his family. Flying is a luxury. Most of the time he drives around the state, performing his duty as an ambassador of Alabama basketball with maintained excitement night after night. The evening was long and tiring. He spent Wednesday doing paperwork, recruiting, scouting, and planning for the rest of the week's practices. During the day, he played a variety of roles: administrator, inspirational speaker, coordinator, captain, fundraiser, coach, surrogate father, and supporter. I grew tired just watching him.

BY THURSDAY, November 4, Gottfried had decided to give the starting point guard role to the freshman Meade.

"We're in trouble if he's not starting by league play so we should give him 12 starts to prepare for the league," Gottfried said to the other coaches before practice.

Kelsey disagreed with Gottfried, and he boldly stated that he was not afraid to fight for his argument. (During this conversation, I was once again amazed by Gottfried's encouragement of an open dialogue with his staff. Like Jim Harrick, he sits in the middle of his staff during games to better receive their thoughts.) Kelsey was concerned about Meade's confidence during the season when he would make the inevitable freshman mistakes and be potentially forced out of the starting role. Kelsey believed the better decision was to make him earn the job by his play, giving him more confidence. Neither man could have guessed that the point guard position wasn't Meade's best role regardless.

"Tom should go get a resumé and find his own job," Gottfried jokingly responded.

Gottfried was not joking later, however, while in the coaches' locker room. He was irritated with Matt Minor—who had called a play in practice that day.

"Tell Matt that the check for the assistant coaching job he does is in the mail. The next time he wants to coach, tell him what happened to Adam Stevens when he tried to coach this team," Gottfried said. I laughed at this remark. Gottfried didn't.

The next morning, Meade complained of back pain early in practice. He had a back spasm, but Morr hoped that an injection before the exhibition game tomorrow would solve the problem. Gottfried faced the reality that he might not be able to start Meade.

Other complications occurred afterward. Grizzard inadvertently hit Haginas in the face during a non-contact drill. Haginas complained of blurred vision and blood on his teeth. Half the guys in practice were fighting laughter because it was a non-contact drill that disabled "Hag." Meanwhile, Cotton entered with the aid of crutches. (Pearson earlier told me that Cotton had described his pain as "excruciating" in a strained manner as if the pain was disabling his ability to speak. Pearson's sarcasm about Cotton's injury reflected a growing sentiment on the team.) Morr stated that Cotton had reported his pain level as ten on a scale of one to ten, with ten being near the worst agony that a human being could feel.

(I later asked Morr how he felt about this. He responded by saying that he was familiar with worker's compensation law and that this kind of thing would have gotten him fired by an employer.)

"I should give him some magic rub," Gottfried said so that Cotton could hear.

Gottfried showed mock surprise and extreme excitement when Cotton walked around twice without the crutches.

Given Meade's back problems, Morr had lost his sense of humor.

"We have nine people practicing, seven of whom are scholarship players. [Long pause] I've talked to Schea's parents more than my own parents recently. If I get fired, I truly won't be surprised," Morr said.

Growing frustrated with Grizzard's lack of toughness at this point, Gottfried said to me loud enough for Rod to hear, "Rod should be sent up with your boy, Bobby Knight, to toughen him up for a little while." (Gottfried and his staff often enjoyed teasing me about my special appreciation for Bobby Knight's coaching ability. When Indiana wins, one would think our staff does not read the newspaper. When Indiana loses, I become instantly popular.) The strategy underlying that remark was probably that a player's coach like Gottfried should be appreciated and performed for because he chooses not to be extremely harsh like Knight. Or maybe he wanted Grizzard to know that it could get worse.

With an exhibition game looming, Gottfried brought the team into the player's lounge to discuss the opponent as he would do throughout the season with the help of videotape.

The session was less formal because the upcoming game was against a traveling team, and the outcome would not count on the record. Arnelle Hamilton, a former Gottfried player at Murray State and a local television reporter, joined the team. He remarked about the high quality of the facilities.

(Gottfried had the player's lounge and the adjacent locker room completely redecorated. It was desperately needed. Two new sofas and two matching large chairs surround a big-screen television and entertainment center. Pictures of past Alabama basketball greats cover the wall. The eyes of McDyess, Sprewell, Horry, and many others looked down on the team.)

"If you give me a reason to put a curfew on this team. I'll put one on it. If I ever hear that someone sees one of you past 11 or 11:30—if somebody walks in and says 'hey I saw Schea Cotton at the disco last night at 2 A.M'—on the night before you play, then what you're telling me is that what we're doing here is not real important. If you're that kind of player, then you're on the wrong team. You need to go somewhere else and play. I want guys that are serious about what we're doing. You've got to have discipline. There's nothing that you need to be doing after 11:30

at night that you can't do in your apartment. I want you in bed getting rest. I may call you and see how you're doing. I want to treat you like adults, but if you behave like a child, then I'll treat you like a child. Tomorrow, we're gonna shoot at two o'clock. We will typically walk through a lot of what the other team does, but we're not gonna do a lot of that tomorrow." Gottfried stopped, interrupted by the ring of Hamilton's cell phone. Gottfried's eyes opened a little wider.

Hamilton was teased before the lecture continued.

"This team we're playing tomorrow has some good players. You might remember Clifton Cook from Texas A&M. Jeron Roberts is playing with them. Roberts averaged about 22 a game with Wyoming. They've got a bunch of real good ex-college guys. They've got Litterial Green. Litterial Green came into Pauley Pavilion when he was playing for Georgia and lit us up for 38. That was with Magic Johnson sitting in the front row. That's the team you're playing tomorrow. So we shoot at two o'clock. We're gonna eat at 3 o'clock at Bryant Hall. We'll go right from here to there. At about 3:30 or 4 o'clock in another room—it's not mandatory—if you want to come, we're doing a devotional. I'd love for you to come. If you don't, that's okay too. Don't feel pressured to be there. And then at 6:20, be taped and ready in the locker room. We will usually meet 40 minutes before the tip-off of all home games."

6

Exhibition Season

"Shoot-around" or "walk-through" is more formal than those names might indicate. It is a simple practice the morning of the game. The assistant coach charged with scouting the opposing team directs the players to defend certain plays that the opponent has been using in previous games. Although the team has defensive tactics that it uses regardless of the opponent, the hope is that seeing the plays will prepare the players to apply those tactics better to the opponent's tendencies. Also, some defensive tactics will vary.

For example, a poor perimeter shooter will obviously be guarded differently than an effective one. Tactics will also change based on the overall tendencies of the opponent. If a team does a phenomenal job of entering the ball to the low-post area around the basket, then there might be emphasis on a certain tactic to disrupt their strength, such as having the guards sink toward the low-post or asking the guards to be super active while pressuring a potential passer to the low-post. A great perimeter shooting team might use many screens far away from the basket. So there has to be a strategy to negotiate those screens to challenge the dreaded assault of three-pointers. "Walk-through" allows the coaches to polish the team's defensive approach for a specific game. The session is also called a "shoot-around" because the other principal activity is shooting. The hope is that mind and body will be better able to perform five hours from now because of these earlier repetitions. That day's "walk-through" focused very little on the opponent. If Litterial Green scored 38 points in the game, Alabama would be 0-0 regardless.

The pre-game home meal was served at Bryant Hall. It looked much different than usual. The tables were covered with nice silverware. Steak and chicken were the entree options. By design, the room is relatively quiet. I had to watch my tone of voice once or twice during the meal when Gottfried intentionally irritated me with a comment to test my temper.

With his appetite nonexistent, Scott loaded his plate anyway. He nibbled for a while. Finally surrendering to his inability to eat, he asked for a to-go plate. Shane Kelley, a baseball coach for the Kansas City Royals, joined us for the meal. He was scheduled to be the guest speaker at the devotional.

Team chaplain Bill Overstreet would deliver most of the devotionals throughout the season. (Home devotionals are held in the large room outside the Bryant Hall cafeteria. All the players attended the first devotional.) Kelley told the team that an athlete needed a third of his preparation for competition to be spiritual. The players listened quietly. (With no intention of investigating the fundamental beliefs of our players, I wondered if they all remained for the first devotional because they would be embarrassed to bolt. Gottfried had aggressively pushed the notion of a voluntary devotional with a separate room. He feared the legal consequences of confusing the players by having the devotional seem mandatory.)

The results of Cotton's bone scan had not returned. Morr believed that he was very capable. Gottfried asked Cotton in the locker room before the game if he was ready.

"I don't think I'm ready to go," Cotton replied in a very soft tone.

Gottfried walked out hurriedly and slammed the door.

Morr told Gottfried that the injection had not helped Meade's back. Two would-be starters would not play. Gottfried struggled to hide his disgust with the situation. The active players could not have guessed their head coach's mood by his body language.

The routine was the same for every home game. John Morr spends the hours before a game waiting for the players to arrive. The players meet Morr at their discretion to have their ankles taped. Every player is dressed in uniform and taped with 40 minutes left before the game. The players are seated in a chair facing a white board when the clock above the board counts down to 40. The chairs are close together, forming a half-circle. While coaches and managers stand farther from the board than the players, Robert Scott used a chair this season. "Look up," Gottfried likes to say. The players focus on the assistant scouting the game who delivers the final scouting report. The left side of the board is covered with the comments about each player on the opponent's roster, keys to success that are unique against this opponent, and drawings of basketball courts with markings indicating some of the planned offensive movements that the opponent has used in earlier games. The assistant coach will address the team on the left-side material. The right side is covered with drawings of Alabama's planned offensive movements that Gottfried has chosen to focus on for this game and keys to the game that tend to be more general. After the assistant finishes his comments about today's enemy, Gottfried delivers the first of two pre-game commentaries about what he thinks the team needs to do to win. He will usually add comments relating to the assistant's scouting report before reviewing his offensive game plan. Then he will make some general comments and a motivational plea for great effort. Gottfried will conclude with the team clapping and coming together. Everybody places their hands together, forming the familiar stack of outstretched arms. The Lord's Prayer is recited. One of the veterans follows with the chant of his choice.

The team hurries out of the locker room with Gottfried behind them, yelling "Warm-up hard." The players jog down the hall. If the photography room is open at the end of the hall, a gigantic picture of a young "Bear" Bryant stares at them. They turn left. The dance team greets them enthusiastically while the ladies finish their stretching. Then the team comes together while jumping up and down, forming a mass of humanity. Finally, they run into the coliseum with the band playing the fight song and the crowd cheering. The assistants generally join the team for the warm-up. The head coach gathers his thoughts alone in preparation for battle.

The warm-up is a routine of fundamentals. Dribbling, passing, and shooting in a formal environment prepares their minds and bodies. The warm-up ends with around ten minutes left before the game. The players jog back to the locker room and sit down.

"Look up," Gottfried says, indicating that he is ready to speak. The head coach delivers his shortened version of a scouting report. The opponent's roster is on the left side of the board again but in bigger letters. Gottfried uses the rest of the board for the final version of five or six keys to winning the game and anything else he wishes to address. The staff and players come together for a final chant. The players hurry out of an excited locker room while coaches grab their dress coats. After the last coach finishes a quick trip to a locker room urinal, the coaches have their ritualistic uniting of hands. Gottfried makes a noise resembling a soldier beginning a marching cadence. The players jog down the same path. Before entering the coliseum, the players begin jumping again to form the same mass of bodies with much greater intensity than before the warm-up. They chant "Bust that head"—or some other chant—as they do so. The team finally enters the coliseum again; the band plays the fight song as they run out.

This routine would be adhered to every home game that year.

Pearson's final scouting report for the Next Level All-Stars was predictably very basic.

"Just like we talked about—three out [on the perimeter] and two in [near the basket trying to post], they'll play a lot of that, guys. They'll look to penetrate in here [dribbling] and get you to help [leave your original assignment in an effort to stop that dribbler]. Then, they'll pitch it to a guy [farther away from the basket who has been momentarily ignored because of the dangerous dribbler moving toward the basket]. They've got a big old white guy, Odoms, who will be down there working very hard on the block. He won't be afraid to put his elbow on your chin. He's gonna be a load down there."

He continued by describing certain plays utilized by the opponent, concluding with out-of-bounds plays. This will be the format of the scouting report all year, but the material was obviously limited for a traveling exhibition team.

Gottfried stepped forward when the assistant finished.

"Purposely, we didn't go over a lot of their stuff. We've got a lot more written down, but I'm not gonna do all that for this game. From day one, we've worked on being in a stance down low. We've worked on talking. We've worked on moving. And I just want you to go out there and play defense. That's what I am going to watch . . . Knowing they're a bunch of guys out of college, they probably ain't taking a long time to shoot the ball. It's going up, fellas. They're probably not going to pass it twelve or fifteen times. Two or three passes and it's probably up."

Gottfried stressed defense and rebounding. He had recruited young talent that had the ability to create their own shots if their teammates were unable to help them find an opening. He did not want that offensively, but it was a viable option. Not being able to guard the opponent, however, was not a viable option. The team was not ready defensively. We all knew it. Pre-season practice could not provide the experience necessary to prepare this group. And like the army officer with inferior numbers, Gottfried attempted to hide his weakness.

He transitioned back into motivation after discussing rebounding, transition, and offense.

"Everything counts. Everything counts. You wanna be a great team? Then, you need to start acting like it right now. We've got a bunch of older guys coming in here. They're 28, 29, and 30 years old. They know how to play. They're big and strong. They are a veteran group. Most of them have played in the NBA or overseas . . . You come in here and have some toughness. Start making a statement about your team." Clapping signaled the end of his message.

While the team warmed up, Gottfried spoke very little, and then only under unusual circumstances. He makes the final decisions about his total approach to the game in the solitude of an empty locker room. (Sharing the room with him as I have done several times, this game was different—he decided to reveal his frustration about his university's treatment of basketball. The Coliseum's parking lot had been closed at

2:30 P.M. for the army of recreational vehicles that utilize the lot during home football weekends. The woman supervising the parking lot would not allow Gottfried to enter the parking lot. He told her that he was the basketball coach. Her response was "basketball what?" Finally, she cooperated. He cruised toward his designated parking spot until he met a barricade. So Alabama's head basketball coach climbed out of his Cadillac and moved the barricade, trying not to ruin his suit. Apparently, the university had decided not to bother with staffing the facility with game management personnel for the exhibition game. Gottfried even played the role of usher when the player's parents had no idea where to sit. Furthermore, the exhibition game has been poorly covered by the local newspaper, the *Tuscaloosa News*. Gottfried felt like his program was being ignored—a common experience for non-revenue producing sports or smaller colleges—but not at the historically second best men's basketball program in the SEC.)

The team returned. He delivered his own scouting report which essentially highlighted critical areas.

"All I know is that I was sitting on the bench in L.A. when he [Green] gave us 38. Magic was right there. He played in the NBA for four or five years. He's gonna be looking to score a lot. He's a strong little guy. And he can shoot it from deep, deep, deep . . . I don't care very much about them. I'm interested in us. I'm going to be watching us closely. I'll take the tape home tonight and break it down to find out where we are . . . We've got a couple of guys out tonight. Everybody step up and play . . . The last thing for every game, guys, is that I can get up here and give you great speeches. We can get all emotional. But you've got to find it within yourself to play hard all the time. When the game is over, look in the mirror and be able to tell yourself that you played as hard as you can play . . . You wanna play on this team? Show me! Talk is cheap, fellas. You make the decisions about who plays—by your play . . . Just make a statement. What kind of team are we? You can be a soft team. You can be a lazy team. Or you can be a hard-nosed, tough team that wants to win. That's the kind of team you ought to be. You guys decide. It's on you."

The team came together clapping for the bonding of hands. The group recited the Lord's Prayer. This routine, also, was followed every game.

An energetic crowd gave the team an enthusiastic hand. Tony Giles, the public address announcer, brought the crowd to their feet with his enthusiastic introduction of the starting lineup which was Grizzard, Dudley, Hays, London, and Martin. Hays made the first bucket of the season, and the Tide built a substantial early lead despite several fouls. Gottfried decided to substitute liberally with Towns, Walker, and Haginas. The substitutes killed momentum. Defensive intensity disappeared like the air leaving a deflating balloon. Towns launched two perimeter shots that missed the goal—probably nerves. From point blank range, Haginas fired an airball of his own with a flip shot that he used too often last year from the coaching staff's point of view. As the game progressed, the team fouls continued to mount—a product of slow footwork unlike the early fouls that were errors of aggression. After shooting 11 of 15 from the foul line, the Next Level All-Stars trailed only 34-31 at halftime.

Before Gottfried addresses the team at halftime, the coaching staff always has a brief meeting. For home games, the staff meets in the players' lounge. Typically, the staff has a short conversation while Gottfried makes brief comments to the players on his way to the restroom. Then the coaches and Gottfried bounce their ideas about the particular game at each other before going to talk to the players. If the team is playing well, these meetings can be relaxed, even fun. If the team is playing poorly, this time is most often tense and frustrating. Regardless, those minutes during halftime were always spent trying to maximize the other team's problems while trying to minimize Alabama's.

Boatright and Baker gather statistics during the game so they are usually busy tallying the numbers. When Gottfried enters the staff meeting, he always wants the statistics. That game, he was concerned about his team's 35% shooting in the first half.

"We've missed a bunch of shots," Gottfried said, scanning the stats sheets.

However, a moment of deep thought about the opponents' comeback changed his focus. "We lost our defensive intensity by subbing everybody."

After a few more minutes of deliberating, Gottfried and his staff walked toward the door of the locker room.

"You better get some life in your game. Some enthusiasm. Have some fun and get excited about playing. That's the one thing you've got to do. [Yelling] Man, get down and play and have some fun! Good night! You guys run up and down like it's a morgue out there. Holy Cow."

Next Level had success with a play initiated by a screen for a dribbling Green where he has been able to turn the corner with an edge on his defender and break the defense down by forcing other defenders to help. Gottfried discussed the negotiation of that play. He finished the way he started.

"Get excited about playing!"

Despite 22 points from Rod Grizzard in his first game wearing an Alabama uniform and 21 from the veteran Hays, the Tide never landed the knockout blow in regulation. Five for 13 foul shooting in the second half did not help. Meanwhile, Green carved the Red Elephants, playing high screen and roll with Ray Thompson, a former Oral Roberts player. Green and Thompson combined for 34. Also, the Tide continued to struggle with its defensive footwork, fouling repeatedly. As the game neared its conclusion, Green began taunting the Tide players. His energy translated to the rest of his aging traveling team. Hays tried to assert his veteran leadership and help the Tide prevail, sinking one of two free throws to tie the game at 65-65 with 51 seconds remaining. Regulation time expired with the score tied, 65-65.

The defensive woes continued in overtime, as the Tide surrendered 11 points in the short five-minute period. Dudley, Grizzard, and Hays, who had combined for 53 of the Tide's points, fouled out of the game. With the Tide trailing by two and time running out, London drove the paint, spun, and scored on a spectacular play to send the game to double overtime. Martin, who had played every minute of the game, remained with London to lead a team now missing all five of the men who would have started until injuries changed the script. Remarkably, the Tide somehow managed to own a one-point lead with time expiring in double overtime. Next Level's penetration broke down the defense one final time and Jeron Roberts, a former Wyoming Cowboy, shot Alabama right between the eyes on a three-pointer from the corner. A humiliated Tide was defeated in an exhibition game by a group of journeymen who had certainly not been prepared for a passionate fight when the night started.

If the outcome was a forerunner of results to come, I needed to purchase a specially made safety seat and buckle up for a scary ride.

Gottfried walked into a quiet locker room—the sound of defeat is the silence of a locker room after a loss. Some of the players' heads were tilted downward.

"Look up. Foul shooting was the difference in the game. Some of you guys who can't make 26 out of 30 so you're running everyday. You need to be shooting more. You've got to practice your foul shooting all the time. If you can't make free throws, it's hard for me to play you. If you need to come early and shoot an extra hundred, then you need to come in the morning and find a way. We should be a great foul shooting team . . . We had a lot of chances to win. We just didn't. [Extremely long pause and you could hear a pin drop on the carpet] Opportunities, fellas. What you do with your opportunities makes all the difference. [Another long pause] I'm gonna find five guys that will get down and play some defense. Five guys that will rebound. We can talk about running the fast break and that crap, but if we can't guard . . . we're not gonna have a good year. It will be tough to beat folks . . . Games always come down to defense, rebounding, and foul shooting—all the time. Tonight, we didn't do those things very well. We didn't do 'em very well at all. Why do we have so many guys foul out? Because the referees are terrible? No! Because you're not down and moving your feet . . . Maybe we're not running enough. I can fix that. We've got ten fouls in both halves before you can blink. We just whack guys. Put our hands all over a guy and push 'em. Foul 'em. That's why they're shooting so many foul shots. Litterial Green is fat and dumpy. He's fat and out of shape." Gottfried's disgust over the loss was apparent.

After finishing his post-game message, Gottfried typically gives his assistants a chance to speak. His staff had nothing to say that night. They concluded with a prayer from Hays who was considering a career involving the church. This was probably not be the only prayer involving his team that Gottfried offered.

There's nothing like a Saturday morning practice at 9 A.M. after losing an exhibition game. On my one-hour commute from Birmingham, I pondered how many Alabamians would read their sports page close enough on the day of an Alabama football game to learn about the exhibition embarrassment. It was no surprise that Coach Scott was the most excited guy in the gym, proclaiming that he would "get after somebody today." I guessed that Scott did not sleep well with that defeat. The practice had a tough tone. Gottfried had the team running sprints early in practice after failing to contest several shots.

Clay Pruitt, a manager who had captivated the imagination of players and staff with his sometimes unusual mannerisms and an often observed high energy approach to his job, purported to be working after only two hours of sleep. David Harrison, a visiting recruit, kept him awake until 5 A.M. playing Nintendo. Hats off to Harrison. Most visiting recruits that are awake at daybreak are participating in more risqué activities.

One of the players reported a leg bruise to Morr. It was worse than Cotton's, but the player decided to play despite the injury because he didn't "want to be like Cotton." The status of Meade's back strain had not changed overnight. Cotton practiced, telling Morr that he was "sucking it up today."

Gottfried placed emphasis on increasing the intensity of their offensive transition. The team was running especially hard in the flanker drill when Cotton suddenly pulled out, limping over for support from the rail separating the floor from the bleachers.

"I want a cortisone shot, but the training staff can't give me one," Cotton said.

While Meade peddled on a stationary bike and Cotton hugged the rail, Scott continued to feel especially energetic, standing up and moving about for long periods of time. Student trainer Kyle Rasco approached Cotton for a consultation. Rasco worked for Morr.

"It's balls to the wall and you gotta suck it up at some point and go," Rasco said.

Cotton did not respond.

Gottfried slammed a ball down to the floor, urging Grizzard to finish with a dunk. "Grizzard! Go up there with some authority!"

Scott fed on Gottfried's energy, jumping out of his chair to coach guys on their defensive stances. Scott's sons, Robert Jr. and Daniel, were watching their father today. Robert Jr. explained to me that his dad had been struggling to eat or drink.

"Start concentrating, fellas," Gottfried insisted at the beginning of the free-throw period. While the players attempted to improve their foul shooting, Gottfried engaged in a long conversation with Cotton.

The visiting recruit was invited to join the team huddle at the end of practice.

"This is David Harrison . . . Where's Clay? Clay, my man had you up until five o'clock in the morning," Gottfried said, triggering raucous laughter.

He concluded practice with a brief statement. "If you're one of those guys running everyday, then you need to be shooting some extra free throws. Get better at it."

AT 2 P.M. on Sunday, Cotton practiced while Meade could not.

The second and final exhibition game was the following day against the Herzegovina Bosnia all-star team, Club Siroki. Richard Dumas, who seemed destined to help the Phoenix Suns to an NBA Championship in '93 before encountering substance abuse problems, played for Club Siroki. Like any other exhibition game the preparation focus remained on the home team. While Hays attempted to lift spirits in the drills, Gottfried spent some time with Meade to keep his mind focused on the team.

Cotton had a big wrap covering the area below his knee.

"It's a placebo with no purpose. It makes him feel comfortable,"

Morr explained to me.

Cotton's bone scan was negative. I asked Morr if he thought it had anything to do with Cotton choosing to practice.

"I don't have a clue. Maybe he's run out of excuses," Morr said. Morr then went on to report that Cotton's father had requested copies of every test that Morr had conducted on Schea.

"I've been trying to get Cotton's issues done. I'm spending so much time on the kid that it's not even funny."

"How is Cotton's rehab going?" I inquired.

"How do you rehab a nonexistent injury?" Morr responded.

Pearson exploded about one of his pet peeves, interrupting our conversation.

"[Yelling] Nobody's opening their mouth! These guys can't see in the back of their head! Call out the screen."

The previous day's efforts to intensify the offensive transition was not paying dividends. The staff was edgy, frustrated.

"I want some guys that will run; If this batch can't do it, I'll recruit some guys that will," Gottfried said.

Kelsey had grown weary of the guards failing to pass the ball to his post players and let them know it. "Erwin, get so open that it embarrasses these guards. I'm tired of Doc and Schea making excuses."

Cotton whispered a response.

Kelsey read his less than receptive body language.

"[Yelling] I'm tired of hearing your excuses, Schea! Make another excuse!" Kelsey exploded.

Cotton seemed challenged by Kelsey's brief tirade. Minutes later, Cotton exploded off the ground, attacking the basket with reckless abandon. Haginas slid in his path late to commit a blocking foul, and Cotton crashed to the floor after reaching an incredible elevation for a man of his size. A worried silence clutched the gym. Morr went to the injured player. The trainer and player engaged in an unpleasant exchange, and Cotton amazingly walked off the floor, rejecting Morr's help. His rugged style of play and certain superman acts like the one we had just witnessed combined with his injury history created the great enigma that was (and still is) Schea Cotton.

Robert Scott arrived with Daniel and his daughter Rahshae. He would have been much more comfortable in bed. If Mark Gottfried or Cynthia or myself or any other caring party could have made the decision for him, he would have stayed in bed. But Scott always called his own shots. The ugly truth, in retrospect, is that we were all selfish because we celebrated his coming by expressing an overwhelming joy to see him everyday. Not that a change in Gottfried's attitude would have impacted the situation. Gottfried told Scott when he was diagnosed that his job was safe if he never came. If every person in the world who loved him had told him to stay home, Scott still would have fought to join the players everyday. That was the kind of person Scott was.

In what seemed like a rejection of Kelsey's theory about the team's difficulties with passing the ball to post players, Gottfried exploded about lack of work by the forwards.

"[Yelling] They don't want it! They do not want it! So don't give it to 'em! Just shoot it every time! Don't give it to 'em. They just want to stand up and be small and not post up for the ball."

When Cotton jumped back into practice, he did so with a vengeance. He shot the first pass that he was thrown and drilled a 22-footer. On the following offensive trip, he rocked Hays with a hard, legal screen and followed it up with a forearm to Hays's chest. Minutes later, he shoved Haginas in the back, jolting the big forward. Cotton nailed Moss with a forearm moments later. Moss responded with a fierce forearm to the delight of his teammates. Gottfried ended the scrimmage immediately after Cotton drilled Hays again with a borderline screen.

After shooting free throws, Cotton hesitated to join the team huddle.

"Step in here, Schea. Come on. I like you competing. I want you competing. And if you're really competing, then every now and then you're gonna lose your temper. But any team of mine will leave that right here. When you walk through that door and head back there, it doesn't go anywhere else. We're all trying. We all get frustrated and lose our temper. That's fine. But you don't carry it off the gym floor with you because I won't let anything eat this team up, fellas. We will become a strong, strong unit. The game tomorrow night, guys—they're gonna be shooting jumpers and running around, kicking and grabbing you. They'll play dirty and that's just the way European guys play. I've been over there about five times and played against a bunch of teams. After tomorrow night, it's a whole different ball game. We need to come and play strong defensively and start playing the way we want to be playing. Anything over there, Coach Scott?"

"Come ready to play tomorrow," Scott said from his chair. "Just come ready to play."

At the shoot-around on Monday, Morr reported to Gottfried that Meade planned to play.

"And Cotton?" Gottfried asked.

"I don't have a clue."

Cotton had distanced himself from most of his teammates and Morr. Morr reported that Cotton had been grumbling about Haginas under-cutting him in practice, claiming that Haginas did it on purpose. Gottfried's speech apparently had not moved Cotton to leaving stuff on the court. To be completely fair, however, I would have bet my car that the rest of the players were complaining about Cotton when they went home, too.

Kelsey scouted Club Siroki. The scouting report had changed radically because news arrived that Dumas suffered a serious injury and would not play. Kelsey warned that the Tide faced another test against constant and determined dribble penetration.

Gottfried chose this shoot-around to comment on motivation.

"Don't wait for the coach to get you excited about playing. That's your job. Get yourself mentally ready to come out here with great focus and attention. We're not jacking around here."

Because of the first game embarrassment, the club found itself surrounded by a sense of urgency unexpected for the exhibition season. Kelsey's discussion of defending their penetrate-and-pitch action had an urgent tone.

Gottfried oozed with confidence about his knowledge of the opponent. "Typical European team, guys. The next thing you know they'll start dribbling and just try to break our defense down." Concerning the Tide's defensive effort, Gottfried reminded the players that he would review the film.

"If anybody wants to come over to my house at midnight tonight and watch the film, you're more than welcome . . . They're a dribble penetrating team. Guards. Forwards. All of 'em . . . What they're gonna do, Erwin, is stand out there and look at you eyeball to eyeball and try to dribble by you. You just have to have your feet on fire and not let him turn the corner." Dudley nodded his head in acknowledgment.

After Gottfried called them "lazy" because of all the fouls committed against Next Level, he turned to the offensive end. He discussed every option in his high-post offense—a technique that he uses as a simple reminder. He also emphasized entering the ball to the low-post.

"Get down there and put some pressure on somebody."

While the teams warmed up, Gottfried and I stayed in the quiet locker room. He would have preferred not to speak, but humored me by asking what I thought about the game.

"I think they'll get better," I responded.

I was relieved when he did not continue because he would have been laboring to do so.

The team returned.

"Share the ball. If my teammate has a better shot than me, I give it to him. Be an unselfish player. The world is a lot more fun when we are unselfish. Compete . You don't get any do-overs . . . We don't expect you to play without making a mistake. You'll make 'em. That's fine. So will we. Just go play." Gottfried clapped to signal his conclusion. "[Yelling over everybody's clapping] If you can't get excited about playing, you don't need to be at the University of Alabama! Let's go!"

Just moments into the game, Scott set the tone by harshly scolding Dudley for being out of position defensively on the weak side of the floor. So much of college basketball boils down to the awareness of your defensive players when the opponent has the ball on the other side of half-court. The so-called man-to-man of the college game is loaded with zone principles. When people talk about the NBA being a different game, the main reason is that the NBA has a rule that penalizes the use of the standard college man-to-man defense. Scott had zero tolerance for Dudley momentarily disobeying the team's rules on this matter.

Concerned about Meade's injury and unwilling to reward Cotton, Gottfried used the starting lineup from the Next Level game. Two three-pointers by Grizzard and adequate defense sparked a 14-four run to open the game. Hays found his rhythm early, making five of six shots in the half. Cotton entered and shined with several impressive passes and two for three shooting while Meade reacted like a freshman with three massively ugly misses. On the defensive end, Club Siroki's penetrate-and-pitch action paid dividends as Edl Vulic drilled four three-pointers and Damir Vujanovic made two of his own.

With about five minutes to play, Gottfried called down the bench for Cotton to send him back into the game. His eyes nearly popped out of his head when he realized that Cotton wasn't there. (Morr was stretching Cotton in the hall.) After Gottfried was informed about the Dennis Rodman-like situation, Cotton was not retrieved to enter the game. Cotton emerged alongside Morr with 3:10 remaining. Finally, Cotton re-entered the game with just over a minute to play.

By halftime, a lead that was 31-20 had shrunk to 39-36 despite an impressive half of 51.6% shooting and allowing Club Siroki only one free throw attempt. Boatright quickly summarized his shot chart displaying where on the court both teams attempted and made shots.

"We're shooting the lights out. The problem is that they just score at will. Are we that bad defensively?" Gottfried asked his staff.

The staff admitted that their team was just that bad.

"The problem is that we can't pressure the passer because they all just beat us off the dribble. So the passer just sits out there like Joe Montana and waits for guys to come off screens and hit 'em. We can't pressure anybody. Rod can't. They'll just go right past him. They'll go past every guy we've got."

The staff chat ended quickly. Gottfried's initial words to the players projected unhappiness.

"They're shooting 46 percent from the field as a team, guys. Forty-six percent. Forty-six percent. The problem is not on the offensive end, fellas. I really don't know what to tell you. We can play way back on 'em and let them get a running start at you. We just can't guard 'em. Everybody comes to help and they just drop it off and zip one through there. If we can't find a way to not allow a guy to penetrate by moving our feet, then it's not looking good . . . We've got to get down and guard 'em, fellas! Just guard 'em. [Moving his feet vigorously as a demonstration] Slide, slide, slide. We come out and Terrance Meade—they just go right around him. They just dribble around everybody. [Screaming] Good night, guys! We're better than that. We're better . . . Maybe I'm not coaching you enough . . . [Yelling] Are we gonna guard 'em or not? Can we?"

The players responded by only allowing five points in the first 6:36 of the second half. A dunk by Cotton opened the half and five quick points from Hays helped engineer a six-point lead. However, a Vujanovic three-pointer was followed by another 33 seconds later courtesy of Zlat Bacurin. One minute later, Vujanovic made it an eight-two run, tying the game at 49. Gottfried predictably tried to stop the bleeding with a timeout. The Tide finally showed life. Cotton took over the game, scoring 13 points in a 16-two run over a four-minute span. Cotton's lightning-quick first step and his willingness to absorb contact yielded free throw after free throw. The Tide cruised down the stretch to an 80-70 win. London capitalized on Meade's injury at the point guard position with six assists against only two turnovers. More importantly for London, the team got high percentage shots and had less turnovers than assists. Meade played only four minutes in the second half.

Despite the win, Gottfried abstained from any celebration.

"I'm glad that we won, but we've got to get better. We've got a long, long way to go. We've got a lot of work to do, fellas. From now on, they all count. And it just gets harder and harder."

7

The Earth Grains Mistake

November 10 was the first day of the early signing period. During this window of time, athletes can sign official letters of intent to participate for colleges. Gerald Wallace signed to play with the Tide, but Gottfried respected Wallace's decision to keep the news quiet until Wallace's official signing ceremony on the 11th. The players were assured that Wallace had chosen Alabama. The only question remaining was whether he would enter the NBA draft. Only a player with Wallace's ability could grab so much attention and respect from the current team.

After resting on Tuesday, November 9, Wednesday practice was preceded by a film session in the player's lounge.

"Here we rotate and help. We get beat, but we rotate and stay in the play," Gottfried explained, extolling the virtues of alert defensive helping with the aid of film.

We all watched the television screen as Gottfried paused, rewound, and fast-forwarded through numerous plays. The staff was frustrated by a play where Doc Martin was chased down by a defender in a one-on-none fast break.

"Doc, you've just got to get out in front of people and stay out there. You're three feet in front of the guy. The next thing you know he's right there with you. If he knocks the ball out of your hand, you're gonna miss an opportunity to score. Let's go out on the floor."

Scott moved easily around the floor. He looked relaxed for the first time in weeks. He had two private sessions with Cotton, undoubtedly giving him some much-needed pearls of wisdom.

A drill became complicated when Gottfried specifically asked the ball to be reversed (passed around the perimeter to the other side of half-court) three times. The ball was never reversed. Gottfried eventually turned around and walked away in frustration.

My personal favorite drill, take-the-charge, helped increase the intensity of practice. (I'll never forget how big Gottfried's eyes were when he found out that I had been instructing a take-the-charge drill in the adjoining gym of his Murray State summer camp for youth. For the record, Kelsey and Pearson had given me permission to use the drill.) Overeager Matt Minor ran over Tide players without restraint. London coached his teammates on protecting their testicles by covering them with two hands while absorbing the blow—that is a leader and a friend.

In war rebounding, Hays fell and twisted his ankle severely. A hush on the gym floor. The team contemplated the loss of its vital player and his desperately needed experience with the first two games of the season coming up on the weekend. Morr helped Hays off the floor, and practice continued. Hays suffered on the sideline from intense pain and limited mobility. The senior knew the poor timing of this injury.

"I must have the worst luck in the world," he said, mumbling through the pain.

Morr's diagnosis was a strained tendon. Gottfried walked over to check on Hays repeatedly. Hays was by leaps and bounds the one man that the team could not afford to lose.

The Earth Grains Classic hosted by the Saint Louis Bilikens immediately appeared like a more adventurous weekend than Gottfried imagined when he scheduled the event for one so-called exempt game. The NCAA mandates that teams play only a certain number of games with the exception of certain events that are granted exempt status. The Tide was scheduled to play Northern Iowa on Saturday in its Classic Opener and Saint Louis on Sunday. Saint Louis was the favorite on Sunday regardless of Hays's status, playing in the Kiel Center where the Bilikens had ranked among the top 12 schools nationally in average attendance for four of the past five years. St. Louis had won 76 of its last 90 home games! They have had moderate success in a conference with substantial past and current prominence—Louisville, Cincinnati, and Marquette have won NCAA titles while Memphis, Houston, and Depaul boast near-misses and national notoriety. In the American division of C-USA, St. Louis is the one school out of six that has not reached the Final Four.

Pearson scouted the opener. The players began working against Northern Iowa's offense. UNI's Robbie Sieverding posed a perimeter threat which meant the players would be hearing his name in their sleep after four days of preparation. Unfortunately for the Tide, the Panthers from Cedar Falls also had a 6-foot-11, 260-pound center who would be difficult to defend if Hays couldn't play.

Cotton practiced hard all week. He punished Davis on a hard charge to the goal, leaving Davis with a bleeding mouth. He punctuated a hard practice with a spectacular dunk. Cotton's sudden emergence had many skeptical teammates and staff members rethinking his ability to contribute. Grizzard continued to struggle defensively. Grizzard's limitless potential combined with his deficiencies had Gottfried confused. He knew that Grizzard could be an NBA player one day—even an NBA All-Star—but the player seemed to be struggling mightily just to adapt to the intensity of the college game.

Gottfried concluded practice. "Go to study hall. Stay on top of your grades."

Thursday's buzz revolved around the preliminary word from the team doctor, Dr. Jimmy Robinson, that would have Hays missing about two weeks with a strained tendon. That would have included three games, including a test against Weber State who beat North Carolina the previous year. Hays vowed to return earlier.

Senior Alfred Moss was suddenly forced to prepare for extensive action in the front court. Moss found himself stuck in the war rebounding drill for an unusually long period. He could not seem to grab the rebound that would free him—a bad sign for a guy who needed to have major rebounds in the coming weekend.

Daniel Scott walked into the Coliseum. After hearing me say Daniel's name, Boatright directed Matt Minor to set up his father's chair on the sideline. Kelsey labored to improve Moss who couldn't satisfy his demanding coach in a post-defense drill. On the opposite end of the court, the guards witnessed a familiar theme.

"[Yelling] You can't take a day off, Rod," Pearson barked emphatically.

Robert Scott entered the building. The moment seemed symbolic because Scott had taken the role of Grizzard's defense counselor in conversations with the rest of the staff. While altering Grizzard's defensive mentality became more and more prioritized as a team need, Scott begged for patience. Scott did not want the player's substantial offensive confidence to be damaged by a barrage of criticism. Scott stood on the floor, watching a frustrated Gottfried refrain from exploding.

"Rod, I don't want to seem like I'm always getting on you, but you've got to find a way to get down and guard somebody."

Reminiscent of the previous day's collision, Cotton nailed Walker in the mouth on his way to the basket. Blood dripped out of Walker's mouth as he walked alongside Morr.

"Damn. Schea messes up everybody's grill. My teeth feel like they've been pushed all the way up," Kenny said as Morr checked his teeth.

Both Davis and Walker would have been called for fouling Cotton on those drives.

Gottfried talked about the team's first road trip at the end of practice.

"We'll have sandwiches after practice. We'll go right from here to the airport. Wear something casual and nice. Stay away from jeans and tennis shoes . . . When we get up there, we'll go to the hotel and check-in first. There is a real nice restaurant that we're going to. So I want you to bring clothes that you can feel comfortable wearing in a nice place. Take that black coat. Even if it's not so cold, it could be cold up there in a day or two. Anything else, coaches?"

"It's Clay's birthday," Pearson said with a smile.

"Clay! Clay! Clay!" the team chanted.

"Look at me, guys. When we go on the road, we'll have some fun. But it's a business trip. We're going up there to win two. We are going to win two. I don't know if Jeremy will play. If he doesn't play, then you're one down. One of your troops is down and you've got to pick it up. That's part of being a team."

Pearson's scouting report on Friday sounded familiar. Pearson loves to be thorough, mixing the other team's statistics with their offensive tendencies to grab the players' attention.

Gottfried later worked on potential situations. Introducing a situational drill where the Tide has the ball with two seconds left and trailed by one or two, he told the most dramatic story of his senior season when Alabama scored in that very predicament to beat Florida.

Walker required a root canal from the collision with Cotton so he couldn't practice. Morr was unhappy with Walker for not wearing his mouth-guard. Walker relayed to me his suffering from incredible pain since the procedure. Walker, who has a phenomenal sense of humor, was angered when I attempted to humor him—it was too painful to laugh.

The team gathered in a huddle. As he often did, Gottfried taught with the aid of a game on television from the previous night.

"Who watched the game last night? Iowa had the ball with 40 seconds left in the game, and UConn is playing great defense. UConn guards them from 35 on the shot clock to eight. The ball goes inside and Khalid El-Almin goes in and whacks the guy. They only had to play defense for six or seven more seconds. At eight, you need to buckle up and not bail them out."

Practice ended.

"Make sure you're with someone who knows how to get to the airport."

DRIVING across town to board a chartered airplane makes commercial flying seem like Chinese water torture. The plane ride can be turbulent, but parking and boarding are wonderfully simple. The flight attendant even pretended that she wanted the team to win.

Our St. Louis hotel was a stone's throw from the famous arch. After eating at a great restaurant selected by Boatright (Boatright is a St. Louis

Cardinals fan. On a last minute maneuver by Pearson, Boatright and Pearson hopped a private jet and witnessed Mark McGwire hit his 62 home run of the season, breaking the record.), the team returned for the typical film session on the eve of a road game.

Pearson handed out a copy of the scouting report. Joe Breckinridge, a 6-foot-6, 230-pound junior, seemed to be the UNI team leader. Breckinridge averaged 11.4 points and 8.2 rebounds last year.

"Breckinridge, No. 32, is a burly looking, skin-headed white guy. He's hard-nosed. He's gonna come out and throw the first punch. He led the league in rebounding last year. Look to take a charge from him. Play him for the drive. He did not take a single three-point shot last year," Pearson explained. He continued by describing every player that they expected to play against.

Gottfried began discussing their sets and tendencies with the use of the film. We watched a play where an opposing player approached a UNI double-screen (two players standing side-by-side) and the defender stopped moving.

"I don't know who 31 is for this other team, but that's the sorriest— [rewinding the tape for a second look] watch this joker on defense. 'I just ran into the screen and quit.' Bucket. That won't get it done," Gottfried said.

UNI suffered the loss of its leading scorer over the summer.

"This guy right here is gone. He smoked too much hooch this summer," Gottfried said, triggering laughter throughout the room.

The film ended.

"We'll get you up at about 9:30. We'll eat at ten. Find a way to turn your lights off about midnight and go to sleep. Watch some T.V. and get some rest."

"They've got some weapons. We don't want to let them hang around," Pearson said as the players stood up to leave.

Saturday, November 13 had finally arrived—a new season.

THE TEAM seemed sluggish at the morning shoot-around.

"Did they get enough sleep last night?" inquired Scott.

One would have thought that the impressive Kiel Center would excite this young team. The 665,000-square-foot center seats 20,000 for basketball games. Built in 1994, the contemporary glass and concrete structure aspires to be ultra-modern.

Hays did not feel comfortable with the sideline view.

"You would not believe how hard it will be for me to sit out. This is the first game that I've missed in my career," Hays said. I could tell he was upset.

The team ate the pre-game meal privately in a hotel banquet room. While breakfast and late-night burger bars are buffet-like, hotels serve a full course pre-game meal. Chicken and steak are the entreé choices. After the meal, the team returned to their rooms until loading the bus around an hour before the game. An optional devotional was conducted by team chaplain Bill Overstreet. I pondered whether anything that Gottfried or Pearson had said could ignite this ball club against a Northern Iowa club that the Tide players would not have been able to distinguish from a community college based on name recognition. It was a neutral floor game with a bunch of newcomers and Hays on the bench. I pondered disaster.

Watching a television in an unoccupied locker room of the Kiel Center, our video coordinator Patrick McDonald and I spent the minutes leading up to the pregame ritual celebrating Alabama's nailing the coffin shut on Mississippi State in football.

It was finally time for Pearson's final scouting report. The material seemed very familiar—as it should have at that point. Gottfried wanted to quicken the pace of the game, hoping to have more transition play that would favor his team's athleticism advantage.

"Put heat on 'em everywhere. Get up and pressure . . . When we get it, push it. Push it."

Later, he addressed the critical area around the basket which would be harder to defend and penetrate without Hays.

"The whole key to game is the paint—like the red zone in football. We have to be able to find a way into the paint. We have to keep them out of it."

After the warm-up and final lecture on sets and options, the stage was set.

"In college basketball, we get 27 games. It's not like the NBA where they get 80. They all count. In March, they total them up to find out who wants to play in the big show. Come out and play."

Cotton had earned the starting nod and would guard UNI's sharp-shooter, Sieverding, to begin the game. London had apparently wrestled the starting role away from Meade at the point guard position. Dudley started in place of Hays. After months of building doubt about Haginas having a prominent role on this team, Haginas found himself in the starting lineup of the opener alongside Grizzard.

The season began on an ominous note when Andy Woodley, a sophomore guard who averaged 1.9 points per game last year, drilled a three-pointer. The UNI Panthers took control of the game, stretching the lead to 13-4 and dominating the paint. Grizzard and Cotton appeared shaken. Everything changed when Martin replaced Cotton and seemed poised to save the day, making shot after shot on the way to 13 first-half points. The Tide also improved defensively, managing to give UNI fewer second chances. The pace of the game was slow, but Gottfried's team led at halftime, 36-30.

"Twenty minutes, fellas. Don't you think it will be easy. I guarantee you it won't be easy. They're sitting over there licking their chops because they've got a shot at you."

With Martin on his way to an incredible seven for eight shooting game, including three of four from the three-point line, combined with adequate team defense, Alabama seemed to be on the way to victory with a 50-41 lead midway into the second half despite being out-rebounded and out-hustled for several loose balls. Even Sieverding had been de-fended very well. Suddenly, my favorite warrior, London, experienced a nightmare sequence. London chose a poor angle around a screen and failed to contest a Sieverding three-pointer that cut the lead to six. London turned the ball over, leading to an easy transition bucket. The lead was four. London turned the ball over, leading to another easy bucket. The lead melted from nine to two quicker than a thief running from a cop.

The closing sequences of the game featured a series of critical rebounding situations with UNI seemingly claiming every ball. The Tide could not seem to muster any intensity against the lesser known team from the lesser known league. The Panthers cruised from a 67-66 lead with 2:58 left, pushing the lead to a comfortable margin down the stretch. Alabama had nearly lost all hope, trailing by four in the closing seconds when Meade made a desperation three-pointer to cut the lead to one. With three seconds left, the Tide needed a foul or a steal. Cotton's assignment caught the ball and dribbled out the clock, triggering a wild celebration from the Panthers of little-known Northern Iowa, a 74-73 winner.

A shocked group of men returned to the Alabama locker room. Gottfried had just been strapped with one of the most embarrassing losses of his career.

The staff had to be devastated by the timing of Hay's injury and the youth of their team, combining for terrible circumstances in the opener.

Deafening silence gripped the locker room. This was not the typical silence because Gottfried usually interrupted that very quickly. In a long basketball season, he generally saw no place for the locker rooms of "Bear" Bryant's setbacks where football players appear to have lost a family member after a tie. (That "I feel so bad I want to jump off a cliff" approach is my preference.) He paced back and forth in the front of the room. He had always won and very seldom been strapped with an embarrassing loss.

Finally, he struggled for words.

"I can't tell you how disappointed I am. [Long pause] This game will always humble you. I have been humbled tonight. Nobody will roll over for you. Nobody. You got outworked." Gottfried's tone was bitter.

The bus ride (or plane ride) after a road loss is always a time for evaluation. The next day would likely bring an 0-2 start to the season. With Louisville, Arizona's tournament, and two other NCAA tourney teams from last year remaining on the non-conference schedule, the Tide seemed to be headed for a horrible non-conference year if they didn't improve dramatically. Five or six non-league losses seemed very possible and that would mean probable destruction of the regular season given that SEC wins are very hard to find. Of course, Hays would return and help the team, but Cotton and Grizzard, who were expected to provide the bulk of the offensive help aside from Hays, had combined to shoot five for 24.

The staff gathered for a midnight film session in Gottfried's hotel suite. Scott was awake and alert. His face looked sunken. I told him that I wished he would get some rest, but he was too deeply disturbed over the loss to sleep. In fact, Scott was the most energetic man in the group. I think the only reaction that he used when faced with adversity was to respond with force.

The environment could have been mistaken for a funeral parlor. Gottfried started the tape.

It was awful. The best shooters on the team couldn't hit the basket to save their lives. The defense was worse. "We made their post people look like a million dollars. Our post defense was terrible," Gottfried complained.

After the tape finished, Gottfried announced that Meade would be given the starting nod at point guard because he represented the future. There was little room in the statement for argument.

THE SUNDAY game against St. Louis had been billed as the match-up between friends and fellow assistants on the 1995 UCLA national championship club. Pearson was not concerned with articles concerning the friendship between St. Louis head coach Lorenzo Romar and Gottfried in the Sunday morning *St. Louis Post Dispatch*. Instead, he dwelled on the revealing words of Kevin Boone who wrote that, "Despite boasting what one national hoops publication calls the sixth-best recruiting class in the country, Alabama—from the powerful Southeastern Conference—was outhustled and consequently outrebounded, 45-38."

Kelsey and I had it out over the scheduling decision. I made it known, for the 145th time, that the Earth Grains Classic was a poor scheduling decision. Kelsey was disgusted, angrily disagreeing with me.

"Shaq, if you can't beat Northern Iowa, who are you going to play?" Kelsey snapped. (The team called me Shaq. I am 5-foot-11. The name came from an argument six years prior wherein I defended Shaquille O'Neail as a great basketball player. The name stuck. I never acknowledged the joke.)

"You planned to take a very young ball club out here to St. Louis for your first two games. St. Louis is too good at home. It's not even a tournament situation where we could be playing a terrible Air Force club today. We come out here and get ambushed. It was a terrible schedule given the rest of our non-league games," I said. The exchange was spoken in a whispered tone, out of ear shot.

"Shaq! You're always talking about playing at home. [Chuckling sarcastically] If you come out here and go 0-2, you're doing something wrong."

"Well, you better buckle up because today is a long shot and the rest of the non-league schedule might break your back."

"We just got beat by Northern Iowa on a neutral floor. I realize we may have some problems."

I wasn't through with him. "I'm just glad we didn't play Winthrop in Tuscaloosa last night. I'm glad we didn't build some confidence for our guys with a routine win. I'm glad we're out here at the Earth Grains Classic."

"I'm not sure if we could have beaten anybody last night, Shaq."

Gottfried scheduled an 11:30 A.M. film session that he would conduct before the noon shoot-around. He used a calm, disappointed tone to generalize and make a series of comments on play after play.

"Get your head out of your butts. Wake up. Get excited about playing. We lost. I don't like it. You don't like it. But it's one game. They all count the same."

He proceeded to deliver a harsh and detailed criticism of the previous night's post defense.

"We made them look like millionaires. They're getting lay-up after lay-up because we were gambling in the post."

"We've got to execute in the high-post and take what they give us . . .You can't force a play . . . We have an answer in our offense for everything the defense takes away."

The screen showed UNI score in transition.

"Let's see who runs back hard here. Look where that dude is and where Sam is. Sam's almost one step ahead. Look where they end up. Sam just gets beat in a foot race. Bucket. Those baskets count, guy."

London suffered his decisive collapse. The tape never lies. I looked at London but could not see his face clearly.

"We haven't got a shot yet since we were up 9. Now it's a whole different game."

Cotton appeared to be lost in the woods on a defensive trip. His assignment looked to be a ghost.

"On this one right here, Schea, I think you just quit on the play. I don't know what happened. You're just in a daze. I don't know who you're guarding. I don't think you know."

UNI grabbed an offensive rebound and scored.

"They get another shot and score. We can't keep playing like this on this end, fellas. We're helpless."

Moss was screened.

"Fight through a screen, Alfred. You ran into a body and quit."

UNI hustled to a loose ball.

"We need to come up with a ball on one of these kinds of plays."

UNI hustled to another loose ball.

"We just can't get a loose ball. They come up with it again."

The videotape ended. The players were probably thankful when the focus shifted to St. Louis. Kelsey scouted the Billikens and went over their personnel and offensive tendencies. While Kelsey handed out a written report, Gottfried shifted the focus back on his team.

"It doesn't come down to major things. It's the little things."

Gottfried stepped aside and let Scott speak. Scott presented an emphatic and eloquent summary of last night's debacle.

"If you're guarding a big guy that's hard to handle, make sure you find a way to block the guy out so that the guards can rebound. Do whatever it takes to make sure that your man does not get the ball. We never did that last night. They almost had more offensive rebounds than defensive rebounds. Twenty-two offensive, 23 defensive. That should never happen! To me, that's a sign of being out-toughed and outhustled. We never want to lose games like that. I would rather people shoot lights out to beat us. It came down to a battle of the hustle."

The shoot-around allowed a demonstration of several of the post-defense concepts that were discussed in the film session. The staff tried to eliminate the gambles to attempt steals by the post-players that lead to lay-ups. St. Louis (SLU) beat Air Force, 78-70, the night before. (The low-key atmosphere of shoot-arounds allowed me the time to learn valuable information like the origin of the St. Louis mascot. A picture of the SLU Billiken reveals a creature with all the features of a human except an oddly shaped head with gigantic cheeks and large, oddly shaped ears. Created in the early 1900's as a bank and statuette, the Billiken had national popularity for about six months in 1910. A St. Louis sports writer determined that the SLU football coach, John Bender, resembled the original Billiken. So he drew a caricature of the coach in the form of the Billiken and posted it in the window of a drug store. That drawing is a SLU Billiken.)

"The good thing about basketball is that you don't have to wait seven days to come back and play after a loss. Deep in my heart, I know that we're gonna be a good team," Gottfried concluded, ending the shoot-around on a positive note.

Academic advisor Rod Asberry and I walked across the street to see the bottom of the arch before loading the bus. Asberry was strapped with the pressure of monitoring every player's academic progression. Boatright served as Asberry's connection with the staff to oversee every single academic twist and turn for every player. I can almost guarantee that Boatright and Asberry knew more about the organization of every class taken by every player than half the other students in those classes. If a player fails to deliver in the classroom, Gottfried will be looking to Asberry for a thorough explanation. Every time a player missed a study hall or tutorial, Asberry was ordered to notify the staff. Boatright was charged with the responsibility of knowing when a player was talking to a co-ed, making him five minutes late to class. For violations of the rigid rules, the staff punishes. Pearson has a particular fondness for the punishment phase of the academic program. He likes to schedule early morning "parties" that typically involve a test of mental and physical stamina. The players hate these "parties." Asberry and I often laughed about his reckoning day when the grades would be posted at the end of the semester.

Kelsey seemed especially prepared for St. Louis. Because Romar was coaching at Pepperdine last year, Kelsey watched some of their film to gather tendencies. He knew that a win could stop profuse bleeding. Justin Love, a 6-2, 210-pound senior guard, served as the Billikens' weapon of choice. Love scored 27 against Air Force. He was their leading scorer the previous season, averaging 13.7 ppg (11th in Conference-USA). Kelsey warned about Love's ability to dribble penetrate and make jumpers while floating forward in the air.

Gottfried began.

"All I want you to do tonight is loosen up and play. Don't be afraid to make a mistake. Just play like you know how to play. Sometimes I feel like I'm locking you up. [Pointing at Rod] You're a good player. That's why you're here. You're all good. Just play. [Pointing to a board filled with notes and plays] Sometimes all this stuff makes you think so much that we're not down and playing. Relax. Have some fun and play basketball."

In the remainder of his speech, Gottfried placed great emphasis on a play that Romar often milked. It is a play that the Tide used, but Gottfried spent an hour the previous evening moaning about how much better Romar's team executed it. He asked his group of young players to ignore the raucous road crowd.

Over 11,000 Billiken fans were excited about the new Romar era. Meade made his first start in hostile territory. The remainder of the starting lineup was the same. To the crowd's delight, Justin Love and the Billikens immediately seized control. Love outscored the Tide eight-seven during a 17-seven St. Louis run to open the game. Two early turnovers by a rattled Meade and two more by Grizzard and Cotton excited the Billiken faithful. Gottfried brought London into the game and the Tide's energy turned. Grizzard had his first confidence building experience of his collegiate career with two straight three-pointers to drag the Tide back into the game, trailing 22-19 at the 10:38 mark. Walker, who checked into the game very early, began scoring when he hit the floor and finally gave the Tide a 31-29 lead with under five minutes to play in the half.

The Billikens grabbed control at that point, closing the half on an 11-4 run to capture a 40-35 lead. Love was dominating, and the shot chart revealed many Billiken shots very close to the goal. The play that Romar and Gottfried shared was killing the Tide.

"Look at their shots. That's the difference. They're all around the basket." The rest of the staff simply shook their heads.

He entered the locker room, talking. Loudly.

"They're beating us with our play! We should know the play! I gave it to him! All the big guys have to see this coming!"

Faithfully playing the role of the eternal optimist, Gottfried concluded by finding hope in his team's apparent peril.

"They're shooting 55 percent from the field and we're shooting 35 percent, and they're only up by five."

Love jumped all over the Tide to begin the second half, scoring seven points in a nine-two Billiken run, pushing the lead to 49-37 at the 16:48. Love had dribbled to create his own shots, drawn foul after foul, and shared the wealth on his way to eight assists. The Tide began to smell like toast when Alfred Moss scored eight straight Alabama points, cutting the lead to 57-49 at the 11:12 mark. Martin converted a three-pointer to trim the lead to six at the 9:57 mark. Love countered with five points in a six-zero run to make the deficit 12 with 7:35 to play.

The SLU pep band taunted Gottfried all day.

"You know, Lorenzo, don't you," the band chanted as if Gottfried was lucky to have coached with Romar at UCLA.

Gottfried became irate when Alfred Moss was mugged on his way to the basket, and no intentional foul was awarded. The crowd responded to his outburst.

"Bobby, want-to-be, Bobby want-to-be, Bobby want-to-be," the pep band chanted in reference to the temper of the legendary three-time NCAA champion coach, Bobby Knight.

Alabama's final flurry came on four straight points from Cotton to cut the lead to five with 2:09 left. But Cotton was whistled for a costly offensive foul, and Dave Fergerson netted four foul shots with under a minute to play, sending the Tide home in absolute disarray, 78-70.

As the clock ran out, the crowd chanted "O and 2! O and 2!"

Gottfried reacted to this predictable loss in a more typical fashion.

"Look up. Get your head up. You guys played hard. We got better tonight. We were a lot better tonight than were last night . . . Get your chin up. You've got to decide if you want to become a better team. We've got to come to practice and get everybody going so we can start to build our team. I don't know if we have had thirteen guys practicing on five days this year. We've got to start coming to work and get focused . . . Although our record doesn't show it, I know we're better. It's early in the season, guys. We're a long way away from February. I'm proud of the way you played."

Alabama limped home, carrying a 0-2 mark for only the second time in 39 years. (Hobbs rebounded from a 0-2 start in the '93-'94 season for 20 wins and an NCAA berth.)

There was plenty of blame to go around. The guards had played poorly, the forwards had been pushed around, and the team shooting was erratic at best. In their first two games, the youthful Tide team had missed the vital role that Hays was supposed to play.

Rattled, we left St. Louis with two losses. The coaches were irritable. The players were tired and downtrodden. Doomed from the start, the Earth Grains Classic had been a complete and total disaster.

8

Before Hitting an Iceberg

After resting on Monday, November 15, Gottfried planned a Tuesday film session. Prior to the session, Gottfried learned that Cotton had been complaining of pain associated with a bruise on his butt that would potentially keep him out of practice. Gottfried confronted him in the locker room. The coach asked the player why he did not report his injury to the trainer in the morning according to standard procedure. Cotton answered that he had left two messages with Morr. Gottfried departed in frustration.

The players gathered in the players' lounge to watch film. Before any of the coaches arrived, the veterans decided to have an informal team meeting. Hays began fervently.

"We've got to get it going. I've never been to the NCAA. I want to get there. I'm sure you do too. We need intensity in practice, fellas."

"We've got to be excited about playing," Martin said.

"Make sure you practice hard with enthusiasm today. You know what he wants, and we know what will happen if we don't," Haginas said.

The staff entered.

"We're gonna execute our offense. I'm showing you two different tapes here. If you don't know what we're doing, then learn what we're doing! We're gonna start shooting a better percentage than 35 percent. We shoot 35 percent as a team because we take ridiculously stupid shots," Gottfried said.

The ritual began again. The tape into the VCR, and then images from the weekend appeared on the screen. It was not a pretty sight.

Meade forced a wild shot.

"That's a horsecrap, bullcrap shot—ridiculous to think in college basketball that you can shoot that shot," Gottfried stated to begin a series of disappointed responses to the film.

A wild shot resulted from a lack of early recognition of the time remaining on the shot clock.

"Another terrible shot. We had no idea that the shot clock had wound down. You [Meade] had no idea that the shot clock had wound down. You had absolutely no idea as our point guard how much time was on the clock."

Rod was out of position on a play.

"I don't know if you know anything that we're doing, Rod."

Rod forced a wild shot.

"Off-balance. That's just a horrible shot."

Schea failed to execute a double-screen.

"Schea ain't screening anybody. He doesn't know the offense either."

Gottfried struggled with the VCR controller. It was terrible timing.

"Darron! You've got to get me a different VCR by the next time we watch film!" Gottfried barked in frustration.

The team failed miserably to execute a play.

"We've got a brand new play that you guys put in here where we just run around. You guys don't need me to coach. You've got your own deal going on out there. It's your own program. I don't even know why we practice. Twenty practices. Man-to-man offense everyday."

Gottfried paused the tape.

"Just so we understand—that was the entire first half. That was every time that we had the ball. And we haven't executed our offense yet!"

Haginas missed from point blank range, and the head coach could no longer avoid a year-long issue.

"Make one, Sam. You missed two of them just like that in the game. Concentrate and get up there around the rim and put the ball in the hole."

Alabama ran up the court on a one-pass-and-shoot trip. No passing.

"That should be our offense right there. We ought to just do that every time. Jack around and go one-on-one. That would be sweet."

He stopped the tape, seemingly unable to stomach anymore.

"This goes on and on the whole game. We didn't run our offense. We did not run our offense. And then we come in the locker room and wonder why we can't win a game. If you don't know what we're doing, you better learn it. Don't be surprised come Friday night when you're sitting over there on the bench because you don't know what we're running."

The offensive tape was taken out and replaced with the defensive tape. His reactions were no less critical.

St. Louis scored easily in transition while Meade failed to fulfill his important role as the first offensive player to run back and make the transition to defense.

"They just beat us down the floor. You're a safety, Terrence Meade! You get back and protect the basket."

St. Louis executed their favorite play that Gottfried gave to Romar. Then they did it again.

"They run this play just like we want to run it! The funny thing about them is that they didn't run anything else the whole game. They just got what they wanted with it all night." Grizzard was beaten by the dribbler to the middle of the floor, exposing the entire defense.

Gottfried shook his head. "You want to force them to the baseline, not to the middle. The other way, Rod. Never stopped 'em. Rod never ever stopped the guy."

The Billikens executed the play again. Kelsey, Pearson, and Boatright all winced. I hardly looked at the tape; Scott's silent shivering for the duration of the film kept my attention.

"[Yelling] Why can't we run that? It's the same play! It's my fault I'll guarantee you that! I've done the worst coaching job that I've done in my lifetime! We can't run a freaking play!"

Haginas failed to prevent his assignment from rebounding the ball.

"Sam, you never put your body into him and blocked him out. You cost us another two."

Walker's assignment manhandled him for a bucket.

"He pushed you underneath the bucket, Kenny."

Rod's assignment left him and scored.

"It's your guy, Rod. You completely lost him."

When the film session ended, practice proceeded as if it was the first day. Gottfried taught the variations of his high-post offense as if he had new players. He obviously felt the need to completely rebuild the ball club.

Grizzard moved slowly in a drill after having already been warned about going "half-speed."

"[Yelling] One more time and I'm gonna send you home! You're gonna go game speed or go home! I'm tired of watching half-speed," Gottfried exploded.

Hays encouraged Grizzard.

Cotton did not practice because of his bruised butt. Morr had received a Monday afternoon phone call from Cotton's father who said that Cotton had an appointment with the UAB team doctor. The UAB team doctor happened to be a viable physician within Cotton's health care plan. On Monday night, the UAB head trainer called Morr to notify him that Cotton had been scheduled for a bone scan. He also told Morr that the UAB team doctor recommended against a bone scan, but Cotton's father had scared them into the procedure with the threat of legal consequences. Morr had grown increasingly agitated by Cotton's exclusion of the Alabama staff from his medical treatment. Cotton had indicated that he did not trust the Alabama staff or the medical care available in Tuscaloosa. An exasperated Morr openly considered closing the doors of his training room to Cotton.

I approached Scott about his shivering at the film session. He confessed that he had been very cold all day. Scott hadn't told anybody about his pain. He looked beyond miserable. In addition to everything that Scott was trying to manage (including a ball club that would be feeling his wrath if he had the energy), his mother had been struggling to overcome the medical consequences of a fire that nearly killed her earlier in Autumn. Gottfried told me during a practice break that Scott's mother had died. Scott had not been given the news because Gottfried felt that he would rather hear it from his wife Cynthia in a few minutes. We were all crushed. A great friend had lost his dear mother, and the timing could not have been worse. When Cynthia told Robert after practice, all the remaining life in his decaying body seemed to disappear. Cynthia, Kelsey, and Gottfried attempted to comfort him, but he was devastated. We departed from practice with a heavy heart.

The team huddled on the following day.

"I don't know if you guys know or not, but Robert Scott's mother passed away yesterday very unexpectedly. She went through a fire in her house a couple of months ago. She got some smoke in her lungs. But they thought she was doing pretty good. You guys know Robert is going through a pretty tough time. And that's just a big blow for him. I don't know if this is appropriate or not. But I'd like somebody to take a minute and pray for him."

Hays bowed his head and began praying for the team. "Father, we want to come to you as a team and ask you to watch over Coach Scott and his family. We just wish that you would help them with this great loss. And help us each and everyday to be thankful for our health, Father. If you could be with Coach Scott during these tough times, Father. Amen."

Robert did not show up. Cynthia said that his sisters were looking to him for support and help with the funeral arrangements. She explained that Robert's sisters have always sought his leadership. Robert cried on his way to see his mother's body but had guarded his emotions from his sisters to project strength. She worried about Robert Jr. who was very close to his grandmother and devastated by the loss.

Morr reported that Hays had been working hard to rehabilitate his right ankle strain.

"He has been doing everything that he needs to do and a little bit more."

Cotton had his bone scan. Morr and Cotton were no longer communicating. An exasperated Morr struggled to reveal to me his level of frustration.

"I'm busting my butt for Schea. I've been doing it. He is eating up all of my time. But my time is for Gottfried. It's my job to work for the head coach of Alabama. Not one of its players, no matter how good he is. And that's what I'm going to do."

Grizzard did not appear to be motivated as the practice began.

"Don't convince me that you don't want to play anymore, Rod. You'll be sitting on the bench with me. I can't play anymore either," Gottfried said.

The Weber State Wildcats would be Friday night's opponent. The Wildcats beat North Carolina the season before to reach the second round of the NCAA tournament and would feature one of the best players in America, Harold "The Show" Arcineaux. We had been talking about "The Show" since the game was added to the schedule. Alabama beat Weber State 84-80 in an overtime war last year at the Pearl Harbor Classic. Arcineaux had nine rebounds and 24 points in the losing effort. Gottfried decided to double-team Arcineaux every time he touched the ball in the low-post area. The newcomers seemed impressed when Gottfried described Arcineaux as a top ten NBA draft pick.

Cotton practiced on Thursday after his bone scan was negative. He participated in a scouting report that preceded the typical beginning of practice.

Pearson scouted Weber State and warned about another player before turning to Arcineaux.

"They've got Ghatto—a big, tall guy from Italy. He makes four of five three-pointers on the tape that I'm gonna show you later . . . Arcineaux. The guys that were here last year remember him. He's gonna do everything. He's gonna loop around in here and come post you up. He's gonna step out here and pump fake and then try to drive. Then, he'll step out here and take a three-point shot. He wants to get baskets from just about anywhere. We've got to try and limit his touches. When he does shoot, we need a good contest. Make sure he doesn't hurt us with some offensive rebounding."

Haginas was told that he would guard Arcineaux.

"I better get a lot of sleep tonight," Haginas said in response.

Gottfried gathered the team after the scouting report.

"They're talking a little trash. They feel like they should have beat us last year. At their exhibition the other night, they were all popping off about Alabama this and that. That's good. Let 'em talk some trash. We're gonna come play."

After Gottfried's introduction, Steve Martin hustled in to conduct the stretching. Martin is paid to make elite athletes mentally and physically stronger. His entire working persona is the high energy man who enjoys pain. Rather than acting like a tyrant, Martin's approach is "let's have a bunch of fun while we work like crazy." When he feels tired, he smiles. When the players are hurting, he smiles. His attitude allows him to keep a great relationship with the players while performing his job at the optimum level. He only expresses anger when a player refuses to fulfill his task.

Kelsey played the role of Arcineaux in a drill. Hays jokingly told Kelsey to move quicker during a momentary break.

"You'll get older too one day, Hays," Steve Martin said.

Kelsey and his squad grabbed a couple of offensive rebounds as the practice game continued.

"Can't you understand that you're playing against a top ten pick, guys? We're giving up offensive rebounds! Kenny, if you come out here and play like this, he's gonna get 40 points! And you look at me like I'm crazy!" Kelsey exclaimed.

Walker tended to be very mild-mannered. He gave Kelsey a wide-eyed stare of amazement. Walker was a hard guy to harshly criticize because of his gentle voice and analytical approach to the game. Kelsey constantly pushed him, trying to make him a better player.

Pearson spiced up the post-practice film session with tape of Arcineaux against North Carolina and Florida in last season's big dance.

"You should get a feel for how he scores and where he scores from," Pearson said.

We watched Arcineaux just kill the Tar Heels from every possible angle and spot on the floor. He had similar success against Florida in the second round before falling short.

By Friday, the team was anxious to push the horrible memories from the Earth Grains Classic to the back of their minds. But a disastrous 0-3 start seemed very possible. Hays would return to action which should have steadied the newcomers. Gottfried had changed his mind about using Haginas to guard Arcineaux. He chose Dudley to start the game. The rest of the staff had many reservations about using Dudley because "The Show" would have a tremendous quickness advantage. Gottfried admitted that he would probably change to Martin or Walker very quickly. Gottfried's leaning toward a bigger player was a tribute to Arcineaux's strength and his nine rebounds against the Tide last year.

Scott attended visitation services for his late mother the night of the game, and his absence left a large void in the player's lounge and locker room. Against Gottfried's advice, Scott had promised to attempt a return before the game ended.

Pearson delivered his final scouting report.

"We can't say too much more about Arcineaux. At any time he'll break whatever pattern they've got going and look to go score. He's dying to score. Let's try and keep it off him. Limit his touches. Limit his points. But all of a sudden we can't have Ghatto come in here and do something crazy with 21 points."

Pearson went on to describe several of their sets.

"This guy setting this screen right here is 6-10, 250. He's like a Mac truck hitting you. So we better call that screen out."

"We've talked enough about them. Let's talk about us," Gottfried began. "Let's get down and guard 'em. Finish the defensive possession with a rebound. And let's go push it. Let's get up and down the floor. If you've got an opportunity, take it. Get the ball down there and get somebody a good shot. Attack the basket. Jeremy go down there and put your body on somebody and be a real big target. We'll get it down there to you. Make yourself attractive. And I'll make sure they throw it to you. If we don't have a great shot, take it back out and run your high-post offense. At this point, we've got to execute. That's what we didn't do the other night, fellas."

He refreshed their memories by talking through the options in his offense with the help of the plays drawn on the board before moving toward an exciting conclusion.

"I want to put the heat on 'em right away. Let's go right into their heart. I want the ball moving. Get down and set some screens . . . [Pointing to his offense on the board] I've been around some great teams that ran the exact same stuff. But there ain't no play on the board for you to jump up and get an offensive rebound basket! I don't have to draw that one up! [Clapping] You just have to go do it! Let's go!"

Craig Neal, a scout for the Toronto Raptors, entered the locker room during the warm-up. Neal had come to see Arcineaux. Gottfried shared his pain from last weekend's St. Louis trip.

"I screwed up the schedule. I took a bunch of rookies out to St. Louis for their first two games with only two and a half weeks of practice." Gottfried shook his head in disgust.

He asked Neal about Gerald Wallace's draft status. Neal said that he was probably a middle of the first round choice at this point.

"The all-star games will be important," Neal said in reference to Wallace's performance in the national high school all-star games in spring.

The team returned. Gottfried gave his summarized version of the scouting report, reinforcing his earlier offensive material.

"Team. Team. Team defense. Share the ball. Move the ball. Don't think these guys won't compete for 40 minutes! These guys beat North Carolina in the NCAA tournament! You don't just go and beat those kind of teams by accident. If I call on you, be ready."

Gottfried ripped Cotton out of the starting lineup for missing practice. Hays replaced Haginas who had gone from feeling like a critical part of the battle to sitting the bench in a single day. The official crowd of 6,513 was very kind toward the struggling team. The fans had much to cheer about early as the Tide jumped out to an 11-4 lead. Arcineaux seemed disoriented and failed to score. But another problem developed when The Show's sidekick, Eddie "The Thrill" Gill, who averaged 14 points per game last season, nailed his second three-pointer of the game to make it 11-7. From that point at the 13:56 mark, Alabama prevented

The Show and The Thrill from scoring through the rest of the half. The bench finally enjoyed the view of productive basketball as the Tide dominated in every phase of the game. Grizzard appeared to be the confident offensive juggernaut that had been publicized in high school, scoring ten points on four of eight shooting. Cotton joined the conflict with a vengeance, slashing through the lane for a four of seven shooting half. Dudley, Walker, Haginas, and Cotton took turns guarding Arcineaux who finished the stanza with zero points on zero for seven shooting. Martin added five rebounds. Finally, Meade converted a three-pointer with 1:15 left to make the halftime score 38-23.

Too bad for Scott that he didn't arrive by halftime. He would have had something to smile about. The halftime coaches' meeting seemed like a group of guys who just ate for the first time in days. Gottfried looked to Boatright for the shot chart.

"They're six for 25. That's the reason."

The staff entered the locker room.

"Good half, fellas. Good half. That's an NCAA tournament team right there. Don't be content. They're gonna come back. They're gonna come play," Gottfried began.

Gottfried was extremely upset by a Haginas turnover on an aggressive pass with nine seconds left when the Tide was playing for the last shot.

"O.K. Sam! Come on, Sam! I use one of my timeouts to set up a play where we're gonna shoot with five seconds or less, and you try to hit a homerun with eight or nine seconds left. Come on, Sam. You're smarter than that.

"Defensively, good job. We will keep fresh bodies on Arcineaux. Be ready to guard him."

With predictably less to say than usual, Gottfried turned to the assistants.

"Fellas, they're not going away. They're coming after you," Pearson said with a sense of urgency.

Kelsey interjected. "All the post guys need to put your butt on somebody and force them to foul you."

Gottfried began to speak again. "Forty minutes, not 20. They got their pride hurt in the first half. Their pride is hurting. They'll come after you."

The only charge that the Wildcats made, however, was toward the bus. Arcineaux never found his rhythm, finishing one for 13 from the floor. Cotton had a field day, finishing with eight rebounds and 20 points on eight for 15 shooting and punctuating the Tide romp with a thunderous dunk to give his team its largest lead of 24 points at the 5:46 mark. Haginas, Dudley, and Meade combined to shoot ten for 13 from the field, adding 24 points. Grizzard punished the Wildcats with seven rebounds and 19 points. Walker grabbed seven rebounds, helping the Tide win the rebounding war decisively, 51-31. Most importantly, Alabama held Weber State to 31.6% shooting. Even the feared Ivan Ghatto went zero for three from the field. Scott walked in the building with 3:32 left and received a standing ovation from his players as he found his place on the bench. That kind of warm gesture is seldom seen. The players appreciated Scott, and they wanted him to know it.

The Tide won, 81-61.

A happy locker room buzzed with positive energy.

"I thought we would practice tomorrow, but you earned a day off tonight. Good job, fellas. Now you know what can happen when you get down and guard somebody."

The players immediately started discussing rides to the Alabama-Auburn football game tomorrow in Auburn. Gottfried sensed what they were considering and discouraged the lengthy drive to the tiny rural town snuggled up to Georgia.

". . .Thank you, Father. Thank you for showing us that if work together, we can reap victory," Hays said in a closing prayer.

The only negatives for Gottfried to discuss in the post-game press conference were 23 turnovers against 11 assists (five turnovers, zero assists for Meade) and a rare bad night for a recovering Hays who was two for nine from the floor with zero rebounds in 22 minutes of play. I knew that in the back of his mind, the coach had to be pondering how long he could live with a starting point guard who could not protect the basketball. To the media he admitted regretting the trip to St. Louis.

Doug Segrest of the *Birmingham News* inquired if Gottfried had heard that future opponent Samford beat St. John's earlier that evening.

"Yes. It's another dumb scheduling move on my part."

Several of us made a glorious trip to the Plains to watch the football team whip the rivals on their home turf. It was a great time.

SUNDAY's practice started with a film review of Friday night's game. The film session was very mild compared to the previous scathing film session. Kelsey scouted the next opponent: Tennessee Tech. Practice began with the assistants and managers walking through several Tech plays.

After Kelsey finished, Gottfried put his spin on Tech.

"They came in here last year and we got 'em. They went out and signed a bunch of guys. Trey Ferguson—you guys from around here know him—is from Birmingham. They signed a junior college guy named Larrie Smith that a lot of people were recruiting. He had big numbers in junior college. He's about 6 foot 5—real crafty and strong. He had 18 points and 13 rebounds in one exhibition game and 20 points and 12 rebounds in the other one. Heard is the guy you will start on Doc. Last year he was third in the nation in three-pointers made. He's letting it rip. Shooting it. Shooting it. Shooting it."

Robert Scott entered the Coliseum. His body appeared to be very small. All of us noticed his rapid weight lost. He had buried his mother the day before.

Stinnett talked to me during practice about an innovative surgery performed by a Boston specialist. In Morr's odyssey to find a solution for Stinnett's condition, he had learned that Stinnett could be a candidate for the surgery. The player was to travel to Boston for a Sunday appointment where the doctor would determine whether he qualified as a candidate. If so, he would stay in Boston for the procedure. Almost everybody around this team had guessed that he would never recover. He had become a guy who everyone felt sorry for behind his back. Morr warred for a solution. He often admitted that Stinnett's injury had been frustrating beyond belief. Combining the stress associated with Cotton and Stinnett, Morr was a dark horse to land in a mental hospital.

Martin promised Gottfried that practice would be intense in exchange for the free day on Saturday. Pearson was the most intense guy in the building because defenders were being continually rocked by screens.

"Call out the screen! We're trying to pressure the ball, and we get belted every time. Nobody talks! Nobody talks."

Sunday concluded with a film session on Tech. Kelsey analyzed the tendencies while Gottfried tried to stress how much Tech had improved since their 26-point loss in Tuscaloosa.

"Don't look back and say we should have done this or that. We've already got a couple that we're looking back on. Bring everything you've got every night."

SEC Championship game tickets would be sold on Tuesday. Gottfried stopped on the way back from Monday's lunch to invite the students camped out in front of Coleman Coliseum to the game. He wished aloud that he could give them some free food. They were afraid to lose their place in line, however, and passed. The scene in front of Coleman Coliseum defined a phenomenal collegiate environment—frisbees flying through the air, music blaring, and pizza everywhere on a perfect sunny day. The scene inspired Tech head coach Jeff Lebo to tell the media after the game that "there were more people outside waiting for tickets for the football game than there were in here."

Scott and I sat in the players' lounge before the game. He moaned and groaned occasionally. Enduring constant pain was his life now. He never spoke about his pain. He did not verbalize the occupying army of evil cells in his stomach, or his aching soul having said goodbye to his mother. I no longer said silly stuff to make him laugh anymore. He only felt pain when he laughed. But he could still make me laugh.

"Shaq, will Fred Moss get a rebound tonight? Can he get one?" Scott inquired rhetorically with a grin.

Scott sent me in with instructions to signal for him when Kelsey started the scouting report. He was frustrated when he missed Kelsey's first sentence.

"Come on, Shaq. You could've gotten me quicker than that."

Scott found his seat behind the players. Kelsey gave an extremely thorough report. This was the fifth consecutive year that the Gottfried staff had faced Tennessee Tech. The Golden Eagles from Cookeville play in Murray State's Ohio Valley Conference.

Kelsey finished and Gottfried began.

"Listen up. Have I got to be the kind of guy to rant and rave and go crazy or are you ready to guard 'em? The guy, Heard. He can shoot it and he can play. I'm not gonna sit up here and tell you that he's third team All-American, but he's flat-out good. If they've got a chance to win it's because he and the other guard are scoring . . . Run your offense. It will help you. It will help you have a better shooting percentage. The offense is all a read. [Pointing to the board] If this guy can't get open at the wing—which would be frustrating if a team like this could take that away and if you can't get open at the wing spot maybe you're not good enough to play—but if the wing is not open, you know your options . . . Every game you play in NCAA basketball is an NCAA tournament game. They all count. Am I right or wrong? If you want to play in the greatest show on earth, they all count. You can't afford to take a night off. You can't afford to not bring your a-game. We've already got ourselves in a hole. We're gonna get out of the hole. It's just like football, guys. We can throw the ball and run all around. But at some point in the night, I've got to line up like this [he dropped into a three-point football stance], and look at you eye to eye and shut you out. I've just got to get a stop. That's what sports are all about. Let's go."

After the warm-up, Gottfried finally closed with a request for self-motivation.

"Don't ever expect somebody to force you to play hard. If you're that kind of guy, you need to find somewhere else to play. That's got to be a self-check. As a player, 'I'm playing as hard as I can play, coach. No matter who the coach is. If the coach changes tomorrow night, I'm playing hard!' Now let's go to work!"

The starting lineup remained the same. Cotton's performance against Weber State had not removed him from the doghouse. Bird lovers were offended early in the contest as the Golden Eagles were slaughtered mercilessly. Dudley, Martin, Hays, Meade, and Grizzard scored while the Eagles managed only three points at the 12:35 mark, making the score 26-3. Game over. By halftime, it was 54-27. A whopping twelve Crimson men played in the half and ten of those scored, including D.J. Towns who made a three-pointer. The single dramatic moment developed when Davis reached the foul line. The bench waited to erupt for his first college point, but the adored walk-on missed both free throws. Cotton boasted the Pleasantville stat sheet, going three for three from the field and four for four from the line to manage ten points in only 11 minutes. Meade shot three for three from the three-point line, adding nine points. Dudley went six for six at the foul line on his way to ten points. The Tide shot 68%. A helpless Lebo told the media after the game that the Tide would have beaten "Duke or Connecticut by 20 points" if they shot that percentage for a game.

Although Tech shot 25.8% in the half, Gottfried was frustrated by a few easy Tech baskets created by Cotton being out of position.

Gottfried talked to his staff before addressing the team. "Schea started gambling. He screwed up our whole defense. We started gambling and taking ourselves out of the play."

Scott wanted to use Tech for practicing offensive execution. "Games like this help you. We need to run our offense all the way through continuity."

The staff entered the locker room and Gottfried did not seem on the verge of patting anybody on the butt as a gesture of gratitude for a 54-27 lead. A coach must always guard against a collapse.

"I want to play defense the way we teach everyday. [Pointing at Cotton] You started to gamble. [Pointing at Grizzard] You were not ready to play defensively. They're starting to get open shots. I don't want that! I don't care if we're up by a hundred. I don't care if the score is two hundred to nothing. We play our way. Everything we do is like building a house. We're starting to build a foundation . . . Rod Grizzard, you catch the ball on the wing and see a double-team coming. You lifted the ball up and got straight-legged rather than getting down where you can be a player and ripping it through! I might have to step through a double-team. Be smart, Tarik. Ninety feet from the basket—they're in the double bonus—you foul the guy and give them two points . . . Here's the deal. We've got 20 minutes left in the game. For 20 minutes you play with the best effort you've got and we'll take tomorrow off. If you don't, we'll practice for three hours tomorrow."

The Tide could not find the net in the second half, shooting ten for 30. Tech's offense improved in a hopeless attempt to rally. Heard finished with 19 for the Golden Eagles. Dudley finished with 10 rebounds and 16 points. The Tide won 91-72 after a second half with all the drama of growing grass. Jim Bakken entered the game, sparking some cheers for the walk-on.

"[Clapping] Good effort, guys. We're taking tomorrow off. That wasn't the greatest half, but they shot the lights out. I know it's hard to keep your concentration." Gottfried was appreciative for his club's recovery from 0-2 to 2-2.

THE TEAM regrouped on Wednesday, November 24, to prepare for their opener against the Centenary Gentlemen in the Alabama Basketball Traditions Classic which would begin on Friday in Tuscaloosa. Scott surprised everyone at practice with his enthusiasm.

"[Yelling] I'll tell you what. If someone comes out of a stance, [pointing at the section letters at the top of the large building] I'm sending you to touch some P's or B's up there. Now stay in a stance!"

In the huddle, Gottfried introduced practice with a reference to the Tech devotional given by Dr. Levan Parker who was Grizzard's coach at Central Park Christian High School in Birmingham.

"Great devotional the other day. Some of you guys didn't come and that's fine. Dr. Parker talked about having faith in yourself and your ability—being confident. He did a great job . . . A couple of things about our game, fellas. We've still got to set more screens. We're not setting very many. You guys scored 91 points with nineteen turnovers. Cut that in half." Gottfried proceeded to a mathematical game which illustrated that the team could have scored 105 points against Tech instead of 91 if its offensive mistakes were cut in half.

Practice began and Grizzard could not shake Jim Bakken who prevented the scholarship player from getting open at the wing.

"No offense to Jim. I love Jim. But if you can't get open against Jim, you're gonna have a hard time getting open against Auburn, Rod," Gottfried said.

Gottfried mentioned the leading Gentlemen Ronnie McCollum early in practice as a motivator. McCollum was a lethal scorer from Fayette, Alabama, averaging 30.5 points per game. The coach warned that McCollum would be thrilled to face the Tide because Fayette rests about 45 miles from the Alabama campus and the junior guard was not recruited by Alabama.

"If I called McCollum on Friday at four o'clock in the morning, he'd be wide awake. He can't wait for his shot. He'll have all kinds of fans coming."

Gottfried concluded practice with praise and an invitation to Thanksgiving at his house.

"I liked how you practiced today. You practiced with some intensity. You went with some purpose. You were focused and played hard. If you want to be a great player, then you go hard. If you want to goof around and the game is not that important to you, then you don't . . . Let's talk about tomorrow. Nine o'clock, you guys are taped and lifting. And then you come right over here. It will be about a forty minute lift, then we'll practice. After practice, if you've got your family in town and you want to be with them, that's fine. At my house, we will have plenty of food. I'd like you to come. I just want to make sure that everybody's got a place to go and eat. You guys can hang out at my house and turn on the T.V. and watch games and relax. I don't have anything planned. I know the coaches' wives have gotten a bunch of food together. It should be pretty good."

A voice in the huddle announced that Walker was expecting a pie from his mother courtesy of UPS.

"I can't wait," Walker said with his eyes beaming.

Martin stepped forward.

"We need to do something for Project Angel Tree. Any suggestions are welcomed. We need to raise money. It does not mean you have to give much. A quarter would be appreciated. The money goes to a child whose parent is incarcerated."

"That's a great, great thing, guys. It's a chance for kid with their parent in jail to have something for the holidays," Gottfried said.

While millions of Americans watched Macy's Thanksgiving Day Parade, the team lifted weights and practiced. Meanwhile, Chaney Boatright, Elizabeth Gottfried, Edie Kelsey, Ashley Pearson, and Cynthia Scott had prepared a feast for the team. Coleman Coliseum manager Steve Wilson set up tables and chairs in the Gottfried basement. Bama Dining, the university dining service, set the tables. The entire team visited the Gottfried's where they enjoyed a wonderful Thanksgiving meal. I missed the gathering to be with family.

Most of the players spent the afternoon watching football in their coach's home. Walker fell asleep while the others watched the television.

Becky Hopf, who was the media relations contact for the team and the associate sports information director, solicited comments by the team about what they were thankful for on Thanksgiving.

"Waking up each morning. My family," Scott said.

"Having great coaches like Coach Scott and Coach Gottfried who support you on and off the court no matter what," Grizzard said.

"I'm thankful for living . . . There are a lot of people who can't say that who I've grown up with, and it does make you think and learn to appreciate what you have," Cotton said.

"I'm thankful for being able to play basketball at the University of Alabama," Dudley said.

Walker shared an embarrassing moment with Hopf.

"I was 11. I made fun of somebody for how much they'd eaten and how full they got, and I was laughing when a macaroni and cheese noodle popped out of my nose."

The dinner and afterward festivities were perhaps the highlight of the season. The team had pulled together, if only for a short while, and the coaches seemed content. The afternoon wasted away with laughter and companionship.

Mal Moore, who had been named the new athletic director days prior, appeared at the tournament luncheon on Friday. Moore wasted no time in showing his support for Gottfried's program. Moore has probably earned more football national championship rings at Alabama as an assistant coach than anybody in history. Moore's seven national title rings gives him three more than Joe Paterno and Bobby Bowden combined. Moore, who is an extremely articulate and intelligent man, was the logical choice for the job. He will do a great job of uniting the Alabama cause. Gottfried congratulated him on winning the position.

The coaches from LaSalle, High Point, and Centenary delivered entertaining speeches while their teams ate. William "Speedy" Morris shared some self-deprecating humor that was every bit as funny as television commentators have described Morris over his 14 years as the men's coach at LaSalle.

The Alabama team was not allowed to eat lunch at the tournament luncheon according to NCAA rules. (And where would we be without the guiding hand of the NCAA? The NCAA should legislate the number of bowel movements that a scholarship athlete is allowed for a given week. That would be as useful as half of their regulations.) The luncheon was just the daily effort that Gottfried's staff made to ensure compliance with the almighty power.

Pearson delivered the scouting report for the Gentlemen at 4:50 before the 5:30 tip-off.

He ended the scouting report quite ominously. "McCollum is coming in here ready to jack it."

Gottfried followed.

"If we press, somebody better get to 32 [McCollum's number]. He shot twenty-nine times the other night, fellas. He ain't waiting for you."

Gottfried seemed somewhat relaxed during the warm-up. With the non-conference schedule waiting for him in the coming weeks, he would have very few relaxing moments on the horizon. He often admitted anger about his scheduling decisions privately.

The final message that night had become a recurring theme.

"You can be the kind of player that needs the coach to get up here and give some great speech. I can throw my coat up against the wall. We can have timeouts where I do all kinds of crazy stuff because you need the coach to get you to play hard. Or you can be the kind of player that is playing no matter what. No matter who I play. No matter what time of day it is. No matter what day of the week it is. I play as hard as I can play. That's all you can do as a basketball player. Don't bank on me to get you ready to play. Be a self-disciplined, self-start kind of player."

The starting lineup remained the same. Meade, Dudley, and Grizzard had apparently managed a firm hold on starting positions as freshman while Hays and Martin added experience. Martin would also be asked to defend an old friend and AAU teammate in McCollum.

McCollum delivered the shot attempts in the first half, letting it fly from anywhere and everywhere. However, Martin's long wing span and tenacious defense frustrated him into four for 17 shooting. Ed Dotson's jumper gave Centenary its only lead of the game at 2-0. Grizzard drained a three-pointer at the 18:34 mark to give the Tide a permanent lead on his way to five of eight shooting in the half. Cotton and Dudley combined to shoot seven of ten in the half. Hays shot five for five from the foul line. The Tide guarded the Gentlemen closely, holding them to 27.8% shooting. Another game was decided by halftime, 47-26.

Gottfried walked into the locker room for a brief comment before joining his assistants. "Good half, fellas. I want us to keep playing that way."

In the staff meeting, Boatright pointed to a major reason for the lead.

"We only have three turnovers, coach."

Even Meade managed to have four assists against two turnovers, keeping London on the bench for 16 minutes of the half. The 6-foot-1 London did manage to grab four rebounds in four minutes.

"They have 13 offensive rebounds, coach," Kelsey added on a somber note.

Scott wanted to establish a fast break. "We've still got to have our guys running those lanes hard."

The staff entered the locker room.

"They've got entirely too many offensive rebounds. Guards, long shots produce long rebounds. You have to be ready and run 'em down . . . We have to guard people. I want you to buy in. I can sell and sell and sell. If you want to win and win in this conference, you better be a great defensive team because everybody's got good players . . . Offensively, the ball is sticking. You're an easy team to guard. We've got to move the ball . . . Let's talk about this real quick. Twenty-five seconds to go, Terrance Meade and Rod Grizzard. We're supposed to take one shot. You start feeding the post at fourteen seconds. When we call for one shot, then we're gonna shoot the last shot. At the very minimum, the score stays the same. What happened there was we hit two free throws and he hits a three, and all of a sudden we're down one from the twenty-five second mark to zero. So we'll take the last one even if we just sit on the ball and walk in. Let's build habits and build our team."

The Gentlemen were outscored 16-3 to open the second half, making it 63-29 and forcing their head coach Kevin Johnson to wonder why he wasn't eating leftovers near Centenary's campus in Shreveport, Louisiana, on the day after Thanksgiving. McCollum fired with some restraint in the second half, finishing six for 25 for the game. Gottfried used every active player on the roster. His most stressful moment came when Grizzard refused to go down to the floor for a loose ball.

"You're gonna get hurt if you don't dive on the floor for a loose ball, Rod!" (Gottfried said this to save Grizzard an injury; at that pace, with players diving at your legs, your best bet is to dive alongside them. Otherwise, you risk breaking something.)

The world stopped for the Tide bench when Davis canned a free throw to make it 88-62 with 1:51 remaining, giving him the first point of his career. The veterans had seen this guy make a million baskets in two years of wide open gunning in practice. He had finally made one that counted. Martin's defense and Cotton's offense (20 points on seven of ten shooting) helped bury the Gentlemen. Meade, Dudley, Grizzard, and Hays also reached double figures. Moss shot four for six from the field. Walker grabbed seven rebounds. The Gents finished with only 37.7 percent shooting for the game. The Tide cut the Gents' offensive rebounding from 13 to seven in the second half. Cotton even managed only one more turnover than assist. Since St. Louis, he had been whistled for some traveling violations after his lightning quick first step. The only negative of the game was Hays sitting down early with a slight ankle injury. Morr's preliminary guess was that he would be ready for the game the next day.

After a brief congratulations, Gottfried shifted the team's focus to LaSalle who were the favorites in the later game to reach the championship game of this tournament.

"Let me tell you something about this team tomorrow. This is the year that they've been waiting for. When Donnie Carr was a freshman, he started off his career with four straight games of scoring thirty points. And now they've got a bunch of seniors around him. They think they'll be good this year. They're in the A-10 with Temple and folks like that. I've talked to a few coaches in that league, and they tell me that they're gonna come after us. They play hard . . . Watch some of this next game if you want. Then get something to eat and go get rested."

The staff stayed for the next game, scouting LaSalle. We were entertained by an exchange between 6-foot-10, 285-pound Garrett Bragg of LaSalle and High Point's 6-foot-11, 240-pound Geordie Cullen. The mammoth Bragg crushed Cullen with a thunderous elbow to the face. After Cullen finally gathered himself, he returned the favor with a short jab at Bragg's testicles. Gottfried and I were particularly captivated by the colorful display of emotions by the big fellows. Bragg's Lasalle Explorers won the war, 85-62, but Bragg must have been experiencing unusual soreness in the morning.

Gottfried had not forgotten in the huddle after the Saturday shoot-around.

"The big white dude, Bragg, is kinda dirty in my opinion. He's really big. I don't want him baiting you into punching him. [Demonstrating the blow] This big white dude gave the High Point player a real good one in the face. And Bragg ended up getting popped in the nuts. You can't let yourself get baited into that stuff. Play hard and physical, but don't throw punches. The NCAA will take you out for a game."

Kelsey scouted the Explorers, and we walked to the player's lounge for a short film session. The tape revealed an athletic team that liked to dribble penetrate into the defense. When we returned to the Coliseum at 6:20, Gottfried reiterated Kelsey's concern about LaSalle's dribble penetration.

"[Demonstrating a dribbling action] At any time they may just get it and start to bam, bam, bam. You've got to be able to contain somebody."

LaSalle was the most tradition-rich basketball program that the Tide had faced—more storied than the great majority of the SEC. LaSalle won the 1954 NCAA Championship with one of the greatest college players of all time, Tom Gola. Gola also coached the Explorers to a 23-1 record in the '68-'69 campaign. The Explorers' home floor is Tom Gola Arena. LaSalle competes in the fairly impressive Atlantic-Ten which has won many big NCAA tournament games over the past ten years with Temple, UMASS, Rhode Island, Xavier, and George Washington. Temple has been no stranger to the Final Eight. Rhode Island under Jim Harrick also reached the Final Eight. UMass reached the Final Four.

Before the final warm-up, Gottfried tried to impress upon the team the caliber of LaSalle "This is a good team, fellas, from the A-10. They're gonna have a good record at the end of the year. It's a game tonight that could help us get into the NCAA tournament. Trust me. This one could help big time. Get yourself down and ready to play . . . I want you to warm-up hard, fellas. Don't jack around when you're shooting lay-ups."

Scott and I sat alone in the player's lounge during the warm-up. He was in terrible pain. He moaned and groaned like somebody was cutting his guts out with a dull pair of scissors. Two of his great friends, Bruce Sokol and David McCloud, entered. Scott immediately tried to stop making noises.

"Coach Scott is feeling rough, guys," I said, understating the situation, hoping that they would realize quickly that he was aching like hell.

"I just don't want to live off pain pills. I've got to fight it. I've got to fight it." Scott struggled to say the words. It often hurt for him to speak.

His visitors were concerned and very nice, but I feared that he hated the pressure of having to speak because he respected them so much. When he was struggling, I usually just asked if he needed anything.

Sometimes it seemed like a burden for him to reply.

The team returned. I walked behind Scott into the locker room, hoping to be able to catch him if his body collapsed. He summoned all his strength and composure to carry himself without alarming the players about the severity of his pain.

"Look up. Doc, you've got Carr," Gottfried began.

Giving Martin the assignment of guarding LaSalle's best scorer, Donnie Carr, further cemented his position as Gottfried's favorite defensive player. The coach spent the bulk of this lecture on defense before his general comments to close.

"Have some courage. Dive on the floor. Get an offensive rebound basket. Get some steals. Get some fast-break points. Get some shut-outs. Get a deflection. If you're playing hard, you're gonna do all those things if you have courage."

Gottfried had apparently found some stability in the starting lineup which remained the same. For the first eight minutes, Hays seemed like the only player on the floor for either team, scoring time after time. Hays performs so gracefully when he finds his rhythm. His 6-foot-11 body spreads wide to seal the defender on his back. He catches the ball and smoothly raises his back, feeling the defensive posture of the opponent for a clue. If he has space, he will quickly turn with one foot planted in the same spot and score with a jumper. What had not been showing up in the stat sheet during the last three wins was the poise that Hays added to the team when he was on the floor. His confidence calmed the youngsters. That evening, Hays had found a higher plain—pump faking and drawing fouls, running the floor hard and scoring in transition, stroking jumpers and foul line shots, charging the basket with authority. Hays carried the Tide to a 41-28 halftime lead with 24 points on nine of ten shooting.

After a very positive staff meeting, Gottfried emphasized a few negative points from the team's defensive effort.

"Away from the ball. We've got to be in a stance and ready to fight through some screens . . . Again, you've got to be down and always seeing it if you're away from the basketball . . . We started the game off by going for every pump fake known to mankind. We were flying around and all of a sudden they're inside us. . . . It's all about your defense. I care about the other end. But right now, I care about your offense about half as much as I care about your defense . . . That ain't Rick Mahorn and Bill Laimbeer out there setting screens. Get your body down and get yourself ready. Fight through picks and talk and help one another. That's how we're gonna become a good team."

Hays was fouled just 16 seconds into the second half, matching his career high of 26 points by making both free throws. Only 20 seconds later, Hays hustled down the floor to convert another offensive opportunity, but his body was clearly off-balance while jumping. His landing was very nasty—a violent twist and a tumble so obviously damaging to his left knee that the entire bench stood up expecting the worst. Writhing on the floor in agony, Hays was the focus of a silent crowd.

(Minutes later in the training room, Dr. Jimmy Robinson decided that Hays had torn the anterior cruciate ligament. Hays's season ended in a violent flash. Morr attempted to comfort Jeremy and his devastated mother, Sharon. The player's father, Ronnie, and his new bride, Dina, appeared to be trapped in a state of shock. The tears flowed freely for Jeremy and Sharon. Jeremy's grief was intensified by his knowledge of the consequences—surgery, excruciating and lengthy rehabilitation, and an altered basketball career. Dr. Robinson and Morr immediately offered hope in the form of the great likelihood that the NCAA would grant Hays a medical redshirt that would allow him to repeat his senior season. Hays desperately needed another season to help his chances of playing in the NBA. Apart from the individual concerns certainly racing through Hays's mind, he probably considered the fate of this young team jolted toward a path of inevitable disaster. The Tide had lost the one player that it could not lose. Already destined for 4-0 with Hays and 0-2 without him, conventional pre-season wisdom had been that Hays would be the absolute key to a successful season. Hays's exit seemed like the ship hitting an iceberg, damning the voyage.)

Alabama went on to hammer LaSalle, 85-70 in a Pyrrhic victory. Walker replaced Hays and shined with five of seven shooting. Dudley and Grizzard combined for 25 on 11 of 17 shooting.

The Tide rolled with a gaudy shooting percentage, 61.1 percent. The deserved winner of the MVP trophy for the tournament was Hays.

Ronnie comforted his son in the locker room until the game ended. The injured player had already decided to come back next year after having his ligament surgically repaired.

A triumphant but somber team walked into the most quiet winning locker room imaginable. Every player walked over to Jeremy's chair one by one to offer their support. Gottfried allowed the focus to remain on Hays for several minutes. When he began to speak, I wondered how hard it would be for this ball club to continue without its senior leader.

"The season goes on. The season goes on. The whole time we play, guys, I know what I want out of you. Offensively, I know you can play. But five guys, whoever they are, should be playing shut-out, balls-to-the-wall defense for 40 minutes. I'm gonna play guys that play defense, and we're gonna shut people out. There will be nights when we won't score. It won't go in. We had one of those up in St. Louis. It just wouldn't go in the hoop. Win, lose, or draw—the five guys on the floor are going to be busting their balls defensively. Does everybody understand that? There should be no mistaking it. You can get pissed off at me. You can bitch at me. You want to come sit in my office and talk? I'm gonna get five guys constantly down and working, working, working. That's the way you win championships. That's the way we won championships at UCLA, Murray State, and when I was a player here. It's on the defensive end. Now you're playing a team on Thursday night—trust me—they can't wait to play you. They were fifteen and one in their league. They won twenty-five games last year. They went to the NCAA tournament. They had five juniors start last year, and they've got five seniors starting. They shoot it well, and they're very smart in how they play. You and I both know that they're 45 minutes down the road, and they're dying to play this game. But so are we. This is an NCAA tournament team coming in our gym that opened up the season by beating St. John's. Okay. That's what you've got . . . Everybody's got to buckle up a little tighter now. Stay together. Stay strong. Good job. Let's pray."

Gottfried asked Matt Minor to say the prayer. He wanted somebody praying for Jeremy.

"God, thank you for this team. We're thankful that we're the kind of unit that when one hurts, we all hurt. Touch Jeremy and be with him. Comfort him."

Dr. Jimmy Robinson appeared in the post-game press conference. He shared the staff's optimism about a medical redshirt for the injured senior. Asked about whether the sore ankle that benched Hays during the Centenary game was a contributing factor, the doctor responded rapidly.

"No, not at all. The mechanism of his injury was the classic mechanism that we see for that ligament . . . When he landed and planted, the knee shifted as soon as he planted. He felt the pop and went down and buckled basically."

Gottfried's session with the press also centered on Hays.

"I'm really sad for him. It breaks your heart. That's part of sports . . . I saw the knee twist pretty hard. Watching it happen, my stomach just got warm because I knew it was gonna be a serious injury."

He was asked about Walker as the replacement.

"That would put four freshmen out there with us. But that's life. We all like to avoid obstacles like that. That certainly makes it harder. But some of these young guys have to step up and play. They'll be counted on even more right now. We started the year with only eleven scholarship players because Travis Stinnett is not healthy, and this knocks us down to ten. So we're obviously at a point where we can't afford too many more injuries. But we've got to overcome it."

(Everyone in the media room knew that there were other questions that could be asked. Are you beginning to accept that this season is doomed? Was a potential terrible season a price that you were willing to pay for a possible great season next year? With the recruiting gurus calling Gerald Wallace a superhuman, and your best player suddenly returning for a repeat senior year and the youngest club in America, how hard will it be to focus this team while everybody talks about next season? You've called your scheduling "dumb." How many regrets do you have about your scheduling now? Are you worried about the confidence of these youngsters in the long term? How will your relatively small freshman front line starters deal with the phenomenal athletes on your schedule?)

I talked to five people outside of the basketball program between the LaSalle game and the Monday practice for Samford. All of them immediately mentioned next season—a potentially magical result of Hays's injury combined with the anticipated one-year college career of Wallace and a seasoned group of players who would be baptized by the fire of a presumably horrific season. They all dreamed about next season being a potential trip to the Final Four.

My only thought was that Robert Scott may not have a next season.

9

Robert's Last Birthday

On the Monday before the Thursday game against Samford, Scott missed practice to begin a round of chemotherapy. The athletic director arrived like a concerned head of state greeting his depleted army in a distant land. Mal Moore's first address to the team began with an introduction from the head coach.

"He won't tell you, but I will. He's got seven national championship rings. Seven. He's somebody I really respect, and I'm glad he's in this position. So I wanted to give him a chance to say something to you guys."

After the introduction, Mal Moore began. "First of all, I wanted to say how much I enjoyed the tournament this weekend and your winning. Jeremy, I enjoyed watching you play in the first half. I'm so sorry that happened. But hell, we got a win anyway. Let me say that I coached for Coach Bryant—I guess for 19 years and then Coach Stallings. The most beautiful thing about coaching is that a group of men can form a team. And a beautiful team is one that can put five people on the floor that play as hard as they can play every minute that they are out there. That's what a team is all about. Same with football. Put eleven men out there that lay it on the line for 60 minutes. It's amazing what will happen if everybody will play hard for every minute of the game. A great conditioned team is a thing of beauty. People that can play in the clutch and play when it's tough and play in the big games—hell, that's what it's all about. And that's why you work hard in practice. I tried to tell something to our football team today [which was preparing for the SEC Championship game]. I said that today's practice in preparation for Saturday's game is the most important. Because if you don't get it done today, that day is gone. When you get to the game, everyone wants to win. If you're not prepared, hell—it's hard to pull it off. When you waltz out here to practice, let it be important everyday. It takes all hands. The people that are not starting are just as important. I'll back you anyway I can. I appreciate your efforts. I wish you the best with the season. I hope you take a genuine pride in your academics and maintaining your eligibility. If you're not doing that, you're letting your team down because they've got to be able to count on you. Are y'all ready to do some business? Then by God, let's go."

"Thank you, Coach. [Pause] I take offense because people ask me about Jeremy and start talking about next season," Gottfried said in a lengthy huddle session.

"This season, baby. This season," Moss said.

"Let me tell you what you're playing on Thursday night. It's basically Princeton. Disregard the name Samford. Because you guys are playing Princeton. The guy used to coach up there. They back-cut you to death. It's constant motion. If you fall asleep, they're getting lay-ups. I'm gonna show you some tape. They did it to St. John's this year. St. John's guys are standing straight up and twisting their heads around—it's cut back-door and lay-up all night. It's Princeton. You ought to just put Princeton across their jerseys."

Having watched Princeton closely over the years and coached against the Princeton Junior Varsity, I knew that the difficult thing about defending a team in Samford's motion offense with their great shooters is defending the three-point line while simultaneously defending the basket.

The only hope for the defense is that the intermediate jumper off the dribble is becoming a lost art in basketball. (As Pearson always likes to mention, the playgrounds and gyms of America are not filled with guys pump-faking a three-point shot and dribbling to take an open 16-foot jumper.) The tremendous value of the three-pointer and the theatrics of the slam dunk captivate the sport. Against Princeton, we tried to fly like mad men through the air to three-point shooters and use the rest of the team to sink off people and guard the basket—never ever try to aggressively deny a pass that is more than ten feet from the basket. If you overplay on the perimeter against Princeton's motion, you're dead—they charge through the back-door and stab you in the back.

Gottfried disagrees with players flinging themselves in the air to contest a three-point shot (the method Wimp Sanderson employed with success). The Wooden way is to stay on the floor while challenging a shot. By staying on the floor, you are assured that the possible rebounding situation will be a five-on-five battle. Disciplined shooters follow their shots and know best where the rebound will go. Everything about Gottfried's approach to basketball rests on the time-honored fundamentals that Wooden still preaches. Everything, that is, except for the slam dunk which has become a necessity. Gottfried clings to the fundamentals. A truly magical event was watching Gottfried teach the fundamentals of basketball to a group of youngsters for the first time. In an amazingly short period of time, he can teach the entire game of basketball. He just has an amazingly strong foundation in his thinking about the game.

Given his appreciation for fundamentals, he was scared to death by Samford. Tuesday's practice was an endless array of compliments.

"They're crafty . . . All their big guys can dribble and move around well . . . If you relax, they will expose you."

Medical issues were buzzing around practice. Scott appeared amazingly energetic just one day after beginning chemotherapy. Also, we received outstanding news from Boston. Having been approved for the procedure, Stinnett underwent surgery yesterday and the preliminary indications were very good. Morr may have finally caught his ghost. Hays would undergo surgery the following day and face a four to six month rehabilitation.

On the other hand, news on the floor was not encouraging. Pearson coached his scout team into several back-door lay-ups. If Pearson and the scout team could huddle for a few minutes and get easy buckets, what can a Samford team do that practices this stuff around the clock?

That Wednesday, December 1, practice featured a nervous Gottfried still pouring the compliments on thick.

"They brought everybody back from last year. They were third in the nation last year in three-point field goals made. All five guys aren't afraid to shoot it . . . They work three hours a day going back door. Their guys probably go nothing but back-door in the summer. They're gonna get some. I hope they get none. But they're probably gonna get some. If they do, don't get all distraught and embarrassed. This group has been playing together since they were sophomores. Don't give 'em a whole bunch. They will also get some three-pointers. Those are the two ways they're trying to score. It's perpetual motion. If you fall asleep, especially away from the ball, boom boom—somebody's cutting and you get exposed."

The lunch conversation today centered on who was favored in the game. Gottfried told the media early in the week that Samford was the favorite. When Jimmy Tillette, the Samford coach, was told by the media about Gottfried's opinion, he was upset.

"We're the favorite against Alabama? . . . Let's keep things in perspective . . . we're getting paid to go there. They're going to hand us a check before we leave. That's what I'm not sure people understand. They're playing us because they're paying us money and they expect to win."

GOTTFRIED's theme at lunch was that he could not believe that he had scheduled Samford. One obvious reason was that Samford's name and basketball history demanded no respect from his players. As much as people like me had tried to excite the players about beating Samford, we knew that the players were not looking forward to playing them. On the other hand, the Samford players would be sky high against the big state school that controls the fan base in the state. Alabama is the team of Robert Horry, Antonio McDyess, Latrell Sprewell, and Derrick McKey. Samford is a tiny college with a pretty campus. As Tillette correctly stated, the Bulldogs were being paid $25,000 to take the bus trip from Homewood to Tuscaloosa. The entire scenario transformed an eternal optimist in Gottfried into a distraught-ridden worrier who seemed doomed by fate. He dealt with the same situation last year when Alabama beat South Alabama where his father is the athletic director. He dreaded that game and hardly celebrated the win. But he was five times as anxious about Samford.

Kelsey pushed his forwards hard. He sent a message that the intensity of the post-defense needed to improve. (He certainly missed Hays. We all did. I could tell the team was having a hard time filling the void left in his wake. Fortunately, his surgery was successful.) "Kenny, you're making it easy for him," Kelsey yelled.

The team huddled around the head coach at the end of practice.

"They beat St. John's. They had two jump shots to beat Dayton. Dayton turned around and beat Kentucky the other night. They're gonna come in here hungry. You know the deal. It's an in-state deal. They're right down the street. They're talking about bringing five thousand people with them—all of that kind of crap. It's the Super Bowl for them."

At the Thursday shoot-around, Gottfried began diagnosing the enemy's offense for what seemed like the ninety-ninth time. Pearson described their personnel. He described the brother of his ex-teammate and friend, Boyd Kaiser (brother of Wade). (Wade appeared in Sports Illustrated when his grabbing a pivotal loose ball gave the Tide momentum in an incredible upset over the '94 Arkansas team that would become one of the all-time greatest teams, winning the NCAA title and only dropping two other games. Wade would be cheering for his brother's Bulldogs that night.)

Gottfried closed the shoot-around with a final plea.

"This game is on Fox which is pretty much all over the country given the satellites and all. So bring it. Bring it. Bring it. They beat St. John's. We've got to bring it."

Game time came around and Scott was not to be found. I called his house and found out he had been experiencing tremendous pain through the late afternoon. At 6:20, he still had not arrived. Given that this has been the most thorough preparation for an opponent, Gottfried used more time prior to warm-up on his team.

"The whole key is that you need to get a bunch of offensive rebound buckets. They're not pushing it. They don't want this game to get up in the nineties. Everybody but the safety must crash to the rim . . . Push it. I want to look up and see you guys running the floor. Come down the floor hard . . . You guys know that we've got Jeremy down and I don't know if Coach Scott will be here tonight. He ain't feeling very good today. All I am asking is that you play as hard as you can play. Warm up hard."

During the warm-up, I went to the player's lounge where I saw Scott's shrinking physique on a couch. He was groaning and grunting. I asked him if he needed anything. He could barely respond. Minutes later, Gottfried entered.

"My man is here," Gottfried said with a wide grin.

Scott slowly rose to a sitting position. Gottfried embraced him with a soft hug.

"You don't have to be here you know. You should be in bed."

Tears began flowing down the cheeks of the seldom emotional Scott. I saw his tears and tears raced down my face. I called on all my strength to refrain from sobbing. A single giant tear flowed down Gottfried's face.

"I just want to be here so bad for these players, Mark. But I don't want them to see me like this."

Gottfried tightened his hug and motioned for me to join them. I did.

"They'll be so happy to see you. But if you went home, they'll understand, too," Gottfried said softly.

Our embrace ended quickly. We were not exactly three personalities that you would ordinarily find in a group hug.

"I know Shaq is ready for Samford," Scott said, chuckling.

(I had been teased for months for trying to motivate the players at lunch about Samford. According to what I had been saying, Dudley expected to play the Lakers.)

The players returned. The head coach returned to his duties. The players decided to pledge allegiance to their fallen leader. Hays's number 52 was written on the sweatbands, tape, and socks of the players.

Gottfried sent the team out with a reference to Hays's situation.

"Be the most unselfish team in the country. Compete! You never know when last possession will be—when you can't play the rest of the season. I'll guarantee you they're coming in here with everything they've got," he said, igniting loud clapping.

Walker replaced Hays in a starting lineup that remained the same otherwise. The Bulldogs jumped all over Alabama, executing exactly like the Tide feared—patiently grinding the clock until nailing a three-pointer or cutting back-door for an uncontested lay-up. Thanks to guard Reed Rawlings, Samford led the Tide by 12 at the 14-minute mark, despite amazing intensity from Coach Scott on the bench who seemed to have risen from near death. While the rest of us on the bench were disgusted, Scott stayed in the game intensely. He reflected so much Alabama pride. His irate eyes clearly revealed the angry adrenaline shooting through his body. He alone seemed determined to win.

Samford dominated, continuing to score easily and the Tide couldn't respond on the offensive end. The officiating crew had apparently made the decision that Cotton's signature first move toward the basket with the ball was a traveling violation. Cotton turned the ball over time after time, landing him on the bench. The Bulldog halftime lead was 43-27. Samford shot 57.1 percent from the field in the half—a humiliating scene for Tide faithful. The typical opinion of Alabama people was that pride alone would drive the players to prevent lowly Samford from waltzing in and bullying Alabama. Wrong.

A quiet and humbled coaches' meeting told the story.

"They're 16 for 27 from the field," Boatright stated.

"Schea's got five turnovers," Kelsey said.

"We've got to cut down on penetration and take away all of Rawlings's threes," Gottfried said.

"They're eight for 17 from the three-point line," Kelsey added.

Pearson remained silent, bewildered and infuriated by the results of his scouting.

Scott's silence was deafening to me. His team's lack of defensive intensity contrasted with the price that he had paid to be here tonight inspired feelings of rage. I had to remind myself that this was a young team playing without Hays, its leader.

The staff entered the locker room.

"Get your head up. Don't pout. It's time to play," Gottfried said.

The head coach decided not to explode on this young team. He urged Martin to guard Rawlings with tenacity and decided to deny their high-post player who has been feeding their cutters effectively. He would begin the half in a press to increase the tempo. He stressed patience and ball movement on the offensive end.

"Twenty minutes is a long time. Just keep getting good shots. Get a good shot. Get a shut-out. Get a good shot. Get a shut-out. Get a good shot. Get a shut-out. Don't rush . . . They played the greatest half that they can play. Now you've got to come back and give them your best."

The press gave the Tide a pulse, but it was a case of too little, too late. Martin provided the bulk of the offense on his way to a career high 23 points on eight of 12 shooting. Although Grizzard mounted a charge which cut the lead to just six with 6:00 left, the Tide needed a couple more stops to save the day. Just as hope materialized, it just as quickly disappeared. The Bulldogs cruised to a 79-67 win on the strength of 60% three-point shooting in the second half and 13 for 21 for the game. Rawlings finished with 26 including four for six shooting behind the arch. The final minutes of the game served as a Samford pep rally. Alabama's aged 26-game winning streak over Samford snapped in an extraordinarily painful home defeat. A terrible 4-3 non-league start combined with Hays's injury left this team strapped onto a roller coaster bound for a house of horrors.

Gottfried gave a very subdued post-game speech, emphasizing how hard the team played. Presumably, he felt a need to start protecting his youngsters from inevitable failure—nurturing their confidence for the future. Perhaps, he actually liked the team's effort. To the media, he vowed not to surrender.

"Our guys are not going to fold the tent. There's a lot of basketball left for this team."

AFTER A horrible defensive outing, the head coach decided to shift the team's focus at practice on Sunday by switching to a two-guard front for his high-post offense. The timing was ripe for a change because the next game was still six days away at Louisville. Meade's mounting turnovers at the point guard position could be reduced by taking some of the pressure off him with another guard helping him initiate the offense. London played just four minutes against Samford and the question remained whether Meade's mistakes would lead to a second chance for London. Another man looking for playing time was Moss who must have been shocked to play only three minutes against the Bulldogs with Hays gone. Haginas played 25 minutes in a fine performance, scoring ten points on five of ten shooting and snatching eight rebounds.

Monday's practice featured an energetic Scott coaching like crazy for several minutes.

"Come on Fred Moss. I know you're better than that," Scott yelled.

Scott's approach to life seemed to have always been that when he got knocked down to the canvas, he jumped up immediately and started swinging harder.

"We got a lot better today. We're taking tomorrow off. Use it academically. You've got tests coming up. Get yourself ahead. I watched a bunch of tape on Louisville today. That game is gonna be played around the rim. That's the way it always is with those guys. So get ready to play above the rim. Anything else, coaches?" Gottfried asked.

"Keep working hard, fellas. Come in everyday and have your attention on what you're supposed to be doing," Scott said.

Louisville would be a sharp contrast from Samford. Louisville's hall-of-famer Denny Crum won two NCAA titles and continues to frequent the tournament with great athletes. The Tide went from being lulled to sleep by tiny Samford to an almost impossible situation in legendary Freedom Hall against the accomplished Cardinals.

Scott entered the gym on Wednesday wearing a short sleeve shirt and sweat pants. I was struck by how tiny his body appeared. From a distance, his frame was that of a young boy.

Crum was a Wooden disciple so Louisville used the high-post

offense. Gottfried said that preparing for the Cardinals is "like looking in the mirror."

Grizzard still did not respond on the defensive end.

"I can't help you on every possession. You've got to start guarding somebody sometime," Gottfried barked.

Gottfried finally pulled Grizzard out of a defensive drill in frustration.

The highlight of the practice was Davis taking a steal and scoring on a length of the court play. He strutted and beat his chest.

"The team we play Saturday is strong and athletic. They'll have a packed house waiting for you," Gottfried concluded.

DIANE BRIDGES and Amanda Coleman brought Scott's birthday cake from the office down to the coliseum floor on Thursday, December 9. Coleman had earned the respect of the coaches as an office assistant because she could perform at their near frantic pace. The office tends to be hectic because coaches often want tasks completed very quickly (faxes, memos, scouting reports, recruiting papers, scheduling meetings, keeping appointments, fielding phone calls, answering phone calls, all done quickly and efficiently). Bridges seemed quite stressed on most days. She smiled today because everyone had been looking forward to Scott's 42nd birthday party with the team.

Scott hopped around the court on his birthday like a new man. He charged around with pencil and paper to tally how many extra sprints would be run by players for practice miscues.

"That's one for Fred! He didn't talk on the screen," Scott yelled.

The red jerseys were beaten in transition for a bucket.

"That's one for the whole Red team. You didn't get back."

Scott noticed Moss out of position defensively.

"That's another one for Fred Moss. You were out of position. You're gonna be busy after practice, buddy."

The coaching staff, managerial staff, the players waiting to play in the drill, and I were smiling and chuckling. Scott was a pleasure to watch in action.

"Coach, I was right there," Moss protested.

"I saw you, Fred. Sam, where was Fred on the play?"

"I don't know, coach," Haginas responds.

"I ought to run you for that," Scott exclaimed as the coliseum floor erupted with laughter.

Scott continued to roam and nail guys throughout practice.

"Kenny, you've got another one," Scott said as Walker stared at him in complete disbelief.

Those glorious moments allowed the newcomers to sample Scott's energy and intensity at practice. We feared that the youngsters would never see the great Scott that tormented a struggling defensive player last year in Neal Ashby.

Gottfried seemed inspired by Scott's enthusiasm after a Haginas turnover.

"Quit turning the ball over! Twenty-three turnovers against Samford! They're not Vegas! They weren't up pressuring us. We just cough it up. Stop turning it over!"

Teammates bitched at one another in a late practice drill.

"Start blaming each other! That's a real good solution," Gottfried exclaimed.

Practice concluded on a very serious note.

"If you want to be a great team you've got to concentrate from start to finish everyday. You can't fade in and fade out. You can't be soft. You can't turn the ball over just because you're tired. I give you opportunities. Nothing is in stone as far as who's playing when and who's subbing in and out. Those decisions aren't in cement. They change everyday. And if you don't bring it everyday, don't come in there and bark at me one day because you've got your opportunity to show the coaching staff who needs to be playing. That's just life in a nutshell. It's Coach Scott's birthday today. We've got a cake over there."

With everyone clapping, Scott stepped forward in the huddle.

"Today in our individual period we had one of our best periods. We rarely missed a jump shot or a lay-up. But we didn't have too much enthusiasm. You guys have to learn to make your own enthusiasm when you're having a period like that. You guys need to look around. The first thing you should see is that we don't have a senior in the gym. You've got a chance to do something great. The future looks so good. But you've got to bring some stuff of your own. The coach can't get you up everyday. Guys were hitting jump shots left and right. This gym should have been full of enthusiasm because Alabama is improving. We can't pep you up everyday. You've got to bring pep in here. We could go 0-30. If one guy tells me that we didn't learn something by going 0-30, that's a guy I don't want to talk to. I feel like when you go through a game like Samford that if you haven't learned something, you're either a conehead or a cowhead or something. All I'm saying is bring some enthusiasm in here. If we didn't love you, coach would have already lined up and shot your asses. [Loud laughter from the team.] Shot you right in the head. We may go to Louisville, and it won't work out. But I guarantee you that if you keep loving each other and keep bringing your own enthusiasm and keep saying that I appreciate and love Rod Grizzard, and I love Schea Cotton, and I love Jim Bakken, and I love the guy that scores the points, and I love the guy cheering on the bench—if we keep that love up, we're gonna be the best in the country one day. You better believe it. When you go over here to get a piece of cake, the squares are already cut up. So don't cut my name up. I don't want to hurt you." Scott's last comment triggered booming laughter.

On his birthday and within a five-minute span, Scott captured the essence of this team's current situation and what it needed to reach lofty goals in the future.

The team and staff ate the cake after the customary singing of the birthday song. It was another great moment in the season. A moment of togetherness.

THE COMMERCIAL flight to Louisville lasted forever compared to the convenience of a chartered plane. Pat Trammell traveled with the team. His father, Pat Trammell, Sr., will never be remembered nationally like Joe Namath, Ken Stabler, or Bart Starr, but he was Coach Bryant's favorite quarterback and leader. Trammell led arguably the greatest

Alabama football team of all in 1961. Their national championship run was Bryant's first, and the club personified the mental and physical toughness of Trammell and Bryant. Trammell's premature death after his playing career rocked Bryant like no other tragedy. In many ways, Trammell is Alabama football. As for his son, dad would be proud. He drips with class.

Gottfried spent some time with me to review Crum's career on the plane. Crum could lose every game for four years and still have an average of twenty wins per year. We remembered the Monday night that Louisville with "Never Nervous" Pervis Ellison beat Duke for the national title in 1986. How Crum's success must have bothered Kentucky fans during the Wildcat title drought between '78 and '96!

Alabama practiced in the Cardinals' campus practice facility at 8:30 P.M. We were appreciative of the heat in the gym situated below the Louisville student center on a cold Kentucky night. Scott especially enjoyed the heat because he often suffered from chills. Crum has a beautiful balcony overlooking the court. The basketball office features large glass windows that allow a great view of this modern and impressive facility.

The shoot-around at Freedom Hall could not have contrasted more sharply with the evening's experience in the warm, intimate gym. The 20,000-seat arena also serves as the home of a minor league hockey club. Scott and I were shaking like a vibrating bed in a cheap motel courtesy of the ice underneath the floor. But one has to respect the great history of Freedom Hall which has hosted the Final Four and countless other huge games.

Our return in the evening led to an aged and small visitor's locker room. An old trick to enhance homecourt advantage is to maintain a terribly uncomfortable visitor's locker room.

The condition of this room, however has everything to do with the building's age. Hearing Pearson and Gottfried prepare the team to defend the high-post offense seemed awkward. Gottfried knew that beating Louisville had less to do with disciplined offensive patterns and meticulous half-court defense than it did fundamental full-court play and furious rebounding action.

"This is a great opportunity for us. I want you to play. Don't worry about all this crap [pointing to the board filled with notes]. Just play! Play!"

During the warm-up, the depth of this club's despair crystallized in my mind. Only one other Alabama team in 26 years stumbled to a .500 record through eight games. With two NCAA title banners hanging in Freedom Hall, 19,000 plus cheering, and an athletic Crum team playing at a wide-open pace, these youngsters were almost certainly destined for a 4-4 record. Combine the evening's prospects with a Christmas tournament remaining at Arizona where it seemed like the Wildcats might have a puncher's chance to beat the NBA's Clippers, and you had a non-conference run from hell. For a quarter-century at Alabama, non-conference games have been winning time. Sanderson's only bad team finished 14-17 in '88 but began the season with a 6-2 mark. Sanderson was more shrewd with his scheduling than Gottfried had been with this team. During Hobbs's nightmarish free-fall when he lost 30 of 52 games over a two season stretch before reluctantly handing the team over to Gottfried, he began those seasons 10-0 and 6-2 before free falling. So the lingering question remained. How bad could this season become with SEC play remaining?

After the warm-up, Gottfried emphasized defensive transition against a Cardinal team that would be looking to run. Transition buckets would ignite the crowd. He wanted the weak-side of his defense to watch for lobs. A large crowd feeds off a high pass to a high jumper who slams the ball in the goal.

"Get some loose balls. Get some deflections. Take a charge. That means you're playing hard. If there is a ball on the floor, dive on it. Just like a grenade, I'm gonna help my team. Play through the crowd. It'll get loud." Gottfried clapped for his team to get them excited.

Grizzard had been pulled from the starting lineup. Cotton grabbed his first start since St. Louis. Louisville began the contest in a full-court press. Credit Crum's staff with thorough scouting. Why not pressure a young team that struggled with turnovers even at the point guard position? 19,293 Cardinals went wild early on. Nate Johnson and Marques Maybin of Louisville capitalized with trip after trip to the foul line. Turnovers and fast breaks fed the frenzy. Eight of the nine Tide players that logged more than five minutes of playing time would register a turnover. 14 of 17 foul shooting for Louisville led to a 39-28 halftime lead for the home team.

The halftime staff meeting centered on the obvious—how to stop the whipping caused by turnovers and weak transition play. Gottfried seemed unusually furious when he entered the locker room.

"You thought I was kidding you about getting back! Terrance Meade, you start the game off just jogging! Just jogging like you're playing against some bullcrap team like Fort Payne or some bullcrap team! This is the Louisville Cardinals! They're running on you! I guess I've been talking to a wall all weekend long . . . 18 turnovers. Eighteen turnovers! You're not gonna give yourself a chance to beat anybody with 18 turnovers. [Pointing at the point guards] I've got you two guys with nine from the point guard position! And you haven't been in the game together. So my point guard on this team has nine turnovers! Nine!"

When the head coach opened the floor to his staff, Scott stepped forward.

"Tarik, you're a junior! You've got to be a leader out there. You can't let their pressure take you out of your game."

Finally, the head coach suggested using more back-door plays to combat Louisville's denying the wings very far out on the perimeter. The team looked tired. They all kept their heads up, trained on Gottfried.

"I have no doubt that you can win," Gottfried concluded.

The Tide marched out of the locker room and stopped the bleeding, minimizing the turnovers and the Cardinals' fast break points. On the strength of accurate shooting by Walker, Cotton, and Grizzard, the Tide closed the gap to six points midway through the second half. The deafening crowd finally went silent.

Despite the admirable comeback, the outcome was never really in doubt. Louisville ended the suspense with an 18-0 run keyed by three-pointers and more backcourt turnovers. The crowd roared endlessly.

Losing is always bad, but the insults from the heckler behind the bench are harder to ignore when the home team is beating your brains out. London finished with eight turnovers and zero assists in the horrible performance of a lifetime—the culmination of butchered confidence after having his starting role stripped and his playing minutes carved. Meade finished zero for three from the field with four turnovers, zero assists, and four fouls in 15 minutes. Aside from one for one shooting by London, one could search the world over and not find a worse exhibition from the point guard position. The visiting team tallied a total of 31 turnovers. The Tide wasted brilliant efforts from Walker and Cotton. Walker finished with 16 points and 11 rebounds while Cotton scored 21 points on five for 8 shooting to go along with nine rebounds. The Cardinals won the game, 87-72.

A calm Gottfried addressed his team.

"You played hard. I'm proud of you for that. You just didn't play well. You kept turning the ball over. They were taking charges. We wouldn't take a charge . . . You can't come in someone else's gym or anywhere and turn the ball over thirty times. We just turned the ball over . . . Don't get your head down. You played hard all the way. They trapped us and pressured us and we just wilted like a flower. We just lost our toughness. We just have to get better. We have to get smarter, [looking at Martin] don't talk to a foul shooter when he is shooting. If I'm shooting a foul shot, nobody needs to be hollering at me. I call [press back to the zone] and Terrance Meade walks right out there with no idea about what we're doing. We've got four guys playing a zone and you take off chasing a guy through the lane. Somebody on this team has to organize our team on the floor—step up and lead the team with some direction. We just ran around and let them get loud and folded up." He concluded regretfully, like a storyteller that accepts but dislikes the end of the story.

As most of the Tide's opposing coaches have done in their post-game press conferences, Crum praised the talent of the young Alabama team and predicted future success. While Speedy Morris of LaSalle called the Tide an NCAA tournament team, the latest rosy predictions for this team hinted at a longer wait for success.

"That's a real talented team. I think they've got a real good future. They'll be real good once they gain a little experience," Crum said.

When asked if Gottfried realistically expected this year's squad to begin winning, he refused to accept the wait.

"Now. No, yesterday. We can moan and groan all we want about inexperience. The only way to solve it is to win."

THE TEAM reconvened on Monday to prepare for a Saturday game with UT-Chattanooga. The Chattanooga Moccasins have been represented by fine teams in recent years. The Mocs extinguished Tubby Smith's stint at Georgia quite prematurely in the first round of the NCAA tournament. This edition of the Mocs, however, seemed poised to embarrass the institution. They had charged out of the corner after hearing the first bell and been immediately belted to the canvas on their way to a 1-5 start. In his third year of coaching the Mocs, Henry Dickerson must guess that he will either the turn the program around in the next three to 15 months or watch the school bang the gong on his tenure.

Scott directed the beginning of Monday's practice, implementing his one-two-two drop zone. Gottfried searched for answers to his defensive problems that were magnified by the loss of Hays. Later, the head coach became frustrated with Grizzard's defensive effort in a drill for what seems like the five-hundredth time. I wondered about the duration of the coach's patience with the talented guard's inability to respond. I assumed that Scott had become the pivotal spokesman for Grizzard. Removed from most staff meetings due to his condition, Scott's dialogue with his boss about the team could be observed around practice on many occasions. Scott's body language in those sessions and his comments to me suggested that he begged for patience from Gottfried.

Cotton had meanwhile settled into a period of relative tranquility. Although removed from the team emotionally, his abilities were reluctantly respected. His redeeming intangible as a player was his willingness to force an advantageous angle and take a hard hit. He was awarded 18 foul shots at Louisville and paid for every one. He was still no threat to win a congeniality prize from his teammates.

That Monday, he was frustrated at practice when his team would not pass him the ball after his scoring had them on the brink of winning a competitive drill.

"I don't know why they just don't give me the ball. I'll end the damn game," Cotton said, aloud.

On the next possession, Cotton ended the game with a three-pointer.

"Can't go away from the well," he said, walking off the floor.

The starting lineup typically wore red jerseys in certain controlled scrimmages. Gottfried never hesitated to make sudden jersey changes. Of course, the symbolism of the first-team jersey is a frequently used psychological ploy. The jersey of preference provides a tangible reward during practice. The head coach grew tired of the white team's defensive lapses.

"Hey, white team! Guard 'em! You want to get on the red team? Play hard on the white team!" Gottfried exploded.

Later, the front court players failed to establish low post position, leading the head coach to offer a quick summary of half-court offense.

"Any offense that you run ends up [pointing at the area midway between the top of the circle and the baseline along the three-point arch] with the ball going to the wing [pointing toward the lower part of the painted area], someone down there posting up, and [pointing toward the foul line] somebody up here in the high post. It looks like a triangle. We're not running the offense just to run it. We run it to get a good shot. If you're down in there in the post when the ball goes to the wing, make yourself available. I want to throw it to you. But if you guys don't post up, we won't throw it to you. We'll just take jump shots during the whole game! We'll never go inside! When the ball goes to the wing, be a presence in there! Post up big!"

Turnovers began to mount as Monday's practice slowly grinded to a halt. After the Louisville debacle, the head coach's tired eyes were not pleased when Walker lost the ball.

"[Screaming] You've got some fatigue and you guys like just go soft like a noodle! It's like a hot potato! I've just got to get rid of the ball! Firm up right now and learn how to play when you're tired! Come on Kenny!" The words echoed off the coliseum walls.

Alabama would be playing in Huntsville for the first time against the Mocs. Gottfried wanted to bring the team to north Alabama as a show of appreciation for a supportive fan base in the area. (He plans to implement this the following season as well, with a trip to Mobile.)

After a largely uneventful practice week because exams prevented the meeting of the whole squad, the Friday bus ride to Huntsville featured a film based on the young rocket scientists from West Virginia who were inspired by the great work of Von Braun. The Tide would be playing in Von Braun Arena tomorrow. It was just a coincidence according to Boatright who manages all the details.

The bus went directly to Von Braun Arena for an afternoon shoot-around. In another hockey locker room, an informal survey revealed an arrogant group of students after their exams. Amazing how confident these guys were about their grades! Asberry and Gottfried would be ready to hold hands and skip down the street in togas if these guys were right. A good academic semester would be a nice payoff after a practice week that was crazier than Chinese Checkers—guys coming and going from every direction before and after exams.

Upon entering Von Braun Arena, I began looking for Rocky Balboa who could find a great workout by punching hanging beef in this place. It was freezing. I was glad that Scott had planned to arrive the next day. He would have been miserable there. The color scheme of the seats in rapidly aging Von Braun Arena featured an array of worn pastels.

Hays, who could make this trip unlike the plane flight to Louisville which would have negatively impacted his knee, told me of his strong desire to play during the shoot-around. Apparently, the Samford defeat and the foreseeable whacking from Louisville had been excruciating to watch for Hays.

"You don't know hard it is for me to not be playing. I just wish that I could help them."

Later at the hotel, news circled that several players had been sexually harassed by a party-goer in the hall. She remained in the hall, accosting all the players who had the misfortune of passing her by. The players anxiously avoided her. Just one more distraction for the young men who were trying to rest up for the next game.

Game day predictions about attendance were pessimistic given that the weekend before Christmas might not be an attractive time to watch a 4-4 team trade punches with a 1-5 club even if it was Alabama's first game in Huntsville.

Former Gottfried teammate and roommate Jim Farmer, who was attempting to jumpstart a country music career in Nashville, did appear for the game. Wearing his signature black outfit from head to toe as always, Farmer also appeared on the sidelines at the SEC Championship Game in Atlanta two weeks before. (Last I heard, he was planning on attempting to combine sex appeal and a shrewd marketing strategy to break through as a celebrity.)

Courtesy of early television scheduling, Dave Neal and Barry Booker of Fox Sports Net must have been shocked to broadcast this one from the Von Braun Center.

Kelsey, who claims Chattanooga as his hometown, appropriately scouted the Mocs. So Kelsey researched a former player in Rongie Cowser who left the Tide program shortly after Gottfried took the reigns. The staff knew that Cowser would shoot from everywhere—even if he caught the ball in a convenient parking space outside the arena.

"Cowser, number fifteen, is looking to shoot coming off the bench. Know when he comes in and we've got to get to him. He'll take every shot that he can get," Kelsey said.

The late night, staff tape session revealed that the Mocs' guards struggled against pressure. A problem with which the Tide could certainly empathize. Michigan decided not to pressure the Mocs, and UTC experienced some limited success before buckling.

"SMOTHER 'em. Get up into their jock strap. Put some heat on 'em," Gottfried said.

During the warm-up, I held a flimsy chalkboard while the head coach made his final notes. The motivational material lacked for the 1-5 Mocs so he used the big picture approach.

"I hope we're excited about playing. We're on game number nine already. I'm telling you that you'll blink, and you'll be in your twenty-sixth game. It's not like the NBA. We don't have 80 games. We've only got 27 or 28 regular season games. Don't waste 'em."

Grizzard rejoined the starting lineup. Cotton grabbed Martin's off-guard position for the first time since St. Louis, making the lineup 100 percent newcomers—to call this team young at this point would have been an understatement. Scott arrived before tip-off and fortunately the crowd had warmed up the building some.

Alabama began the game with a gigantic shooting slump but managed to stay close because of adequate defense. With 9:30 remaining in the half, UTC led 9-6. The score did not exactly reflect a Knicks-Heat-like defensive war with phenomenal intensity.

Meade salvaged the half for the Tide, scoring eight points in eight minutes to spark a 17-eight run. Meade's shooting stroke was pure—simple and reliable. Watching him shoot the ball necessitated asking whether all of Meade's problems couldn't be attributed to the staff playing him at the wrong position. He certainly had the talent to be a shooting guard.

Dudley grabbed six rebounds, helping the Tide to a 27-21 halftime lead. Boatright focused on the positive in the staff meeting.

"We finished the half going eight for twelve."

"We started off about one for one hundred," Gottfried responded.

After more input from assistants, the head coach was still puzzled by the lack of scoring. "I like the way we're playing, but we're just missing open shots."

Nevertheless, he asked the team to be more patient with their shot selection. After not having criticized a very good defensive half, he closed on a defensive note.

"Buckle down, fellas. Start the half off with a shut-out. Get another shut-out. Every time they get the ball, think about getting another shut-out."

Six points apiece from Dudley, Grizzard, and Cotton demolished Chattanooga's chances in the first 6:30 of the half, making it 45-30. Gottfried played everybody in the blowout, leading to the dramatic moment of the game for the Tide.

The flamboyant walk-on Davis grabbed a steal and streaked toward the goal in a one-on-none break with bad intentions while the bench waited to explode. The bench would have erupted if Davis nailed a jumper, but a Davis dunk could have sparked a riot. Most close teams desire individual achievement from the players deep on their bench more than anybody. If a player cares about his teammates, it seems natural to want everybody to experience success in a game after working so hard in practice.

But the rushing adrenaline proved too much, and Davis jumped too early, causing an ugly miss. A hustling Bakken trailed the play. He grabbed the rebound and scored, to the delight of the bench.

Dudley finished with ten points and eight rebounds on five for seven shooting. Meade added 15 on five for eight shooting. Cotton led the team with 17 on seven for eight foul shooting. Cowser finished with two for 11 shooting. Alabama hammered Chattanooga, 75-51, and Bakken was the locker room hero.

After the game Gottfried asked a visitor to step forward.

"Let me introduce you to Peter Lowe. He is one of our Board of Regents at Alabama. There are only fourteen of them. They make all the decisions, fellas. This is a big cheese right here," the head coach said, prompting Lowe to speak.

"Y'all played great. I had a fun time watching you. Good luck the rest of the year. You've got a great coach and a bunch of great assistants. I was thrilled by watching you this afternoon. Thanks for coming to Huntsville."

WHEN THE team met again on Monday, Dec. 20, to prepare for a Tuesday game in Tuscaloosa against Alabama A&M, Scott displayed his substantial teaching ability by vigorously showing how the players should position themselves to maintain sight of their assigned player while moving to help from the weak side to various emergencies threat-ening their goal. Having scouted the next opponent, Pearson warned the group about Terrance Vanlier of Alabama A&M—who averaged 17.6 points per game.

"He can play at this level, guys," Pearson said.

Walker would be playing against a high school teammate in Garik Nicholson who was also a freshman.

"This freshman is left-handed. He likes a jump hook. Kenny knows it a lot better than me. I haven't seem him make one or two. I've seen him make ten or 12 in three or four games."

Later, Moss knocked Walker to the ground in a drill.

"Where are you, Kenny?" Scott barked.

"He knocked me down," Walker replied.

"He can't hurt you, Kenny," Scott said sarcastically.

A few minutes ater, Walker lost sight of the ball in his defensive stance—a bad mistake.

"See the ball, Kenny. The ball is gonna hit you in the back of the head," Scott remarked before an uncontrollable chuckle.

Walker giggled.

Minutes later, Scott caught Walker out of position on the weak side of the floor.

"Where are you on help-side, Kenny?" Scott inquired.

"I was there," Walker replied emphatically.

(Note that Walker never sounded belligerent. He thinks the game, and there is a beautiful ten-year-old kid still alive in him that must question authority.)

"Are you calling me a liar, Kenny?"

Walker smiled while the sideline spectators chuckled.

The head coach voiced concern in the huddle after practice.

"I know some of you guys are staying up too late. We took yesterday off. But you came out today and looked a little sluggish . . .That's a sign of immaturity. You've got to get yourself mentally focused . . . You're gonna find that the season is long and your body starts to wear down. You gotta eat right and sleep right . . . We can go to a nine o'clock movie tonight. You can be my date, Alfred." This sparked a volcano of laughter.

(People knock the testosterone-filled world of male team sports, and the negatives are abundant. But there are also special times shared by a group of men who genuinely care about each other. Critics say that the drive to win and make money corrupts everything in sports. That is a lie. When Gottfried asked Moss on a date and everybody laughed like crazy, there was a moment when we all realized that the coach was just a person—a person who likes Moss as a person. I think that I can speak for the great majority of the people around the team in saying that I liked Moss. I did not care if Moss never scored another point. He was the kind of person that I would want for a father, son, brother, or fellow soldier. That is team sports. Then why is winning important?

Striving to win means everything because it is the goal that unites. Within the rules, the effort to win purifies completely. It demands selflessness. When Michael Jordan has already scored 39, and his team-mate has a pretty good look at the basket, the winner passes the ball to Jordan because it is the selfless thing to do. No matter how good the teammate's shot happens to be, it is not better for the team than whatever could happen if Jordan tries to score. For Jordan, the selfless act is the willingness to take individual blame for the team's failure. Furthermore, the striving to win supersedes all racial, ethnic, socioeconomic, sexual, and religious barriers.

The striving to win has lifted African-Americans to hero status on Autumn football Saturdays in Alabama where they were once blatantly oppressed. Even the hidden bigotry that still grips the South slowly erodes away because generations of white children have cheered and adored African-American athletes. So much ignorance has been erased by the ruthless equality of opportunity in the gyms and stadiums of the American South.

And the money?

All we hear about today in the world of sports is the phenomenal importance of money! Obviously, money is important in sports. The Red Sox decided that they could not afford Babe Ruth. The White Sox wanted more money so they accepted a bribe to lose the 1919 World

Series. Today's salaries for pro athletes and big-time coaches are sky high! People complain endlessly about the salaries. The salaries are exactly where they should be. This is a market economy. Americans value sports tremendously.

For many, it is the only escape from a tired and boring existence. Making money has never been based on making some contribution to society that a group of intellectuals would deem to be important. The owner of Krispy Kreme Doughnuts is making a killing. People love his doughnuts. That is America. Let us not lose sight of the great positives remaining in big-time sports.)

The movie idea crashed because the chosen late film didn't not start until 9:50.

TUESDAY's shoot-around brought a warning from the head coach.

"Sometimes you will look at the coach and not believe what he's telling you. Trust me. The team that you're playing tonight is dangerous. They're gonna come in here and shoot it quickly. If they happen to be shooting the ball well, they will press you all night. And it's all-out denial. Trust me. Don't overlook 'em . . . They went into Mississippi State and were beating them right before the half. And they're just balling. They're pressing. They're shooting threes. They're driving and dunking—flying around. That's what you're playing against."

After the game, the plan was that the team would break for a few days before returning to prepare for Arizona's tournament. Gottfried feared that they would look ahead to their break and not concentrate on the game.

"I don't want you to think about going home. Think about that after the game. If we need to stay and practice, we will. I don't want to do that and neither do you."

This was the first meeting between these two schools. L. Vann Pettaway, who accumulated a 292-100 record in 13 seasons of Division II hoops, guided Alabama A&M into the unchartered waters of Division I.

Because the A&M Bulldogs would use a full-court press after every made basket, Gottfried discussed breaking the press extensively before the warm-up. He continued to fight a possible mental lapse.

"They're gonna come after you. They've got a lot of energy. They've got a lot of pride. And they're coming in here to try and whip you. They will press you. You've got to firm up and be smart. You've got to take it at 'em at dunk on 'em."

I was grateful that Scott appeared to be without pain during the warm-up. He had experienced several positive days in a row.

Gottfried's final pre-game words called for massive bonding.

"It's not five players. It's all of us. We need everyone in the room to get where we want to be. We're all together."

The all-newcomer starting lineup remained. A&M controlled the first ten minutes of the contest, but Alabama slowly took over and never relinquished the lead. The home team led 50-41 in the locker room, but the defense seemed to have been left in Huntsville—four different A&M players combined to shoot an amazing eight for 12 from the three-point line.

Because A&M used a zone, Scott suggested in the staff meeting that Gottfried use the age-old technique of posting up a player at the short corner (the area just outside the paint and near the baseline).

"They can't handle anything we've got inside," Scott said.

The head coach's mind was elsewhere.

"Rod Grizzard won't contest a shot," Gottfried said.

"We've got 11 turnovers," Boatright interrupted.

The staff joined the players.

"The name of the game in that half was turnovers. We've got 11. The starting guards have seven between Meade and Rod. Firm up. Get tough with the basketball . . . Rod you're seven feet tall with your hand up. Your guy is about to shoot and you're four feet tall because you don't react by shadowing the ball with your hand. When the ball goes up to pass or shoot, your hand goes up. Let's get high on the floor to overplay VanLier. The guy is four for four . . . Make sure that we keep going to the big guys against their zone. Try to post up in the short corner. That's always available against a zone."

"The first five minutes we need a knockout punch," Pearson added.

Alabama knocked A&M into next month in the first five minutes of the second half. Four lay-ups and two free throws led to a 16-2 run in 5:32. Game over at 66-43. Again, Gottfried played the entire active roster. The bench cheered for D.J. Towns who shot two for two from the field. For a scholarship player, Towns had earned minimal minutes over 9 games.

Martin exploded with four of six three-point shooting and 8 rebounds. Dudley finished with 24 points on nine for 13 shooting to go along with 16 rebounds during a night to remember for him.

A developing trend among opponents was the taunting and banging of Cotton. Cotton's history was such that he did not mind a verbal or physical confrontation. He often said with pride that he felt at home in south central Los Angeles, and thriving in that area meant not backing down ("unless somebody is sprinting toward their car or house for a gun," Cotton said).

So Cotton's big arms were often tangled by an opposing player when he moved without the ball. Reminiscent of Larry Bird and Chuck Person when the Celtics and Pacers battled in the playoffs, Cotton liked a continuing verbal exchange with opponents.

The A&M players were particularly vocal and physical with Cotton. Near the end of the game, Cotton drove the lane and slammed home a fantastic dunk to push the lead to 25. His head turned toward an A&M player.

"Punk bitch," he yelled.

The whistle blew and Cotton was called for a technical foul. Gottfried scolded him. Certainly not a pivotal sequence, but it added spice to an otherwise routine 97-74 win.

After giving his player a short and less than enthusiastic congratulations, Gottfried loudly asked Boatright for the Tide turnover total.

"Twenty-three," Boatright responded.

Apparently that disturbing statistic had the head coach looking forward to the opener of Arizona's tournament.

"Let me tell you something right now so you understand. Delaware was 26-5 last year. They went to the NCAA. They're 7-1 now. They can play . . . Have a good three days off. I'll see you Christmas night at 6:30 P.M."

The team wished Kelsey a happy birthday before departing. The group separated. I went to spend Christmas with my family. I learned later that Scott was in agony the whole three days. He slept and ate very little.

The coming Arizona tournament loomed over everyone's heads.

The 1999-2000 Alabama basketball team and staff. From left, front row: Manager Matt Minor, Schea Cotton, Solomon Davis, Terrence "Doc" Martin, Tarik London, Travis Stinnett, D. J. Townes, Terrence Meade, Jim Bakken, and Head Manager Winslow Armstead. Standing: Kyle Rasco, Scott Hewitt, Darren Boatright, Robert Scott, Head Coach Mark Gottfried, Rod Grizzard, Kenny Walker, Jeremy Hays, Erwin Dudley, Alfred Moss, Sam Haginas, Tom Kelsey, Philip Pearson, Kobie Baker, John Morr, Brent Vinson, and Manager Clay Pruitt.

BELOW: The Crimson Tide at home in fan-filled Coleman Coliseum, during the 1999-2000 campaign.

ABOVE,
Tom
Kelsey,
Mark
Gottfried,
and
Robert
Scott.

RIGHT:
Gottfried,
Scott, and
Philip
Pearson.

ABOVE: Schea Cotton
dunking against the
University of Florida.

RIGHT: Rod Grizzard
shooting against
Auburn University.

Robert Scott, Mark Gottfried, and Howard Pride check the stats at halftime of the Kentucky game.

Gottfried talking to his players after beating Kentucky during the 1998-1999 season.

Halftime in the locker room, with Tom Kelsey exhorting the players. From left, "Doc" Martin, Schea Cotton, and Erwin Dudley. Behind and to the left, Pearson leaning against the lockers.

At one point during the 1999-2000 season, it seemed half the team was injured. From left, Dr. Jimmy Robinson conferring with Alfred Moss, and continuing from L to R: Kenny Walker, Sam Haginas, Jeremy Hays, Travis Stinnett, and Schea Cotton.

CLOCKWISE FROM ABOVE: The Bama fans are in it as Alabama beats Auburn. Trainer John Morr. Mark Gottfried embracing Robert Scott after the emotional win over Auburn. Rod Grizzard talking to Brad Daugherty from ESPN television after the win over Auburn.

RIGHT: Sam Haginas and Robert Scott after a big win over Tennessee.

BELOW: Jeremy Hays presents Scott with a plaque from the team. The inscription reads: "You are the man we all dream of one day becoming. May God bless you as you have blessed our lives."

ABOVE LEFT: Scott during his playing days at Alabama.

ABOVE: Robert Scott, coaching near the end of his life.

LEFT: Scott and Gottfried, enjoying a victory.

10

"We'll make sure you don't die."

The Bank One Fiesta Bowl Classic hosted by the '97 national champion Arizona Wildcats has been owned by the host school. Arizona consistently invites a school from a major conference to their incredible tournament and boasts a 28-0 record. Gottfried had warned me that Arizona does such an incredible job of running a tournament that I would be shocked. I was excited enough to see legendary Arizona coach Lute Olson in his stomping ground. Olson silenced all critics when his Wildcats beat Rick Pitino's last Kentucky team for the national championship.

Scott did not travel with the team to Arizona. We hoped he would feel well enough to join the team before the opener. On the other hand, we didn't want him to push his body to hard by flying across the country. The long commercial flights to Tuscon allowed plenty of time for evaluating this tournament which basically appeared to be a no-win situation. I would have bet my car that Arizona would win the tournament. They were that good and even better at home. Only Duke can argue about surpassing Arizona in the home court advantage department. The Wildcats are simply very good every year. And they do not lose their Christmas tournament. Ever. So the Tide would be traveling home with a nasty 7-5 non-conference record in the best case scenario.

The bad news did not stop there. The Tide was scheduled to open against Mike Brey's Delaware Blue Hens who were in the NCAA tournament the last two years and were planning another trip with their 8-1 record and many veteran players. Brey is one of the hottest coaches in America.

The third disadvantage of this tournament was that the UNC-Wilmington Seahawks had been picked by many to reach the NCAA tournament that year under Jerry Wainwright. Wainwright's teams are tough as nails. The Seahawks would be the Tide's second opponent after an extremely plausible loss to Delaware. The Tide team was going to have to buckle up. It was going to be a bumpy ride.

UPON ARRIVAL in Tucson, the most bizarre situation materialized on our walk from the plane to the terminal. We heard loud Christmas music. It sounded as though a band was playing inside the airport. When we arrived, we found a group of guys dressed in costumes like they were celebrating Mexican Independence Day playing Christmas songs. I admit that I was briefly confused by the situation. This experience differed so radically from a typical airport scene. Another group of people wearing yellow jackets with the Fiesta Bowl trademark lined up to form a greeting line clarifying the intentions of everybody involved. Each team was assigned a yellow jacket person as their guide.

Curiosity overwhelmed me about how our players still leaving the plane would react. Some of the guys were disoriented from a long sleep. Several were excited when they arrived. Others were somewhat alarmed. But one of the funniest scenes that I have ever witnessed unfolded when D. J. Towns, a tough guy who does about 250 bicep curls a day, walked into the airport and glanced repeatedly at the yellow coat people while walking by the greeting line without greeting anybody as if suspicious and angry about the invasive eyes of those oddly dressed strangers. Davis, London, and I nearly knocked each other down laughing.

From the airport, a bus carried the team to Loews Ventana Canyon Resort. On our way to the ritzy location, Gottfried discussed his appreciation for the unbelievable hospitality while warning that "Arizona is just fattening us up for the kill."

That night's practice experience was not very accommodating.

Gottfried became irritated by the length of the trip from the desert resort to campus. He likes his business trips to be very simple. He only wants a few people in the traveling party and insists that they are well known and trusted. Primarily, he wants a hotel near the practice facility and game site. When we finally arrived at the aged Bear Down Gym, he neared his boiling point when he noticed that all the courts were draped with a thick dust. The old building appeared to be nearly abandoned. I accompanied Scott Hewitt to the famous McKale Arena to find towels for urgent operation "Clean this Crap Up Before Coach G. Goes Buck Wild." We were guided by our assigned yellow coat person from the Fiesta Bowl. She was very nice but slightly flustered by Gottfried's obvious disenchantment.

At the beautiful McKale Arena with the signature cactus on the floor, we hustled around the gym to find someone who could help us. Olson calmly conducted practice in his arena. The situation was very symbolic. A veteran legend routinely orchestrated practice with his national title banner hanging overhead in a place of mystique that he built while a young coach struggling to rebuild a struggling program stood irritated in a terribly maintained gym just hundreds of yards away from each other.

After we returned with the towels, Boatright finished the cleaning project—supervising the managers and working feverishly. If the problem was not solved soon, the head coach would not be looking for head manager Winslow Armstead's posterior to chew—it would be the rump of Boatright. Boatright always ties up the loose ends.

(And here is yet another example of the many roles a head coach must play. In the end, everything falls to him. Everything. Uniforms, practice schedules, team diet. Although supported by a great staff, the head coach bears the burden of total responsibility. The responsibilities of a head coach range from the trivial to the crucial. I do not envy the weight they sometimes carry.)

Everything seemed to be settling down when Moss received a sudden call from nature. The Bear Down Gym, however, had no functioning rest room. So Moss hustled anxiously to the McKale Center. Upon his return, the Tide managed to conduct a fairly routine practice in the smoldering heat of a December 26 night in climate-control challenged Bear Down Gym.

The name of Bear Down Gym resembled the message painted on the Arizona football field. In the early years of Arizona football, a player was badly injured in an automobile accident. His message to his worried teammates was "bear down" when times are tough. I hoped, while watching the team practice, that Alabama had heard the message.

THE MONDAY practice before the Tuesday tournament opener unfolded in the McKale Arena. Pearson provided the morning fireworks after Walker jogged back in defensive transition.

"[Screaming at the top of his lungs] What do think this is, Kenny? You've got to run the floor!"

After practice, the players enjoyed the great weather and the resort. Meanwhile, Pearson and Kelsey watched Delaware on film. Gottfried entered the hotel room. After five minutes of watching the film, he appeared to be miserable.

"I could not have done a worse job with the schedule."

The unpopular former athletic director Bob Bockrath actually scheduled this tournament before departing. He had previously worked for the Arizona athletic department. Gottfried had already endured a couple of awkward conversations with current staff in the Arizona athletic department who worked with Bockrath years ago. They wanted to know what happened to Bockrath's rocky tenure.

Gottfried was diplomatic. Bockrath had engaged in a series of activities that received negative feedback from alumni. Gottfried only gave them vague details and allowed them to draw their own conclusions.

"I cannot believe Bob has us out here. [Pause] It's really my fault. I should have planned better. But losing Jeremy . . ." Gottfried stopped in mid-sentence agony.

His body language and words would be entirely positive with his team. This was his only forum to complain or show an ounce of real weakness. Normally, he would be the most optimistic guy in the room. But he has always been a winner, and he hated the reality that his team seemed bound for a bad season.

Brey's Delaware team appeared to be an efficient machine on the tape. They often played four players who shoot the ball very well. They penetrate and pitch with the efficiency of a veteran European team.

The visiting teams departed for the tournament banquet on Monday night. Delaware and UNC-Wilmington were staying at the same resort as Alabama. In fact, the guys who exercised on the road (Kelsey, Armstead, Gottfried, Pearson, and me) all saw Delaware players in the exercise room. The banquet was incredible. An old west theme meant locals in cowboy costumes, dancing girls, and a simulated shoot-out. Players were invited on stage to dance. Towns proved that he could be a social butterfly by dancing more than any player at the tournament. Even Kelsey danced. The shoot-out attracted much attention. Laser guns allowed a winner and a loser, but nobody died. Wearing a cowboy outfit, Olson addressed the group during a delicious dinner. The teams were introduced with highlight videos and loud music. It was quite a time.

THE NEWS at the Tuesday morning shoot-around was that Scott would be flying in this afternoon. We rejoiced in finding that he felt like making the trip, but a round-trip flight across the country did not seem like a healthy decision for him. I was unsure if it was a good idea. Gottfried tried to dissuade Scott from coming, but it was to no avail. Scott would clearly ignore any advice to join his team.

Pearson, in his scouting report, warned the team about how well Delaware shot the ball.

Before the shoot-around began, Gottfried noticed that every seat of the arena was being filled by volunteers with big cards displaying "3." Apparently, the fans held the cards up when Arizona made shots behind the arch. The head coach liked the idea and sent me to gather some information about making the cards. Coleman Coliseum would be decorated with cards at the next home game.

The team returned to the McKale Arena at 4 P.M. for the 5:15 game. Scott had not yet joined the team when Pearson stood before the players in the locker room of Arizona's football team.

"Sprint back on defense. Sprint back. Their big guys will run the floor . . . Find their shooters."

Gottfried stepped forward after Pearson's report.

"Some of you might want to go into coaching one day. I'm not 60 years old. It hasn't been long since I played. When I played, I always knew how I was gonna play. I might not play great. But I knew that I would get down in a stance and guard somebody—set some good screens and play. As a coach, you really don't know how your team will play. All I want for you every night is to not worry about making mistakes because you will make mistakes. We all do. I look back at our ten games. I say to myself why did I not play this guy instead of that guy. That was a mistake. That's part of coaching. We're not perfect. I just want you to come out and get down in a stance and fight and scratch and claw. Be tough-minded. Don't be soft. Play as hard as you can play. Have some emotion. You don't have to be up and running around if that's not your style. But get excited for one another. And go as hard as you can possibly go. If you do, you'll walk in here at the end of the game with a win most of the time. I don't care if it's Delaware or Duke . . . I'll tell you another thing. Everybody in here knows your own game. And you know each other's game. You know what the people around you do best. Go play your game. Do what you do best. And then help bring out what someone else does best. Tarik is one of the best ball defenders in the country. I mean he can get up after somebody. We could go through the whole team. You bring what you bring. You carry your load. 'I'm not Michael Jordan. I can't do everything well. But I can do this well, coach. I'll do it for the team.'"

Scott arrived! He was well dressed as usual and seemed to be feeling pretty well. (This staff seemed to compete for a style award every night.) Baker, Pearson, and I ran over to catch up and see how he was doing. He smiled at our questions and we caught him up to date.

After the warm-up, the head coach put his spin on the match-ups. Walker was assigned to 6-foot-5, 240-pound Mike Pegues to start the game. On a good team, Pegues's abilities towered over his teammates. Averaging 20.1 points per game and 7.9 rebounds, Pegues was a versatile player who knew how to use his strong body. Fearing the perimeter shooting ability of the Blue Hens, especially Kestutis Marciulionis, Gottfried elected not to double-team Pegues.

The starting lineup remained the same. A small and lethargic crowd watched the Blue Hens drill three three-pointers to take a 9-5 lead. Alabama was currently eleventh among SEC teams in field goal percentage defense—and it showed against quality opposition. Haginas, whose minutes and productivity had been steadily increasing, entered the game early and gave the team a spark with four points in four minutes and a power dunk to give the Tide a 24-18 lead with 9:32 left. Two assists and two free throws from Grizzard helped maintain a lead, 29-25. Cotton, Grizzard, and Haginas scored throughout the half, combining for 35, with Haginas finally nailing a desperation three-pointer to make the Tide halftime lead, 44-39. Pegues, Madou Diouf, Marciulionis, Greg Miller, and Billy Wells were all 50 percent or better from the three-point line, combining to shoot seven for 13 for the Blue Hens—talk about sharing the fun.

Kobie Baker offered a thought during a strange staff meeting in a busy hallway.

"Rod turned down some chances to take a charge," Baker said.

Moments later, Baker suggested that the back-door option in the offense should be used more. Apparently, Baker had become more comfortable with his role as an advisor.

When Gottfried addressed the players, he mentioned the back-door option. He also asked his forwards to show (switch to defending a dribbling guard momentarily) on the ball-screens out on the perimeter that were leading to a driving dribbler attracting help and pitching to an open shooter. He turned the speaking floor over to his staff early.

"The problem on penetration is that we're not in a stance. So we're getting off balance. Stay in a stance," Scott insisted.

"When the big guys go to help, they need to go early with their hands up," Kelsey said.

Boatright made a strong observation. The players learned before the season started that a rule change had made the use of a stabilized forearm to defend an offensive player with the ball a foul. However, that night's officiating crew was the first to enforce the new rule in an Alabama game.

"They're calling it. So we have to adjust."

Pearson was offended by the Blue Hens belting the Tide from the perimeter.

"Get to 'em with your hand up, guys. They're over fifty-four percent from the three-point line. Hey, they're not that good."

The half began on a positive note for the Tide as Dudley immediately increased his team's biggest lead of the game to seven by sinking two free throws after being assaulted on his way to the basket. Then, the transition attack of Marciulionis and the Blue Hens changed the game. An 11-3 run mostly via the fast break over the next 3:36 put Delaware in the lead, 50-48. Until the 15:11 mark, Dudley was the only man that had scored in the half for the Tide, leaving the game tied at 50. A toe-to-toe slugfest ensued from this point with both clubs exchanging blows without either team mounting a substantial advantage. Nearly 16 minutes of the second half were played without a lead greater than three held by either school. Finally, the Blue Hens took control on a three-pointer by Greg Miller at the 3:49 mark that gave them a five-point lead that felt like 15. The Tide failed to respond on two missed free throws just 19 seconds later. Cotton made one free throw to cut the lead to four with 2:54 left. But Pegues replied with a dagger—jump-shooting his team to a 71-65 lead with 2:38 left. Delaware cruised to a 76-66 victory, controlling the Tide the rest of the way with solid defense.

(During the agonizing final minute of watching another school from an inferior league whip Alabama, Pearson observed Walker laughing on the bench. After the game, he scolded Walker privately and harshly.)

In the locker room, Gottfried delivered a unique post-game speech. He refused to criticize the team while acknowledging that their failure to execute the defensive game plan and lack of hustle proved to be the difference in the contest. Apparently, he feared a complete loss of morale that could have killed the learning process desperately needed by these youngsters during this winter of their discontent.

"Get your head up, guys. I like how we played. That's a good team.

You got beat by a good team. They'll be playing in the tournament. Keep doing what you're doing. We've got good days ahead of us. We open the half with a seven point lead. Boom! Boom! They get fast break baskets and all of a sudden it's tied . . . I like what I saw. I like how we played . . . We can't relax against any team on the rest of our schedule. You've got to run the floor. We've got to make free throws. We've got to do the little things . . . We've got to get loose balls."

While the team removed its uniforms and hit the showers, Martin and Walker argued. A quiet losing locker room was disturbed by Walker's loud voice which revealed his concern about matters other than Delaware beating Alabama. He had just reinforced the notion that he did not prioritize the welfare of the team. Pearson rushed back into the players' area of the large locker room.

"[Yelling] Shut your mouth, Kenny! Shut your mouth, freshman!" Pearson exclaimed in deference to the junior Martin who had the team's interest at heart.

The players remained for the first half of the Arizona game. The coaches stayed to scout UNC-Wilmington, who would be Alabama's Thursday's opponent after they bowed to Lute Olson's team. Alarmingly, the players' moods seemed to recover extremely quickly after the loss. Without the coaches, the bus ride to the resort featured a very upbeat environment. The players ate dinner after their return. Having accompanied her spouse to the holiday tournament, Ashley Pearson reported that the players were very happy during dinner. A 6-5 Alabama team was outwardly content with losing. This had the potential to be disastrous. Losing in the short term is not cataclysmic. Jerry Jones's Dallas Cowboys went 1-15 before they were three-time world champions and team of the 90's. The acceptance of losing, however, is a cancer. The dismal circumstances of this club and their jovial recovery from being defeated by Delaware triggered contemplation about the future.

Baker and I shared a room. Young and hungry, Baker told me that he wanted to be a head coach in big-time college hoops and win the national title. When asked about what he would do with this team, he shrugged his shoulders and shook his head. (This team had so many problems that a bright person free of responsibility hesitated to venture a guess about handling them in a private conversation. Things were that bad.)

Later that night, Pearson and Boatright found me after a staff meeting. I had been in some staff meetings with Gottfried after tough losses, but this was obviously a meeting to miss. This loss was particularly excruciating for him because he is the kind of person that loves a huge challenge. Not just stimulated by the end goal, Gottfried is excited by the big obstacle. While the Samford loss drove me absolutely nuts because it was Samford, Gottfried was devastated by the missed opportunity to play Arizona in their building. He was crushed because he actually believed that his team could have won. That mentality nearly produced a Murray State win over Duke in the NCAA tourney. That mentality inevitably leads to him scheduling difficult non-league opponents. Indeed, Boatright reported that he was crushed in the meeting. His reaction to this loss says so much about his personality. I could have polled every Division I coach familiar with Arizona's tournament before the event and every one of them would have told me that Alabama's best case scenario was just 1-1. But Gottfried desperately wanted to play Arizona.

Pearson expressed his discomfort with the team's reaction to the loss. Different from the head coach or Scott, Pearson wore the Alabama jersey with pride just five years before. Perhaps the four NCAA tourney trips and two SEC championships of his playing career felt less removed. He vividly remembered how his teams reacted to losses, and it was a vastly different response from how the current team behaved that night.

While the Delaware Blue Hens enjoyed a leisurely Wednesday morning after their win, the alternative schedule for the losers had the Tide players up for an 8 A.M. ankle-taping session with John Morr. Before the ten o'clock practice, Kyle Rasco discussed his regrets about leaving the team. As a student trainer assisting Morr, Rasco left his position before the beginning of second semester which meant UNC-Wilmington would be his last game. He would be missed, especially by Stinnett, for his healthy sense of humor.

"Basketball is in my blood now. I've joked around a lot, but I love everybody around this team. This is a good family," Rasco said.

Unfortunately for those players still attempting to wake up on the losers' schedule, Gottfried's approach seemed to have changed radically after staying up through the night. Apparently, he had decided the youngsters must suffer his criticism to learn.

"If you can't handle what I say, then too bad for you. I look at our team and it frustrates me that we don't execute our offense. It's all my fault."

He commented on the lack of passing the ball rapidly from one side of the floor to the other.

"It goes to one side of the floor and we jack it. At some point this year, [pointing at the point guards] one of you two guys has to step up and play. Seven turnovers from the point guard position. Terrance Meade starts the game by going across half-court and throwing the ball into the fourth row. Guys just come up to you, Tarik, and take the ball from you. I'm telling you that I think you're better than that. But why does that happen? Is it concentration? I can go right through the team because numbers don't lie. Schea Cotton has 19 assists, 39 turnovers [many of his coming on traveling violations whistled on his quirky first step]. Rod Grizzard has 18 assists, 30 turnovers. Erwin Dudley has six assists, 23 turnovers. Doc Martin is the only guy on our a team on the plus side— 19 assists, 18 turnovers. Kenny Walker has zip. Kenny, you don't have an assist yet with 8 turnovers. Sam Haginas has three assists, 20 turnovers. As a team, we have 113 assists, 205 turnovers. We're not giving ourselves a chance to win. It was 64-64 last night. We're in the double bonus with six minutes to go. We come down and have two straight turnovers . . . Then we come to the other end and we're lost. We don't know who we're guarding. All of a sudden Erwin is defending a guard and Rod Grizzard is guarding Mike Pegues on the block . . . There was no defensive transition on at least three plays . . . We can sit around here and moan and groan and bullcrap around about how we've got young players and bullcrap about Jeremy Hays. Screw that!

"At some point, you've got to play. If you're not mentally tough enough to handle all that crap, let's phone it in. We're sitting here 6-5 and easily could have eight or nine wins . . . You were dead tired last night, Sam. Dead tired! And you try to take your guy one on one and turn the ball over. I could see it coming. You could hardly breathe. They came and double-teamed you, Kenny, and it was just embarrassing. The guy just reached up and grabbed it from you. Instead of being down in a stance and firming up—maybe we recruited a bunch of softies. I don't know."

He paused. "Maybe y'all aren't very tough! That's the name of the game with this team . . . All we did at halftime was talk about showing on a ball screen. Show on the ball screen! They come out on their first play after we've gone up seven. They set a ball screen on Rod Grizzard and Erwin is ten feet behind him. Rod fights to get over the top and finally whacks the guy and fouls a three-point shooter! Your job as a post player if your man sets a screen on the ball is to force the ball handler to detour from the hoop. At some point, you've got to start correcting your mistakes. We're making the same mistakes over and over again. It's like October 15th all the time! We don't have one leader on our team. But lead as a team."

Early in the practice, Scott used the showing technique as a metaphor for expressing love of the game, eloquently connecting a technical aspect of winning basketball with the deep caring that the team seemed to be lacking.

"We've got to develop a 'we care' attitude! I care! Now Erwin, let me tell you one thing about defense. I know you're a great kid. I know you love this game. I know you want to be better. But you've got to show me that you care. You've always got to show me! You didn't show on the screen last night. So show! Show that you care." Scott's intensity of thought and feeling reminded me of why I loved basketball.

An intense practice was followed by a film session where Pearson decided to reveal his feelings about the season to date.

"I told a couple of you guys last night. But for the guys who don't know, it's embarrassing to be 6-5 at Alabama. That's embarrassing. We need somebody to step up with some intensity—a spark plug to lead this team."

Scott later unleashed his negative feelings about the team at lunch with Cynthia, the Pearsons, and me.

"Nothing is worse than a happy bunch of losers."

Gottfried canceled all possible fun events for the afternoon. Tourism had been a tentative plan for the team, but the vacation aspect of this trip was over.

While Delaware slept late again on Thursday, the losers' schedule had the Tide bus leaving the resort at 9:15 for the shoot-around. UNC-Wilmington, a 66-51 loser to Arizona, was the topic of the day.

"Have great, great intensity and play hard," Gottfried began. "I'll stop pussy-footing around and be real honest with you. That's what I'm watching. If in my opinion, you're not playing hard, I'm taking you out! Sit down over there! I'm not gonna sit and watch tape of you jogging up and down the floor—watch loose balls roll around on the ground while we're standing. And watch us stand around on offense. Just understand that! We're grown men, and we all understand it. The only opinion in this building that counts tonight is mine. My opinion! If you're not playing hard, sit down."

The UNC-Wilmington Seahawks were a rough and ready group loaded with tough veterans and a freshman shooting specialist in Brett Blizzard who had wanted a scholarship from Gottfried.

"I don't want Blizzard to get off. He wanted to come to Alabama, fellas. He didn't get a scholarship. I know he is lying in the hotel right now and can't wait for the game," Gottfried said after Pearson described the shooter.

The clock had nearly run out on the time allowed by the tournament for the shoot-around.

"Some of the teams in our league have played a bunch of stiffs. You guys haven't. You've played some good teams. This team you're playing tonight is a good team. They're sitting on top of their league. They've already had league games. They went down to Florida and played with them through almost the whole game. Arizona also had a hard time putting them away. They're scrappy, smart, and tough."

I missed the 3:30 bus departure for the 5:15 game. Mike Adams, who owns a clothing store in Decatur and travels to campus often to sell suits

to many key people in the athletic department, agreed to drive me to the
game. We all loved Adams—he is humorous, humble, and upbeat.
When he is expected to join a group for lunch, anticipation of his arrival
truly excites. On the way to McKale Arena, I learned that Adams was a
paratrooper and had jumped out of over 25 perfectly good airplanes. He
had also been a trooper for Gottfried's cause. When Gottfried inevitably
wins and begins to receive attention from tons of boosters, Adams will
not be forgotten because he has supported his teams through the valley.

Having called a former Tide assistant about the Seahawks, Pearson
was told that the Seahawks were "physical as sh—." His scouting reports
reflected that evaluation.

"They will set some hard screens. I'm telling you right now. Get
through it . . . It's a low possession game. So every one is important."

Jerry Wainwright had built a good team with an unappreciated style.
They were extremely patient with the ball, extremely physical with their
screens, and extremely serious with their defense.

"Every time down the floor is a mini-battle. They'll be patient,"
Gottfried began.

After quickly analyzing points of emphasis in his offense, he simplified his message.

"[Pointing at the markings on the board] All this stuff is good. You
better execute it. But I'm interested in our effort. If you ain't playing
hard, you're not playing. We're going to flat out guard 'em. Then we'll
come down to the other end and get great shots."

After the warm-up, the head coach told Cotton to "jump in Blizzard's
drawers."

The all-newcomer starting lineup was becoming a fixture. Another
small and passive crowd gathered to watch the Tide. The game was tied
at 11 after a few minutes of play with both Cotton and his assignment
Blizzard having six points. Meade, then, sparked 15 minutes of Tide
domination. Alabama displayed its highest level of defensive intensity of
the season by far. Meade, Dudley, and Cotton combined to shoot 11 for
14 from the field. London awoke from the dead, playing eight minutes
of furious defensive basketball to accompany one assist versus zero

turnovers and one for one shooting—a three-pointer. Whatever message had been sent by the tremendously disappointed staff and traveling party around this team, the players had responded. The Tide led 37-19 at the half.

A strange feeling of calm surrounded the Tide in the locker room—a feeling that had been missing without Hays in the lineup. The group entered clapping and excited like a group who found something important that had been missing for a long time.

"That's the way you need to play every time you touch the floor—practice and games. Great intensity! Let me tell you something about this group. They're not rolling over. You need to take it to 'em and put a dagger right in their heart," Gottfried said.

The Seahawks opened the second half on a 9-0 run, reviving a contest that seemed to be decided. A 6-2 Tide run, however, on baskets by Walker, Dudley, and Meade pushed the lead back to 13. From that point on, the Seahawks never seriously threatened, inching no closer than eight points behind. The Tide won, 62-45. Alabama held UNC-Wilmington to 34% shooting. Meade finished with 19 points on seven for ten shooting and five rebounds. Dudley scored 15 points and grabbed 12 rebounds. Walker grabbed ten rebounds and shot three for five. London logged 23 minutes of playing time and recorded three assists without a turnover. Cotton added 12 points on four of eight shooting.

"Way to bounce back. We've got LSU in the next game. They're 11-0. It's down there. I sure wish we were playing in this second game tonight. We've had some chances. We're 7-5. Louisville beat us. We turned it over way too much, but they beat us. You've got to give it to Samford. They came into our house and beat us—as embarrassing as it is, they beat us. We could easily be 9-3. We gave a couple away because we didn't run our offense or guard anybody. Now we've got to find a way to get a couple games back that we gave away. We've got to get 'em back—which we can. There is no doubt in my mind. Do you want watch any of this second game?"

The team rejected the invitation and returned to the resort to pack. The plane tickets were bought on the winner's schedule. So the team waited in the resort while Arizona pounded Delaware to win the tournament. Given the time change, the players would be home by around 10 A.M. on Friday. Exhausted by the game and commercial flying through the early morning hours, the very best aspect of the Arizona trip was that it ended with a win. We were able to laugh through airport after airport. Kelsey and I joked about the journey beginning with a ten-minute flight. That had to be one of the shortest commercial hops in America. By sunrise, the players were certainly laughing about everything. The only factor restraining our often hilarious laughter was a glance at Scott who seemed to be too tired to continue.

Scott suffered excruciating pain on the long trip, prompting the staff to successfully lobby for his moving to first class on every flight. He looked to be in so much pain that the coaches were unsure if he would survive the ride. He looked so sick and unhappy. I hated seeing him that way, knowing that he was going to have to wait it out.

"He just looked to be as miserable as a person could be on that trip," Pearson later said.

"I was concerned that he would pass away on the plane because he was hurting so much. His making the Arizona trip at that time represented an unbelievable commitment to the team," Gottfried said to me later. Elizabeth Gottfried—Mark's wife, who sometimes traveled with her husband—also shared Mark's concern.

Robert went home to Cynthia a mess. As always, she struggled to pick up the pieces. She comforted him in every way possible. Her high school sweetheart was suffering. She had been so loyal and caring for Robert throughout their long relationship. In his worst moments, she had committed everything to his battle against cancer.

After resting during the remainder of New Year's Eve, the team began the new century with a practice similar to Wednesday's intense workout. Gottfried must have enjoyed the results. Taking full advantage of the rest, Scott somehow found the energy to lead the charge for his boss. He set the tone in the pre-practice individual drills. Practice was closed to visitors.

"I've got some drills that will run your ass into a wall or skin your elbows up. Let me tell you what you did the other night that almost made me puke! I could have damn died! We had a man on their team laying on the ground. And you let him get back up and post you up! And you did nothing, Kenny! We don't have a time when we can relax. You've got to keep the ball off the block! You've got to stop anybody that drives." This was the emphatic Scott, reminding me of his coaching that I used to look forward to throughout the day.

Scott summarized his desired direction for the team minutes later.

"You guys can either get tough on your own or we can make you tough. It's your choice. If I'm one of you guys, I'm saying that I'm ready to get tough. I wouldn't want to be out here diving on balls. Instead of coming out here and shooting, we can have you diving on the floor and taking charges. We're not gonna kill you. We'll make sure you don't die. We'll make you tough."

Kelsey joined the intensity party.

"If you guys let their guys catch the ball with a foot in the paint, it's done. You better knock their block off. You better knock Swift and Smith out of there. Everybody is talking about how they're the greatest front line in basketball. Strohmile Swift—top draft pick. You better put their butts on the ground. Because I guarantee that if you're not gonna play tough, it will be a long night . . . We want to see them go down. Everybody is talking about how great they are. That's a bunch of crap. We're gonna start playing hard today."

The '99-'00 LSU team had already become a Cinderella story before SEC play. After years of horrible basketball, John Brady had ignited the Bayou Bengal faithful. Their 12-0 start had the nation watching. After pounding the 11th ranked Oklahoma State Cowboys in New Orleans, Brady could have been elected governor—given that their football program has been awful for the great majority of ten years. Treated to two Final Four appearances by Dale Brown, Tiger fans watched miserably while Brown lost his recruiting zeal and suffered an inappropriate and painstakingly long demise for a great coach marked by terrible seasons and drowning spirits. Brady's teams had also been hammered until this one—LSU's moment had arrived. The senior Jabari Smith and junior Strohmile Swift would probably be ghosts on the bayou next year after joining the NBA.

Gottfried continued the momentum of his assistants in the huddle.

"We will practice hard today—probably as hard as you've ever practiced. We're sitting here at Alabama right now 7-5. I hope nobody in this room is comfortable with that. I'm not. I'm embarrassed. I went out to eat last night, and I was embarrassed. I am embarrassed to go out in town. I'm blaming me! I always look at me. I haven't done a good job. I haven't demanded that we run our offense from the first day of practice. I was letting you play. We have a hundred more turnovers than assists. I haven't demanded that all twelve of you guys get down in a stance and guard somebody. That's my fault as a coach. I have let you down in that regard because I haven't demanded what I should demand. But I want everybody to understand that there isn't one guy out here that is more important than anybody else. There isn't one guy that I'm not afraid to sit on that bench with me. And I don't care if you leave! You can leave the program—any of you guys.

"If you won't bust your balls and can't handle me pushing to make sure you bust your balls, then leave this program! Because we're gonna play hard! There will be somebody who buys a ticket to this freaking game that will walk out saying that's the hardest I've ever seen a team play. I'm not gonna sit here at seven and five and watch tapes where I don't think we're playing as hard as we can play—and practice as hard as we can practice. If you can't handle it, you won't hurt my feelings. I'll live. I'll survive without you! You can leave if you can't handle it.

"Mentally, you better be willing to suck it up right now. We're getting ready to go through 16 games where there ain't no easy ones. No cupcakes! No stiffs! You've got to be willing to play through all that. Play through me. We're gonna get down and play defense. You know why we won six of eight games last year in the SEC and beat Kentucky and swept Arkansas? Because we ended up playing some defense and getting down and guarding people. There's a lot of talent around the country, fellas. Walking around with great talent doesn't get you anything. That doesn't get you crap. It's those guys that want to play hard that get it done. To look at somebody eyeball to eyeball and say 'I'm shutting you out.' To fight through a screen and not fall down. To get a rebound. To look at a guy who catches the ball at the top of the key and make sure he can't beat you off the dribble right or left. He can't break our defense down! That's the way we're gonna play.

"Don't think I'm bullcrapping you! I don't really care if between now and two weeks from now our roster goes from 12 to eight. If four of you want to quit, then quit. The eight that are left—we're gonna bust our balls. Whoever is left on the team will bust 'em. We're gonna walk in the locker room every night after a game and sit in here exhausted because you gave everything you had. There's a bunch of teams out there around the country that will like some soft sissies. I'll find you one! I'll get on the phone and find you one to transfer to. That's fine with me. But on this team, there is some pride! Maybe I shouldn't have played here. It's not good for me to be the coach here! But I wore your uniform one time! And so did a lot of dudes, fellas. We take pride in that jersey! And people say we're young. Bullcrap! I don't care how young we are! We don't need to lose to Delaware. I don't care if they've been in the tournament five straight years! Northern Iowa and a bunch of bullcrap.

"[Pause] You're gonna make a decision, fellas. We'll find out a little bit today. [Pointing at his heart] Who's got something there and who doesn't? There's a league across campus that we call the rec. league. And they don't care who wins and loses. You don't have to play hard. And they'll take you. Stay in school. I'll let you keep your scholarship. You can go right over there and play. Nobody cares who wins. You can get 50 a game. You can walk around campus and feel big time. [Yelling] But not here! This is a whole different deal out here! Here we go."

Practice began with one of the most basic drills in basketball. The players slid full court in a defensive stance. Gottfried sent the message that the team had to be totally reconstructed. He added an offensive player pretending to dribble without a ball in a one-on-one full court situation. Gottfried became upset with Rod's defensive stance and his sliding.

"Get out, Rod. [Pointing to the top of the Coliseum] Go to the top three times."

Haginas struggled.

"Sam, go touch the top three times."

Pearson was sick and felt miserable. When he observed Haginas slowly progressing up the steps, he summoned every ounce of strength in his ailing body.

"[Screaming] Run, Sam!" Pearson produced an incredible noise that did not seem possible for a guy with substantial sinus problems.

Minutes later, Pearson was still not satisfied with Haginas's pace.

"[Yelling] Come on, Sam!" Pearson exclaimed without the benefit of the strength lost in his initial scream.

Finally, Gottfried tired of Haginas's slow attempt to finish.

"Let's go, Sam. Get back in line," Gottfried said with disappointment.

The guards worked on double-teaming Smith and Swift. Grizzard reacted slowly.

"Go to the top, Rod."

Grizzard appeared to be tired while climbing the steps.

"[Yelling] Hey Rod! I'm tired of you not running hard!" Gottfried exploded.

With his son Daniel watching, Scott displayed unbelievable intensity in a war rebounding drill.

"Alfred, you're up here hugging him like he's your girlfriend."

Minutes later, Walker could not grab a rebound.

"Damn! That's not basketball! I can get Daniel over here to block out better than that. In fact, Daniel will do better than that. Get out there Daniel. Show them how to rebound."

Walker still could not grab a rebound.

"Kenny wants to be killed! He wants to be killed!"

Practice continued with explosion after explosion by Gottfried. He finally turned his biggest cannon toward a target of choice—knowing that his players felt that Cotton had been given favored status. Cotton was beaten off the dribble.

"[Screaming as if Cotton was at the top of the coliseum] Who can you guard? What's your limitation? How come you can't guard anybody?"

Scott finally paused for a break and sat down. His thin body would be very sore in the morning.

Grizzard failed to challenge a highly predictable jump shot as the shot clock expired. Gottfried almost lost it.

"The shot clock is running out and you just let the guy have an open shot. [Screaming] That ain't physical! That's mental! That's mental weakness!"

Practice continued with phenomenal intensity. During a spirited five on five half-court defense drill, Gottfried invited Scott to bring his chair down to the baseline to help him coach. Scott agreed with pleasure and excitement. I had fallen head over heels in love with that practice. The intensity and the pace were unbelievable.

Minutes later in a wing denial/get open at the wing situation, Pearson lost his patience with Grizzard's inability to get open.

"[Yelling] Come on, Rod!"

Finally, Pearson fired a rocket pass to the spot where Grizzard should have been. The ball nailed a table and bounced over the railing and disappeared into coliseum seating. Attracted by Pearson's energy, Gottfried jogged away from the forwards on the opposite end. Immediately, the head coach diagnosed the situation as Grizzard still failed to get open.

"[Screaming] Can't get open! Can't get open! Can't get open!" Gottfried shouted like a drill sergeant.

Minutes later in a feed-the-post drill, Cotton and Meade tangled while Cotton attempted to establish post position. Seemingly on the brink of a fist fight, they were reluctantly separated—two guards in Cadillac bodies ready to clash.

In a five on five offensive drill, a wild pass nailed Scott for the second time today. I gasped for air at the sight of the impact with his fragile body. He buckled with pain.

"[Yelling] Take care of the freaking ball!" Gottfried scolded—less patient when a ball nailed his assistant than when it hit him.

Scott took over the practice minutes later. He taught his drop zone.

"Good," Scott yelled with such passion and urgency that the word seems to have a higher meaning.

"We've got to pick it up. That's the only way we'll win a game. That's the only way." Scott's session cooked with energy.

After the grueling workout, Gottfried required "17's"—usually reserved for earlier in the calendar.

Having explored the coliseum steps, Haginas and Grizzard angered the rest of the team by missing the required time. Grizzard rested on the opposite side of the floor from the finish line, refusing to return to the line for the mandatory repeat. Bakken approached and encouraged him to continue.

"Come on, Rod. Sh—," Bakken said.

Watching Haginas on the verge of puking, I remembered that Morr had said earlier that Haginas was somewhat ill before practice.

London attempted to motivate Grizzard from a distance."[Yelling] We can want it for you, but we can't put it inside you. You've got to want to. You're in the same shape as everybody else. You started conditioning on the same day as everybody else."

Martin, Meade, and Walker joined Bakken on the opposite side of the floor to motivate Grizzard. He refused to respond. Bakken finally grabbed him and carried him across the floor.

"Sam is sick. He's doing this sh—. You can do it," Bakken said.

Given that Davis, Pearson, and Haginas were fighting colds and Boatright had remained at this practice with a flu only because it was obviously the most important workout of the year, the entire group was suffering on many levels.

The team eventually began running again, except for Haginas who was excused by his illness. Grizzard stopped quickly. The other players finished on time and would be excused.

"You pay a price everyday if you want to be good. If you can't handle it, it's fine to leave. I'll still love you. I'll get on the phone and help you out. We'll get you a scholarship somewhere. I won't be down on you. You can walk right out of here. Everything we do is stepping up. It's stepping up. If you don't want to be a part of it, that's fine. Rod, you're gonna get that. I don't care if you rest for half an hour. You will get it today. You can stay here all day long if you want to. Get it done. Good job. Take tomorrow off," Gottfried concluded.

Several of the players remained with Rod until he attempted the sprints. Fifteen minutes later, Dudley and I urged him to the finish line while a sick Pearson kept the time. I think you have to be a mean person to dislike Erwin Dudley. Well after an excruciating practice, he cheered for a teammate who had cost him an extra series of sprints.

AFTER A badly needed rest day, the Monday before the Wednesday game in Baton Rouge brought another closed practice. Gottfried embraced the increased intensity of his workouts when he exploded after nobody cheered when Martin absorbed a charge.

"The guy takes a hit for our team and nobody says anything! You've got to be unselfish to do something special."

Minutes later, Grizzard absorbed a charge! A shocked group of people on the gym floor cheered as if a baby had been saved from danger. The lengthy round of applause reflected the rarity of the event. Perhaps the coaches were finally reaching him. He smiled in recognition of a needed step forward in his development as a player.

All day Scott wore a heating pad over his mid-section where he tended to feel the most pain. He could not produce the energy of his Saturday coaching. Haginas also seemed to be feeling the impact of Saturday's workout combined with his cold. His lack of effort became a continuing issue through practice.

"Can you play, Sam?" Gottfried inquired early in practice.

"I'm waiting for you to play, Sam," he said later.

"It's on you, Sam. You can either decide to play or not."

Haginas continued to suffer through practice.

Grizzard failed to grab a loose ball.

"[Yelling]Come on, Rod! You've got to get on the floor for that. With five minutes to go in Baton Rouge, will we fold up the tents or be strong?"

Moss manhandled Walker from behind for a rebound.

"Kenny, you better put an elbow in somebody's throat who is sitting behind you if that's what it takes."

In the closing huddle, an eternally optimistic head coach used the only spin that he knew.

"We've got a chance to do something special. We've got a chance to have a special team. But to accomplish great things, you have to give of yourself. You can't worry about your stats and points. We've got to be the most unselfish team. You've got to care about your teammates and encourage them. If a guy has a great game and you have a stinky game, then be happy for him. We're about to start league play. It's the best league in America. But you didn't come here just to play in these games. You came to win 'em . . . We're going down there to win. They're 12-0. You played in Louisville before 19,000 and St. Louis before 13,000. You've seen it all. You need to get your mind right to go down and get the job done. 40 minutes. Mentally tough for 40 minutes."

Tuesday brought another closed practice. Kelsey demonstrated some of LSU's plays early on. Walker became confused about his proper position. Gottfried was not amused.

"[Yelling] Kenny, if you don't want to go, we'll leave you at home! You walk in here two minutes before practice every day! You and Schea! The last guys in the gym every day! If we have practice at two o'clock, we're loose and ready to go at two o'clock."

Because Cotton ran half-speed in the flanker drill, Gottfried punished the team with a sprint. Grizzard missed the required time so the team had to repeat. After they finished, Gottfried continued to push the notion that he would not protest Cotton's departure.

"Schea, you won't go half-speed in my practice anymore. You can go do that in somebody else's practice."

At Gottfried's request, Boatright combed the coliseum to boot four spectators out that had maneuvered into a closed workout. Reluctantly, Boatright dismissed Tuscaloosa high school coaching legend and local radio personality Pete Pearson from the building. When Gottfried realized that Pearson was booted, he directed Boatright to run and catch the respected friend of the program. During a later practice break, the head coach insisted that there should be a formal apology for the incident.

Given the environment of the proceeding practices, a relatively uneventful workout ended. It was a technical day. The team had to be sure about their double-teaming strategy against the dominant LSU forwards.

"We're gonna play more people. I want you ball-busting. We're walking into a situation where they are loud and wild and fired up."

He shifted gears at the end of practice. "I want to congratulate you on our grades. Unofficially, you have the highest grade point average as a team since our updated records begin. You have set the standard academically. Special congratulations to Hays with a 3.9 and London with a 3.4. London has made a special comeback in his academic life, fellas. That's why you are here—to get a degree. You can screw around and not pay attention to your grades and one day you'll regret it. Several past players have come in here and wasted a free education. I'm working with these guys everyday to help them get a degree because they regret how they treated their classes when they were here. It's sad. It's sad. I expect you to have continued success in the spring semester."

The chartered flight to Baton Rouge felt like a walk down the street compared to the Tuscon trip. The Tuesday night film session revealed an LSU club that appeared to do everything well. Alabama simply had to play tougher to have a shot at winning.

LSU's flamboyant head coach John Brady had suffered through terrible seasons before building his newfound success. He did not sympathize with Gottfried's young and vulnerable team. Gottfried and I happened to be the only people in the hotel gym on Wednesday morning. He rode the stationary bike while taking exception to Brady's comments in this morning's *Baton Rouge Advocate*. The reporter had asked Brady about the Tide's youth.

"I've been there. So am I supposed to feel sorry for them?" Brady asked rhetorically.

Gottfried took offense because he believes in a coaching fraternity. He wants coaches to care for one another. In all fairness to Brady, the SEC is not exactly a warm and fuzzy league. It is mostly multi-million-aires coaching against multi-millionaires in a game of whoever loses gets fired and watches their huge salary go up in flames. Brady had been knocked around like the neighborhood punk. So metaphorically, he worked hard on a strength program, and he was looking to beat the hell out of some kids.

Waiting for the morning shoot-around to begin at the Pete Maravich Assembly Center, the Tide stretched outside their locker room while LSU finished practice. Brady noticed the Tide and sent his managers over to push the Tide back into the locker room. Gottfried experienced the feeling of the four guys he had kicked out of his closed practice a few days earlier.

It is easy to understand Brady's hunger to succeed, fear of failure, and lack of compassion for the rest of the schools in this power league. His selection as the LSU coach was something like Apollo Creed initialing selecting Rocky Balboa as an opponent. From '91-'97, Brady coached Samford without reaching the NCAA tournament. He was only 89-77. LSU had struggled mightily in Dale Brown's twilight years, but it was still the school of two Final Fours and Shaquille O'Neal. An excruciating search for a head coach led to many embarrassments for the Tigers. Big time coaches did not seem interested. Finally, LSU seemed to stumble into hiring a family friend—the buddy of athletic director Joe Dean's family. However, Brady had surprised everybody and lifted the black cloud from big revenue-producing sports at LSU. Gerry DiNardo accomplished the same trick in '96 when the Tigers were finally represented by a good football team. (Although Brady, I'm sure, hoped his long-term fate will be better than that of DiNardo who was chased off campus by an angry posse after returning the Tigers to the trash can over his last two seasons.)

The Deaf Dome would certainly earn its nickname given the number of students that arrived an hour before the game. The best thing about losing for a long time is that winning seems more special for the fan base. Percentages were stacked very heavily against an undermanned and struggling Alabama team on the road against a juggernaut in the most exciting SEC game for LSU basketball since early in the first Clinton administration.

Obviously excited by the challenge, Kelsey delivered the final scouting report. Normally a very good communicator, Kelsey was at his best that night. Earlier in the week, Kelsey essentially picked a Tide win in that game, and I could not prevent my reflex reaction which was to look at him as if he claimed to be the King of England. The defensive key would be how well the Tide could recover from leaving an LSU wing player like Lamont Roland to double-down on Swift and Smith when the ball goes inside. It is not rocket science to understand that when the ball-handler is double-teamed and he manages to pass the ball, the rest of the offense has a four on three edge momentarily. The recovery or rotation is everything. On the other hand, if either Swift or Smith catch the ball close enough to the goal, both could tomahawk dunk over a double-team.

Gottfried began with a lineup change.

"Doc, you're starting tonight in Rod's spot."

Martin would start as the designated double-down guy, leaving Lamont Roland when the ball goes inside to help with one of their monster forwards.

"No dunks for Swift, Erwin. Zero. We want to make him catch it and score over our defense, Alfred."

When he finished the technical discussion of his offense, his voice was filled with an excitement unlike any moment before a game this season.

"We came down here to play hard! If you're not gonna play hard, come sit with me! Don't moan and cry and call your mommy and daddy because I'm playing the dudes that play the hardest. [Pointing to the board and yelling] Erase all that crap if you want to! It's about us playing hard!"

The team clapped louder than ever before while bringing their hands together. Random voices chanted "SEC! SEC!"

After a rowdy warm-up colored by hecklers yelling unpleasant thoughts at the Tide, Gottfried gave his brief summary of the scouting report. Brian Beshara was a shooting threat.

"Schea, you're not leaving Beshara . . . We're covering down off Roland. Recover to your own."

Before concluding, he warned that he would try to press and retreat to a man-to-man defense. LSU preferred a half-court game. He emphasized that he wanted no Tiger dunks.

"[Yelling with great intensity] Loose Balls! Dive on it! Your hands are up and active! Get a deflection! Take a charge! Everybody playing hard! Hard!"

The team came together with a fever pitch of enthusiasm. If there was a light at the end of the tunnel for this campaign beyond a puncher's chance at the league tournament—if there was a chance for renewal, it could have been discovered on the bayou. Perhaps the greatest thing about Division I college basketball is the endless possibility of a season. Unless the school plays in the few conferences like the Pac-10 or Ivy League where league tournaments do not determine the official league champion bound for the big dance, hope springs eternal until the season ends in the league tournament. Almost everybody is nine or ten wins in a row away from a national championship—not unlike college football, except the drama begins at the end. Moreover, if the school competes in a true power conference like the SEC in the '90's, then a good conference season almost insures a ticket to the dance. The SEC has the best winning percentage by far in the NCAA tourney since 1994. Opportunity was not the problem for the Tide.

The Deaf Dome roared their approval of its conquering heroes having returned home to battle after the great victory in New Orleans. Alabama immediately quieted the crowd with a 6-0 run. Walker and Dudley absorbed charges from Swift and Smith. Cotton attacked the basket for the first four points of the game. The Tide proceeded to display its best basketball so far. Aside from a few costly mental lapses, the defense appeared sturdy. Meade shot the ball with supreme confidence, singlehandedly taking over the half with critical shots that gave the Tide leads at 17-8, 20-12, 30-25, and 33-28. Cotton appeared to be determined that the SEC learn about his abilities as he slashed through the lane to shoot four of five in the half and pushed the lead to 39-28 at the 2:14 mark. The Tide controlled the first stanza, 41-32. Meade's 15 points on three of four shooting from behind the arch led the way. As a true freshman in his first half of SEC play, Meade outscored Strohmile Swift, Jabari Smith, and Brian Beshara combined. Smith, who played like Magic Johnson in the last game between these schools when Alabama won a home thriller, had not scored. I credited Walker, Dudley, and Moss for impressive defensive play against the Tiger forwards.

With little critiquing required after that half, Gottfried warned that LSU would make a furious effort.

"They will come after you like nothing you've ever seen. If we don't guard 'em, the roof will blow off this place."

A spectacular half had revitalized Scott who seemed willing to play against the Tigers himself as he urged the forwards to block out.

"Fred, Jabari shouldn't be able to get around you without knocking you down. He couldn't get around me without knocking me down!"

The second half began with Smith powering to the basket repeatedly for five straight points. A raucous crowd sensed that their 12-0 Tigers had simply been toying with the Tide. But a Cotton free throw and yet another critical three-point play from Meade on a drive to the basket stopped the Crimson bleeding. Beshara answered, cutting the lead to 45-40. Another Smith basket whipped the crowd into a frenzy. Cotton restored the five-point lead on an emphatic dunk at the 16:47 mark after an inbounds pass. Then an agonizing 3:41 went by without either team scoring. The next basket would be critical. Starting a freshman front court against arguably the best front court in America, the Tide had managed to lead most of the way. The setting was incredibly ripe for an LSU run. When LSU cut the lead to one, the Pete Maravich Assembly Center seemed to be on the verge of losing its roof. Gottfried did not wait for the upcoming media timeout. With a timeout at 12:01 left in the game, the Tide was in deep, deep trouble.

When Swift gave the Tigers their first lead 26 seconds later, an LSU pep rally had begun. The Tigers completely dominated every phase of the game for the following nine full minutes. Trailing by nine points with five minutes remaining and the shot clock running out on a Tide possession, all hope seemed lost when Cotton nailed a 25-foot jumper at the horn to cut the lead to six. A Meade free throw cut the lead to five before the Tigers answered with a 4-0 run keyed by a Torris Bright offensive rebound basket. Trailing 68-60 with 2:08 left, Grizzard nailed a three-pointer from the left wing to delay the last nail in the coffin. Suddenly, LSU breezed by the Alabama press and Beshara raced down the floor to throw a pass that appeared to be too high. Amazingly, Swift flew like Superman to grab the ball and slam dunk the Tide, exciting the crowd beyond description. The Tide bench suffered through a Cajun party until the final horn. We finally hurried to the locker room while Brady raced across the floor to emphatically thank the student section. 78-66 was the final tally.

Gottfried addressed a devastated locker room. A window to redemption closed tonight faster than Michael Johnson in the '96 Olympics.

"We've been here before, guys. That shouldn't happen to us. We've got to play, fellas. Young and all that bullcrap—you've got to play. We got to about ten minutes left in the game and you didn't play. Erwin, you quit playing, son. You quit playing defense. You play the guy great in the first half, and he operates in the second half like you're not in the game. [Long pause and the all-too familiar sound of the LSU pep band rubs salt in the fresh wound] We can't make it back to the defensive end of the floor. We can't block a guy out. Rod didn't block a guy out. We've got to be mentally tougher. When I get a rebound down there, I better firm up and put an elbow in someone's mouth before I give the ball away. Mentally tough! I'm not giving it to you! I can't just let 'em pop it right out of my hands.

"[Long pause] Shoot, you come down here and play so well in the first half. You start the second half and quit playing. We ran the same offense in the second half. The same thing as the first. We don't cut hard all of a sudden. The crowd gets loud. We don't cut hard and move. [Long pause] The mental side of the game is four or five times more important that the physical side. [Long pause] Kenny, in this league, if you're gonna get the ball around the bucket, you need to take it up and dunk on somebody. You've got to get buckets. We just had a total collapse. Collapse! You're a lot better team than that. Way better than that!

"[Another long pause] We've got to start correcting the mistakes.

We've had enough games. We've played 13 games. Big defensive trip, Tarik, and we didn't block out. You've got to guard the guy in the back of the zone, Alfred. Sam, you've got to quit fouling. You come right into the game and foul—then turn the ball over. You're better than that. You're better players. And we're a better team. You come in here and score 41 points in the first half and play like you did. That shows how good a team you are. [Long pause] I've never seen you play like that, Erwin. You played scared tonight, son. As good as you are, you were scared to play in the second half. [Long pause] It's a broken record. We've got to start correcting our mistakes. [Long pause] Take a knee, fellas."

Hays said a kind prayer, but the Tide had needed him in another capacity.

THURSDAY'S practice began with a different tone. Gottfried must have felt that his damaged team needed to be stroked.

"Believe me when I tell you this. We're close. We're close. We're close to not being just—we're close to being real good. What we have to start doing is getting better in the areas where we have hurt ourselves. Because you start taking away their offensive transition by sprinting the floor and having our safety. We start taking away defensive breakdowns like when we gamble on Beshara. We start taking away possessions like when Rod comes in the game, and we're not sure who he's guarding, and Beshara just loops down and dunks. We didn't talk. We start taking away unforced turnovers. We start taking away free throw second chances. There's about four times when you don't block anybody out, Tarik. You had about four chances down there to move somebody into the third row, and you don't. Those are not talent issues. We let one get away last night. The name of the game last night was on the glass. And the truth of the matter is, fellas, that joker right there [pointing at Hays] got ten per game last year in SEC games. Ten a game. He led the SEC in rebounding. The truth of the matter is that he ain't here. That doesn't mean you have to get ten, Erwin. Although, I think you could get ten a game. I think you could lead the league in rebounding. All of you could get more . . . This game last night was won on the backboard. That was the whole game. We're up 17-8, and they couldn't get a bucket without an offensive board."

We went to the player's lounge to view a tape compiled by Patrick McDonald that showed only LSU's 16 critical offensive rebounds.

"Terrance Meade and Tarik London, you two guys are the worst. Around the basket, you just get manhandled too often. That guy ought to be pushed over to Soloman on the bench," the head coach said, beginning a series of comments on the tape.

"Schea, I see you getting pushed under."

"Rod, you can't be content to sit on the outside. You've got to knife your way through and beat somebody up."

"It's just a war down there, Kenny."

"They saw a weakness in Alabama. They don't even use a safety. They're all crashing because they think Alabama can't block 'em out."

The tape ended.

"The good news is that you played your butt off for a while down there. Today's plan is to have you out of here in 45 minutes. But I'm telling you that for 45 minutes your balls better be working. If not, we may have the whole team running up there today. You're right there. And LSU is pretty good. They're 13-0. But I think everybody on this team knows we let one go. Don't we?"

The players responded by nodding their heads.

Mal Moore visited practice to offer his sympathy. However, Scott had not yet appeared. Apparently, he had suffered through the day. The gut-wrenching loss to LSU certainly did not help his pain.

I ATTENDED another staff meeting after the LSU game. Scott did not make it. The coaches all seemed anxious; they all knew that the team was on the cusp of greatness. But how to push them without breaking them was a major concern.

"With all the problems we've had with Rod, it's just like Robert says, fellas, he can put the ball in the basket. We would have loved to have a player like him last year. If we can't force him to get down and be a player and guard, that's our fault. That's my fault, fellas. I'll accept the responsibility. But the bottom line is that he can play," Gottfried said, kicking off the meeting.

Pearson followed. "And it's not that he's a bad kid. He's a good kid. We just have to find a way to get through to him. If we keep demanding things from him, he'll deliver. We just can't sell him short by not pushing him hard. We're spending his money when we're not getting after him, guys. I've seen some pros. He's a pro. While Robert is absolutely right about being patient with Rod, let's not forget that if Robert were a little more healthy, he'd be passing a little more tough loving around this joint."

"I think it's good that he has such a strong relationship with Erwin. As long as we've got him in the right frame of mind—around the right people, we can teach him and improve him," Kelsey said.

Considering the last few games, the coaches were extremely hopeful. It was inspiring to see them so positive despite the obstacles they faced.

The next two days were critical for preparation. Aside from Auburn, the most intense game of the year would be Saturday against Mississippi State. A recruiting feud between the schools had escalated into a personal war—someone had told Gottfried that the State staff has been using the high probability of Scott's death as a recruiting pitch against Alabama. Although never verified, this made Gottfried furious. He refused to use that information as a motivational tool for the players.

While practice ended with free throws, Scott entered. Gottfried asked his hurting friend to address the team.

"The only thing that I would like to say is that people don't think you can play basketball. They don't think you can win. LSU's coach said this morning that the reason you led at halftime was they thought Oklahoma State could beat them, but they did not think Alabama could. So that's why they were behind—not because we outplayed them. So you guys have to go home and look in the mirror. Look at yourself. Guys, when we come over and tell you that you're not doing something right, we're not just wasting our time to tell you that you're not blocking out. I don't tell you that if it's not true. You've got to start picking it up. You need to realize that we're all on the same page. We're trying to help you. So go out there and execute. When we talk about blocking out, that's what we have to do to win. As soon as you relax, bad things start to snowball. Let's quit talking about being young. Let's get some respect. Like Philip said, it gets embarrassing when we keep giving away games. Last night was our game if we don't give up. We let a team that is much bigger than us out-hustle us. That should never happen. It's time to stop coming to the sideline saying 'my bad.' 'My bad.' 'My bad.' After a while, the season is over and all we've got is 'my bad' on the same plays that we screwed up in the first game of the year. Tell you're teammate that 'I'm blocking out.' Defense and rebounding are things that can happen so easily. That's something you can do every night—hustle and rebound every night. That's just effort. When I don't do it, I'm not giving the effort."

Friday's practice began in the back gym because the women's team remained on the coliseum floor. Gottfried turned the scouting report over to Pearson with a simple thought.

"You better want this one bad," Pearson said.

The head coach interjected a thought.

"Antonio Jackson. He's shooting it every time he gets it."

After Pearson finished, the head coach generalized.

"This is our house. They came in here last year and took one from us. They ain't doing it again. You better put your mind to it right now. They're not doing it again."

Gottfried released some steam by harshly criticizing managers Minor and Armstead.

"Winslow, you better get your guys going. We'll run the managers if we have to."

At the end of practice, Gottfried was tempted to share all his feelings about the next opponent.

"There are not a whole lot of teams out there that—[pause] I shouldn't even say that. I want to come out tomorrow and kick their behinds. Their guys talk a lot of trash. We're gonna come out and play with emotion. This is our house."

II

Ecstasy and Agony

An uneventful shoot-around combined with a routine scouting report could have disguised the passion of this game. However, when Gottfried finally generalized before the warm-up, his message was clear: "If you don't want to play in this game, get out of this program!"

After the warm-up, Gottfried announced that Martin would remain in the starting lineup. Apparently, Martin's defensive ability combined with Grizzard defensive deficiencies had benched the freshman. Grizzard only played seven minutes in Baton Rouge. Gottfried challenged Dudley to battle the 6-foot-8, 245-pound Robert Jackson who was expected to control the middle. Jackson played center for a rugged, aggressive team. Rebounding would be critical.

"Do whatever you have to do. Keep them off the boards. If you have to turn around and face somebody to stop 'em, do it. This game will be won on the glass. Their team might as well throw it at the rim and crash the glass. I want you to push somebody into the third row."

The team left the locker room chanting, "Our house! Our house!"

The MSU Bulldogs from nearby Starkville entered the game 9-4 and 1-0 in the SEC after belting Gottfried's former boss Jim Harrick of Georgia. An emotional Tide team grabbed an early 10-2 lead. After a wise Bulldog timeout and a three-pointer by State's Tang Hamilton, Dudley made a jumper to give every player in the Tide starting lineup a bucket at the 16:27 mark. The Bulldogs responded with a run. Hamilton, the 6-foot-7, 215-pound versatile offensive player who ripped Alabama to shreds the year before, scored repeatedly. Tyrus Boswell, a 6-foot-7, 235-pound Alabama native, entered the game and immediately began manhandling people for offensive rebound baskets. A Hamilton dunk punctuated the State surge, giving MSU a 22-21 lead. The half ended on a long sequence of trading buckets. MSU led, 35-33. Boswell shot four for five while Hamilton was five for eight. Antonio Jackson was zero for five. The Tide shot ten for 12 from the line but only 34.5 percent from the field. The Bulldogs owned the rebounding war, 22-18.

The staff meeting centered on Hamilton and rebounding. Walker had been predictably struggling to defend his assignment Hamilton on the perimeter. If the Tide switched to a guard defending Hamilton, they would be vulnerable to his formidable low-post game. No solution found.

The message to the team was simple.

"The name of the game is rebounding. You've got to want the ball, fellas. Find a way to keep your man from getting it. They've got eight offensive rebounds. Eight! I don't care what you have to do, but you better push somebody out of there."

"This game is a just a rat race. It comes down to who wants it the most," Pearson added.

In a game filled with harsh words exchanged by the opposing players and spectacular athleticism showcased in the frenzy of rebounding action, both teams seemed to desperately desire victory. After five ties and four lead changes in the opening nine minutes of the second half, the stronger and more mature Bulldogs grabbed control of the game. Perhaps too concerned about warring the ferocious Bulldogs on re-bounding action plays, Alabama could not make a shot. Even Meade who has slowly developed into the Tide's sharp-shooter was on his way to three of nine shooting.

Something much more important happened to the group of people wearing crimson that evening. Frustrated by awful shooting and the tenacity of the Dogs, the Tide persevered by winning the physical battles that they had lost all year. Offensive rebound after offensive rebound combined with determined defense kept hope alive, preventing State's lead from snowballing.

State led 53-51 at the 11:03 mark and held that lead all the way until Alabama finally seemed on the brink of extinction, trailing 66-62 with the ball and only 30 seconds left.

A struggling Cotton missed a three-pointer. Dudley grabbed the rebound and made a lay-up to keep hope alive. Trailing by two, the Tide was forced to foul Antonio Jackson to send him to the line with 12 seconds left. The Huntsville native had a chance to break Gottfried's heart.

He made the first free throw despite a wildly cheering student section. The three-point lead almost guaranteed overtime as a worst case scenario for the visitors and certainly made a Tide comeback improbable.

He missed the second. Alabama pushed the ball down the floor. Martin was open for a three-pointer that would tie the game. He missed. Cotton grabbed the rebound and furiously dribbled behind the arch for another shot at a tie. The fans moaned as he missed and the clock seemed destined to expire. Dudley grabbed the rebound but apparently had no time to locate and pass to a potential shooter. Instead, the 6-foot-8 power forward sprint-dribbled to the left baseline to attempt a play that I have never seen even Jordan make. With one foot on the ground behind the arch and his momentum carrying him completely out of a balanced shooting posture, Dudley released the textbook desperation shot before the buzzer sounded. It hovered in the air over the basket. Dudley drilled it. He made it! The bench went mad. However, the coliseum rapidly transformed from wild celebration to silence as the officials conferred about whether his foot was behind the three-point line and whether time had expired. As the moments passed liked hours, the officials finally signaled that the basket counted. Overtime!

After all of Dudley's heroics in regulation, the Bulldogs immediately seized control in overtime. A 7-2 MSU run put the Tide on death's doorstep again at the 3:20 mark. But tenacious defense led by London and four straight points from an unlikely scoring threat in London cut the lead to one with 1:14 left. In a timeout at the 1:00 mark, Gottfried urged his men to dig deep for one more stop. MSU tried the one play that the Tide has struggled to negotiate. The Dogs set a tough screen in the painted area for a player who was diving toward the basket. But this time, the Bulldogs did not finish the play.

A Tide rebound and a thoughtful possession pressured the Bulldogs into fouling Dudley with :26 left! Through the non-league season, Dudley was among the top free-throw shooters in the SEC. He stayed after practice every day to shoot free throws and three-pointers with Pearson. He calmly converted both critical shots to give the Tide a one-point lead. Finally, while the coliseum rocked with noise, the home team stopped the Bulldogs as the clock ticked to :04. A Dudley rebound, and MSU immediately fouled. The freshman made two more. A last-second MSU shot missed, and the Tide beat State, 77-74!

An emotional scene unfolded in the locker room. Hugging and yelling signified a release from what had been a horrible series of months for this team. Something substantially positive had finally occurred. Losing to a bitter rival had seemed imminent, and a loss to State would have been the climax of defeat and frustration. Gottfried engaged in a group hug with his players as five adults jumped around like bunnies. The coaches were jubilant. Dudley received the praise of everybody in the room. After much celebration, Gottfried managed few words.

"I love this team. I have all year. But tonight, I think you grew up some. [Long pause] I don't want to leave the locker room."

After leaving the locker room, I went to find Dudley's father, Otis, who had been telling me all year with the deepest conviction that his son could make three-pointers. When I found him, he was looking for me. His son had only made two three-pointers in the young season, but I now believed that Otis had more insight than Dick Vitale and Billy Packer combined.

The total outlook for an 8-6 Tide team was still gloomy. Other than the upcoming Georgia game, not a single road game in the SEC seemed promising. Home games against four schools legitimately thinking about the Final Four (Florida, Tennessee, LSU, and Auburn) meant that the

Tide would certainly need road wins to have a good year. So the season would not likely change its ill-fated course.

Still, the win over MSU—I'm sure that the Tide coaches and players slept well that night—and the heart displayed indicated that these youngsters still had a chance to record a memorable victory.

On the Monday before a Saturday game at Georgia, Stinnett reported that he had felt much better since his surgery. He boasted a brightened demeanor. On the other hand, the daily report on Scott was not encouraging. He suffered through a painful Sunday before beginning chemical injections in Birmingham.

Gottfried did not like the pace of a preliminary shooting drill.

"Guys, everything has to be game speed. My father would feed me passes when I was little. I always practiced at game speed. There is no reason to practice any other way. If you're not getting ready for the game, then you're just wasting your time."

A rare Wednesday night without a game allowed more time for individual skill development and reflection. Rather than practice on Tuesday, the forwards watched the MSU film with Kelsey while the guards watched the tape with Pearson.

The Wednesday lunch news was bad. Walker had been complaining about his shin. Morr suspected that it was not a problem but had an X-ray done to be sure. Walker had a stress fracture in his left leg and would miss at least the great majority of the remaining games. A thin and young front court was disappearing before our eyes. Walker was the only starter against State who shot 50 percent or better. Little hope remained for a turnaround without him. Furthermore, a talented youngster would miss valuable experience for next year's highly anticipated season. The team suffered yet another setback.

Auburn, who was picked by many in the pre-season to reach the Final Four, defeated Kentucky on the Tuesday night ESPN game. Kentucky dominated the Plainsmen the previous year so a victory over the mighty Widcats signalled that Auburn might not fold again in March like a house of cards. The publicity surrounding Auburn's program this season had reached an all-time high for the Plainsmen in the state. With great seniors like Doc Robinson, Mamadou N'diaye, and Chris Porter, Auburn seemed capable of finally bringing the national basketball spotlight to the state of Alabama with a Final Four berth or even a national championship. So the Alabama program has watched its historically inferior neighbor, Auburn (Alabama leads the overall series 73-46, owns many more NCAA berths and SEC title rings), seize complete control of the state's attention. Even Gottfried watched.

"Did anybody watch the Auburn game last night?" Gottfried inquired in the huddle before practice on Wednesday.

Several guys responded affirmatively. They had been watching too.

"In a tied game, Auburn is at the foul line with forty seconds left in the game with a guy who is an 18 percent foul shooter. The guy is three for 20. The Kentucky coaches are yelling at their guys to block out. He misses both and Auburn gets the rebound. Doc Robinson hits a three and the game is basically over because Kentucky can't get a free throw rebound. Free throw rebounding was the difference in the game. It's the fundamentals, guys. It's the little things. It's the little things. [Pause] You guys may know that Kenny is probably out for four or five weeks. They're putting a steel rod in his shin. So you've got to tighten up and buckle up again. You've got to latch on to one another. You've got to practice harder. You've got to concentrate harder. You've got to rise up and play. Let's go! It's not time to feel sorry for yourself. It's not time to pout."

Morr reported that Walker would indeed have a 16-inch steel rod surgically placed into his left leg. Morr said that the medical community had made great strides with repairing this injury. The trainer's general reaction to the injury was predictable.

"What else can go wrong? I hope we have enough guys to finish the season," he said. It had indeed been a rough year for Morr.

Boatright's reaction reflected the core optimism of his boss and mentor.

"If we drop another guy—God forbid—we'll just keep playing."

Michael Floyd, one of Gottfried's former players at Murray State, dropped by practice. It is not uncommon for ex-Gottfried players to stop by for a visit. He treats all of his former players and staff like family.

"I want you guys to meet Michael Floyd. He is from Mobile. He played for us at Murray State. He's driving back to Murray now for one more class to finish his degree. I'm proud of him for that. That's an NCAA tournament guy right there. He was a good player."

A Thursday film session began the intense scrutiny of Harrick's Georgia Bulldogs. Harrick would need another one of his miracles to energize Georgia's program. Former head coach Ron Jersa was chased out of Athens like a fleeing convict after rapidly stripping innocent UGA (lovable English bulldog mascot) of his hoops success generated by Tubby Smith.

Harrick's team would be the easiest to study. Like all great champions, he would play to his strengths above everything else—know your personnel better than anybody and play to your strengths always (see Red Auerbach, Phil Jackson, Pat Riley, Vince Lombardi, Paul Bryant, Bobby Knight, U.S. Grant . . .). Aside from that all-important principle, he used the familiar high-post offense. Gottfried's staff would never be surprised again by the go-to-your-strength idea. After preparing a ton for the high-post offense, Harrick's Rhode Island team just spread the floor all night and used the superior quickness of their guards to cut Gottfried's team to bits in the NCAA tournament on CBS. Similarly, the handwriting was on the wall for Saturday's game. Harrick had signed two highly physical junior college forwards. With the Tide's front court in disarray, Georgia would look to beat Alabama senseless in the low-post and the rebounding war. Moss, who would probably make his dramatic first entry into the starting lineup on his native soil, would be asked for the performance of a lifetime.

"Evans and Shon Coleman can play around the basket. Believe me when I tell you this, fellas. They will take it right at our throats. To be very honest, their best offense is a missed shot. That's the way they score. Shoot it. Miss it. Go get it," Gottfried said.

The other feared Georgia weapon was a sharp-shooting guard.

"D.A. Layne threw in a 28-footer to beat us last year. D.A. Layne went into Arkansas as a freshman and gave them 36."

Practice began, and Scott had not arrived. McDonald filmed the workout for his benefit. The film would not feature Cotton because of a nagging injury.

I asked Morr what was wrong, and he stated simply that Cotton was "cleared to play." He offered no further insight.

As Gottfried experimented with a four-guard lineup in a scrimmage, Moss hammered three straight dunks for the scout team.

"We've got the wrong guys on the scout team," Kelsey exclaimed.

As practice ended, I found the stark contrast between the intensity of last week's workouts and the preparation for Georgia somewhat alarming. However, Gottfried certainly did not want a boot camp environment in practice. So a minor relaxation was inevitable.

The staff turned up the heat on Friday. Cotton complained that he was pushed in a drill.

"Don't give me that crap, Schea," Gottfried responded.

"They push in the game, Schea," Pearson added.

In a long-pass drill, Cotton failed to score as the catcher. He mumbled about the pass being poor.

"[Yelling] The easiest thing to do in life is blame somebody!" the head coach exploded.

Scott entered and found his chair on the sideline as Gottfried had become flustered by the lack of effort for rebounds.

"We get a little tired and just phone it in. That's cost us about four games this year. Everybody on the line," he said.

At the end of the practice, Gottfried prepared his players for a road trip to face a team that replaced Alabama as the most doomed squad in the league with a humiliating 74-54 home loss to Arkansas, pushing their SEC record to 0-3.

"They will be hungry. They got embarrassed the other night. You better believe they won't roll over for you. They'll come out scratching and clawing. Let's get out of here. We need to get to the plane before 5:30."

The 9:30 A.M. shoot-around at Stegeman Coliseum on Saturday attracted Paul Kennedy who was preparing to broadcast the game for JP television. Kennedy was the radio voice of Alabama football and basketball for a stint in the '80s. Gottfried and Kennedy are friends from their experience as broadcaster and player. They exchanged a warm greeting.

Concluding the shoot-around, the head coach was cautiously optimistic with his team.

"We're playing a team that is questioning themselves. They're 0-3 in the league. Arkansas came in here and got 'em. You need to get after them hard. It will get loud in here. They will make runs. They will fight you for forty minutes."

Regardless of Georgia's struggles, playing on the road in college basketball changes everything. For example, the Tide leads its overall series with the Bulldogs 82-42, but Georgia only trails by three in games played in Athens. (Alabama leads LSU 84-57, but trails in Baton Rouge games, 38-25.)

Pearson did not face a difficult challenge in delivering the final scouting report. The Tide prepared to defend plays that it used. The Bulldogs even happened to use a couple of the same out-of-bounds plays. Gottfried followed by emphasizing the importance of rebounding and low-post defense.

"Have an attitude that you'll take whatever they want to throw at you."

After the warm-up, he continued to mentally prepare the group to a win a road game.

"They'll hit some threes. The crowd will get loud. That's life on the road in this league. Deal with it."

In his last opportunity to play on the campus of his state's school, Moss received the nod for a starting position. Martin, Dudley, Cotton, and Meade completed the lineup. Grizzard rested in the doghouse for the time being.

"I'm so hyped, dog," Moss told me before the game.

Unfortunately for Alabama, Moss seemed to be its only excited player. From start to finish, 5,672 fans on a cold afternoon enjoyed Georgia drilling a lethargic Tide team in every battle of the half. A comfortable Bulldog lead of 37-27 reflected a far more hungry Georgia team.

The staff meeting outside the locker room began with a lengthy period of silence like men inside a funeral home. Without an active player taller than 6-foot-8 and a nucleus formed largely by newcomers, this team simply had to offer a better effort. In its best opportunity to steal a road win, they were being out-hustled. Again. Given Georgia's 0-3 start and their inevitably bad team, Alabama's nightmare seemed to be climaxing. Kelsey broke the silence with a detail that somehow seemed to summarize the season.

"I've got Evans at four for four," he said.

Gottfried turned to the offense.

"Schea Cotton is supposed to be a scorer. He just turns the ball over. The alternative is Rod. You go to Rod and he goes in like we're at the park. He doesn't care about playing. He never bends his knees. He never gets down in a stance. He doesn't do anything."

A gloomy reality for the group was their belief that Georgia was the worst team in the league other than their team.

"They're awful," Kelsey stated.

After a long and quiet staff meeting, Gottfried charged into the locker room and wrote "compete" so hard on the chalkboard that the chalk seemed like it should have broken. Immediately, I knew that the frustrations of three rocky months would explode.

"[Screaming every sentence and every word] Compete! You gotta compete! Hard! [Looking at Schea] I've about had enough of watching you in practice going half-speed! You get in the game and you've got five turnovers! Five turnovers! 'It's the referee's fault! It's his fault on the pass!' No! The bottom line is five turnovers! Find somebody to blame, Schea! Blame me! 'It's all coaches' fault!' That's why big, slower than snot number 51 catches the ball and goes right around you! You gotta play! You come over here, fellas, and you don't compete! Rod, I don't know! Maybe this game isn't real serious to you! I don't know! You come right into the game and instead of being down and ready because he's about to shoot a foul shot, you just kind of stand straight up and step in early! Then, you get the ball going one-on-one and you're just straight-legged like you're at the park! This ain't the park! Casual crap! You gotta get

down and play! Compete and guard them! Schea, we start the game off
by running a play to you! I want you to cut hard and get you a lay-up! We
run guard-screen. You won't even come hard off that! You go half-
speed—just wanting to catch it and go one-on-one! If you go hard, you
might get an open jump shot! But you won't go hard! We get beat down
the floor! [Looking at Martin] D.A. Layne beats you down the floor! Let
me explain it again! Number 32! You don't leave him, Doc! You don't
leave him! 32! You come over here and leave your brain in the hotel!"

Gottfried paused. He breathed heavily through a half-minute break.

"[Yelling] They've got nine offensive rebounds," Pearson interjected.

"Nine offensive rebounds!"Gottfried exclaimed.

"Who's taken a charge for us? Who's tried to take a charge?" Pearson
asked aggressively.

Gottfried was once again stimulated.

"[Screaming] Fourteen minutes and Schea has one rebound! That's
what you call not competing! You see there are other things in the game
than scoring! It's rebounding! It's playing hard! It's taking a charge! It's
getting down and guarding somebody! They're shooting 46 percent and
we're shooting 34. D.A. Layne has 14 points! We'll find somebody in
here that will guard him! We'll start with you again, Doc. If you still can't
handle him, then we'll go right down the line. You can't let 'em
penetrate, Terrance Meade! You can't let them go right into the lane!
Lay-up! Dunk! Give me the shot chart! They've got two shots outside the
paint!" he exclaimed before stopping again.

He calmly covered a few technical issues before suddenly feeling
another urge to erupt.

"[Screaming louder than ever] It's about your effort! Good night! It's
about your effort! They dribble the ball wherever they want to dribble it!
They beat you down the floor and we're in a scramble! We can't run the
floor! If you guys don't want to win, just tell me! Tell me! If you think
they're just gonna roll over and die for you because they suck, that ain't
the game in this league! Everybody can play! Everybody can play in this
league! [Pointing to the plays on the board] It's not about all this bullcrap
on the board! It's about effort! Make a decision to come out and play in

the second half with some intensity and not let those big guys dribble right around us and not let the point guard dribble to underneath the net! Nobody takes a charge! They shoot airballs and we can't get 'em! That's effort! That's not technique! They're quicker than you? They're better than you? They are a better offensive player than you are a defensive player? That's why you can't contain them off the dribble? You better make a decision about your team. Bring everything you've got! If you can't and that's too hard for you, sit down! We'll find somebody that can! And don't come over to the bench bitching at me! Don't be bitching at me! And don't blame everybody else! [Looking at Cotton] That's all you do is blame everybody! Make a decision."

In the movies, the team would have been inspired to a great second half comeback by that speech. But nobody gave Georgia a script. The Bulldogs proceeded to shoot better in the second half than the first, embarrassing Alabama 75-59 without being threatened.

A subdued and devastated Gottfried struggled for words in the locker room.

"You played harder in the second half. But you dug yourself a hole. We just can't go out on the road like this. You have to be mentally ready to go from start to finish."

ON THE plane headed home, Gottfried appeared to be soul searching. With an open bible in his hands and team chaplain Overstreet gently whispering encouragement in his ear, he coped with the loss of his best chance to win on the road.

At the end of the flight, the head coach made a rare motivational plea in the back of the plane. When a formal address about basketball unfolds on the plane, the team has problems. The tone of the speech was somber and sobering.

"You've got to have a fire in your belly to compete. You've got to pick yourself up and get ready to play. In this league, one loss can easily turn into two. If you see someone not working as hard as he should be, pull him aside and get him going. We've got to have some defensive intensity. Everybody needs to go home and look in the mirror."

The team reconvened on Martin Luther King, Jr., Day, Monday, January 17. Morr attempted to help Meade with a tight back. A very tight back had apparently contributed to his shooting slump (two for 13 at Georgia). Walker struggled to ride a bike with a rod in his leg. Stinnett jogged around the sideline. Lifting weights at the moment, Hays entered later to climb steps to strengthen his recovering knee. A brief glance at the sideline during practice could have led one to confuse the coliseum for a rehabilitation clinic.

And amidst all of this, Scott lay on a table with a pillow under his head at the start of practice. His skinny neck lolled about as he fought to stay awake. He had had a rough few days of pain and nausea. He came to practice anyway.

The staff used many full-court drills to prepare for Arkansas. If a team is preparing for Nolan Richardson's Razorbacks, they better be prepared to play a game of constant transition. Richardson's teams control the pace. His philosophy is simple and effective. He is always willing to bet that his team is more conditioned than the opponent. A liberal shooting policy allows his perimeter scorers to develop supreme confidence (*see* Scotty Thurmond putting a dagger in Duke's heart for the national championship).

"Arkansas has taken 200 more threes than anybody else in the league," Gottfried commented.

Practice on Tuesday began late while Moss attended an important class in his quest for graduation. As a partial academic qualifier, Moss could earn back the year of eligibility that was initially lost for not qualifying by completing his degree within four years. Moss had that goal well within his reach.

Kobie Baker mentioned earlier that a phone conversation with Scott had not been encouraging. Baker told me that he thought Scott was suffering too much to attend practice. Baker and Scott had quickly developed a close bond. Baker worked diligently to help the traumatized Scott family by transporting Robert or the children—anything to make life easier. In those miserable days, many men in Scott's position would not have wasted the effort to develop a friendship with somebody who just joined the staff. However, Scott befriended Baker in every way imaginable—before Baker was helping his family. While many highly ambitious and successful people actively choose to associate only with those who have been successful or that can potentially help them, Scott always had time for people like me who could not help him in any shape, form, or fashion.

Scott arrived just before practice and came out coaching. We know that he would sit down soon, but his effort was symbolic—refuse to surrender.

Gottfried has a history with Arkansas, working against them frequently, including the national championship game. He knew them well.

"The way they play is up and down. They'll trap you. They'll full court press you. You've just got to play through it. You can't let them beat you off the dribble."

The film session after practice featured the exploits of freshman Joe Johnson. Richardson had so much confidence in the youngster that he spread the floor for Johnson to create the winning score at the end of games. He had 17 points and nine rebounds in a win over Ole Miss.

The Wednesday afternoon shoot-around afforded Scott an opportunity to have a lengthy private conversation with Martin. Then he spoke to London and Davis. Who knows what knowledge he imparted? Those conversations were private for a reason.

After Pearson finished the scouting report, Gottfried closed on a direct note.

"We can talk about making a good duck move. Basketball is really about playing as hard as you can play. Taking great, great shots. Rebounding the ball. Guarding people. It's not real complicated. You've got to play as hard as you can play."

PEARSON stood before the team in the locker room as the pre-game clock ticked.

"Let's take a charge. We only had one at Georgia," he said.

Gottfried diagnosed their trapping defense.

"If they trap when the ball gets passed to the wing, it becomes backyard football. Somebody is uncovered. You must get open and flash to the ball."

After the warm-up, he asked for a better defensive effort.

"These are the percentages that league opponents have shot against us. 48, 52, and 52. We've got to have a shut-out mentality . . . Give a great, great effort. Don't make me walk in here like at Georgia for halftime. It's not worth that."

A crowd of 7,547 gathered to watch an always exciting game between Arkansas and Alabama. Since Arkansas joined the SEC and subsequently replaced Alabama as the second fiddle in the league to Kentucky, the Tide and Hogs have waged memorable wars. While the Razorbacks have achieved national prominence in the tournament, Alabama has been the jealous neighbor that continues to scrap for its old position—managing a 9-9 record in SEC games against the Hogs.

Moss exited the starting lineup, leaving four guards (Cotton, Martin, Meade, and Grizzard) and Dudley. Never accuse Gottfried of avoiding bold decisions. He embraced Grizzard with a starting nod after the worst game of the guy's life. The Razorbacks are not a big team so the time to experiment with a four-guard lineup was eminent.

Meade nailed two three-pointers to open the game. According to Morr, his back had improved slightly. The Hogs answered each Meade bucket with a three-pointer, tying the game and setting the tone for a half that would have its highest leading margin of four points reached only twice. Meade cut a four-point Hog lead to 1 at the 11:08 mark with another shot behind the arch. Meade's 16 points and vastly improved defense gave the Tide a 30-26 halftime lead. The Hogs were held to 28.6% shooting. Haginas shot two for two, including a power dunk.

In the staff meeting, Baker suggested that Rod was not seeing the ball defensively, triggering a reaction from Scott who finally revealed his disappointment with the player he had up to that point always defended.

"Rod needs to get some damn discipline! He should be through with all that crazy mess. He's not in a stance. He's reaching all the time!"

The staff was also upset by several unnecessary fouls that led the Hogs to ten of 12 foul shooting. The staff entered the locker room.

"Our problem is that we're fouling unnecessarily. We foul the little white guy [Jason Gilbert) and just give 'em four or six points. We're reaching and whacking around there, and he's a great foul shooter. He's not gonna miss 'em . . . [Turning to offense] They're gonna be slapping, swiping, reaching around—take care of the ball," Gottfried said.

Scott could not resist a face-to-face criticism.

"Rod, you're way out there trying to steal a ball from a midget. Stay between your man and the ball."

The feared Joe Johnson, who did not attempt a shot in the first half, led a Razorback surge in the second stanza. A Johnson free throw giving him 8 points in the half at the 13:22 mark put Arkansas on top, 39-38. Cotton answered with two free throws to give the Tide a 40-39 lead after being mugged on a rush to the goal. Meade added another three-pointer, building on a lead that would not be surrendered. Cotton, who continued to be fouled after his lightning quick first step, drained one free throw after another. The muscular journeyman finished the Hogs. He even nailed a three-pointer to expand the lead after the Hogs made a run. Martin added a three-pointer at the 1:44 mark to end any mystery. A comfortable finish ended with a 73-64 Alabama win. Cotton finished 15 of 19 from the line with 26 points and 11 rebounds. Meade finished five of seven from the three-point line, leading to 23 points. London entered the game early for defensive help against the Hogs' quick guards and logged 38 minutes with eight assists, four points, four rebounds, and a steal. The four-guard lineup worked. But would it work again?

Gottfried's greatest coaching achievements have come at the Hogs' expense. The NCAA title game as an assistant, his signature win at Murray State, and the first Tide sweep of Arkansas last season have helped define his career to date.

Why do coaches sometimes appear to be maniacs? Because there is a world of difference between a happy locker room and a sad one. Smiles and clapping filled that one.

"Nice job. We've just got to get better at all the little things. You played good defense. You played smart. Good team win, guys. Real good win. We go through a lot together everyday so that we can come in here and enjoy a win. You guuys just helped Coach Scott sleep better tonight.

"Practice tomorrow at 3:30. Let's get ready to play Florida on Saturday. They've got great talent and they're a top ten team. They got beat at home last night. Tennessee went down there and got 'em. They're coming after you. Way to shoot it, Meade [Applause]. Schea, that's a big three you hit [Applause]. Doc, how about that three, Doc [Applause]."

After the game, Scott jokingly told me to stay on the players the next day because he would miss practice for a doctor's visit.

Thursday brought a predictable lackluster workout.

"There was no life today. You guys have to come out with some life tomorrow. The other night they shot 33 three-pointers. They're coming in here to play," Gottfried said to finish practice.

Kelsey reported on the Florida Gators in the Friday practice. "They love to penetrate and pitch. Their guards are excellent ball-handlers and very quick. They like to dribble all the way to the goal. 6-foot-8 Mike Miller dribbles like a guard and will carve through a defense."

"It's a three-point game and a lay-up game," Gottfried said.

The Gators also had one of the nation's most physical players in Donnell Harvey. Built like a tank, Harvey takes no prisoners.

"A lot of times you guys [forwards] like to fall down when you get pushed. If you want to do that, don't play tomorrow night because Donnell Harvey will push you all over the place," Gottfried said.

Practice closed with tough talk.

"This is a great opportunity for you. We've got to play smart and tough. Donnell Harvey will elbow you. He'll punch you in the mouth. He'll talk trash for forty minutes. He might hit you in the balls. He baits a guy into something in just about every game that I've watched him. They'll bring everything they've got. You better bow up and be ready to play. Don't come in here half-hearted."

THE TEAM appeared tired in the two o'clock Saturday shoot-around.

"Guys, we've got to wake up. We've got the number nine team in America coming in. We've got to get excited."

Before the warm-up, the players seemed to be excited and ready for the game. LSU was experiencing success but Billy Donovan's Florida team had been hyped by the media throughout the off-season. Surrounded by good players, Miller and Harvey were considered to be first-round NBA material before the season started. The Gators were so talented that Harvey was not in the starting lineup. The publicity surrounding their team had certainly reached the Tide players.

"We've got to do a great job of getting back in transition and finding their shooters," Kelsey began. "Florida will push the ball down the floor furiously and find one of their many good shooters for an open shot. They will also utilize many screens for the ball-handler . . . Big guys, get out there in a hurry with a presence to show on the ball screens."

"This is a great opportunity. This is a great opportunity. This is a great opportunity. Let's have fun playing. Let's have fun playing, Rod."

The tremendously talented Grizzard needed to improve to prevent his team from being completely dead in the water. He was currently buried in a six for 28 shooting nightmare. Gottfried's latest approach was to relax the freshman—how rare to hear an individual's name called at the end of a motivational rant.

After the warm-up, the head coach seemed to be ready to put on a jersey.

"Don't be shocked if Harvey puts an elbow down your throat. Don't let him take you out of your game, but you better buck up . . . Pass the ball four, six, eight times tonight. Get a great look. Shoot your shot. Save nothing. They're stopping it every four minutes. I've got plenty of timeouts. Don't save anything. [He turns toward the board and knocks on it as if it were a door] Every now and then, opportunity knocks," he concluded to loud applause.

An enthusiastic crowd of 9,507 gathered after an always popular win over Arkansas. Cotton began with arguably the toughest defensive assignment of the year against Miller. London replaced Martin in the starting lineup. London and Meade seemed to play very well together against the Hogs. London embraced the point-guard role, controlling the team and distributing the ball. Meade seemed more and more like a shooting guard—just get him the ball with a slight opening. Gottfried had begun openly regretting his placing the burden of the point guard spot on Meade. The one area that Gottfried was not lacking in this season was regrets.

Florida started like a great team on a 5-0 run. Meade, Cotton, Grizzard, and Dudley scored in the next 3:37 to tie the game at 13 in a high-paced offensive shootout. Five more minutes of intense transition up and down the floor ended with a 24-21 Gator lead after back-to-back three-pointers. After a rare scoreless sequence, Cotton ignited the raucous crowd with a dunk to make it 24-23. However, Miller, towering over Cotton, led Florida to dominate the rest of the half with Florida leading 40-33 at the intermission. Miller scored 15. Cotton replied with 12, and Grizzard's hoops spirit was resurrected with 11 points on four of five shooting against the best competition of the year.

"We've got to find a way to guard Mike Miller. That's the one we've got to guard," Gottfried said in the staff meeting.

After a long, meandering conversation, the staff reluctantly decided to stay with Cotton guarding Miller while Martin waited in the bullpen. Miller was simply too tall for the Tide guards and too quick for the forwards.

The staff entered the locker room.

"That's one of the best teams in the country out there fellas. You just showed 'em that you can play. Let's keep getting after g'em . . . [Looking at Cotton] You and [turns to Martin] you have to guard Miller. He had 15. He's the one, fellas. In the first five minutes of the half, you have to buck up and guard him. You have to find him in the break. He's getting offensive rebound tips. Against our zone, he got loose. He's the man right now. He walks up to the foul line and makes four foul shots. Our defensive transition is not very good. You've got to find him and be aware. I've got to know who's coming. I've got to get back and find 'em."

The second half began with a Gator threat to run away and hide. Teddy Dupay, who endured humiliation on ESPN in failing to beat Tennessee at the foul line, finally nailed a three-pointer to make it 45-34. Meade connected on two three-pointers to give the Tide a pulse. Meade had an incredible ability to endure the pressure of a big shot when his team was on the ropes. Martin and Dupay exchanged three-pointers to make it 50-43. Productive Tide defense for 3:07 allowed Cotton and Grizzard to cut the lead to three at the 11:41 mark.

When another three-pointer by Meade gave the Tide a 54-53 lead at the 10:30 mark for the first time since 11:10 remained in the first half, the crowd erupted. The Gators responded with a 9-3 run keyed by another three-pointer from a redemption-seeking Dupay. Trailing the mighty Gators by five with under eight minutes to play, Grizzard leaped onto the stage of big-time college basketball with a spectacular dunk and a three-pointer, sparking a near riot by the crowd. A responding Kenyan Weaks three-pointer kept the Gators in front.

Meade to the rescue! A three-pointer capped six straight points from Meade, and a mesmerized crowd roared their approval of a 68-67 Tide lead with 4:55 left. When Grizzard nailed another three-pointer with 2:43 left to make the lead three, it seemed that the highly publicized Tide youngsters would finally signal a major turn in the long-term direction of the program. But the crowd agonized while six straight Gator points from Miller helped the visitors back to the lead, 73-71 with 1:49 left. Dudley tied the game 11 seconds later with a clutch jumper. With the clock ticking under a minute, a Tide stop would put the home team in great position. The Gators missed! Grizzard grabbed the ball momentarily before the Gators' 260-pound center Udonis Haslem ripped the ball out of his hands and muscled in a lay-up as if thrusting his fist through Alabama's chest to rip out the heart and take a big bite. The Gators led 75-73. Cotton attempted to answer with a rush through the lane. He missed after believing that he was fouled. Florida rebounded, and the Tide was forced to foul Dupay with just 16 seconds left. Faced with a similar challenge to the one he failed against the Vols on Tuesday, Dupay calmly delivered the fatal blow with two makes. Even the Tide's best performance was wrecked, 77-73.

A tortured and silent team heard very little from Gottfried. He stood before the group, struggling to place a positive spin on the depth of their despair.

"I know you're hurting. I am extremely frustrated too. [Long pause] But believe me when I tell you that good days are ahead. I don't know about you, but I think we can play with any team in the country after tonight. We've just to find a way to get these kind of games done. We will. Believe me."

12

How To Get a Rebound?

Afamiliar feeling greeted the team on the Monday after the Florida loss. Haginas and Dudley collided violently in a war rebounding drill. Haginas was injured. Kelsey, Minor, Gottfried, and Morr surrounded him and lifted him off the floor. Haginas sat with Morr on the baseline. Kelsey and Gottfried continually left the action momentarily to check on him.

Was another player badly hurt? Brent Vinson, who replaced Rasco in the student trainer role for the second semester, escorted Haginas to the team doctor for an X-ray. Morr suspected that his collar bone was broken. The X-ray was negative, but Haginas did have a separated shoulder. The front court would be even thinner for the upcoming Ole Miss game at home on Saturday. The team was granted a needed rest day.

Scott missed practice on Monday while McDonald filmed the workout for him. When the team reconvened on Wednesday, Scott had not yet arrived.

Cotton went down in a one-on-one from the wing drill against Grizzard. He appeared to have "rolled" his left ankle—fortunately not a serious injury.

Morr was skeptical about the results of Haginas's X-ray. He would have another X-ray again on Friday and a possible bone scan the following week.

A rattled head coach finally reacted to a season of injuries when

Bakken hammered Grizzard who was trying to score on a fast break.

"Hey Jim! Let it go today. We'll beat up on somebody on Saturday." Although Gottfried loved intense practices, he could not bear to see another injury.

A suffering Scott never arrived. He had to be in Birmingham for a screening of his cancerous growth on the following day but planned to return for practice. (Robert was crushed by the loss to Florida, but had found encouragement in Grizzard's emergence. Gottfried, also, was pleased with Grizzard's development and increased mental toughness. It had been a long time coming, but Grizzard had finally come into his own.)

With Cotton nursing his ankle on Thursday, Morr complained of having a starting lineup of his own (Hays, Walker, Haginas, Cotton, and Stinnett) with so many players in rehabilitation.

"I've got my own team over here," Morr said.

Adapting to the lack of depth, Gottfried had Pearson practicing. The coach enjoyed setting some solid screens and feeding the post.

When a television crew entered the coliseum to prepare for the broadcast of the Alabama-Kentucky women's game that night, technical equipment was placed on the sideline in a potentially dangerous position. Gottfried called one of the crew members over.

"Do you mind moving this stuff for just about 15 minutes? We've got enough people hurt."

Accompanied by Cynthia, Scott arrived late into practice. Cynthia indicated that the doctor's diagnosis was not good. Baker reported later that Scott had the rest of the staff laughing in the coaches' locker room after practice.

"Did you see Fred today? I think he would foul his girlfriend if she suited up for the other team."

He had been evaluating the players in a humorous manner, a commonly used stress reliever for coaches. And Scott was so good at making people laugh without hurting anyone's feelings. When he felt like sharing, Scott could have a room nearly crying with laughter.

Cotton and Scott seemed to be rejuvenated on Friday. Scott stood and coached for most of the practice. Having been carefully fitted with an ankle brace by Morr, Cotton joined the early drills. Pearson scrimmaged again, and his practicing had sparked some good-natured trash talking with the players at lunch. More elbows were talked about being thrown over lunch than were delivered by Pearson or the players.

At the Saturday shoot-around, Kelsey voiced his concern about the Rebels' 6-foot-6 Marcus Hicks who was a highly productive low-post scorer for the Rebels. Kelsey scouted an Ole Miss team that just stopped the bleeding with a gigantic win over Auburn. After racing to an impressive 12-1 non-league record, the Rebels had tripped out of the gate in league play.

The Auburn win moved their league record to 1-5 after predictable losses to Florida at home and on the road at Arkansas, Kentucky, and Tennessee. The Rebels' 13-6 record was envied by a 9-8 Tide team just wishing desperately that it could have a win over Auburn.

"They will do a lot of different things to finally have Hicks freed to post-up on the block," Kelsey said.

BEFORE the warm-up on Saturday night, Gottfried was overflowing with enthusiasm, rapidly firing ideas about winning basketball at his team.

"[Excited] Move the ball. It's not sticking in your hands. Take it to the hoop. Penetrate and pitch. Play without the ball. How good are you when you don't have it? That's your shot . . . Eliminate the penetration. If they make 25 three-pointers to beat us, we'll live with that. But no point-blank jumpers and dunks."

Ole Miss did not have a reputation for perimeter play. They were (and still are) known as a rugged defensive team with an aggressive low-post attack that has visited the NCAA tournament recently. The Rebels have answered the doubts about a school that has traditionally embraced the symbols of the slave-holding Confederacy being able to field a good hoops team in today's era. Credit the Rebels' hiring of African-American head coaches. When you have Confederate battle flags or poorly disguised imitations of that flag flying everywhere on your campus during athletic events, you better hire an African-American coach to attract players to your basketball team.

After the warm-up, Gottfried commented on the match-ups.

"Tarik has to get under ball screens in time to keep Jason Harrison from turning the corner . . . Erwin, you've got Rahim Lockhart. He's a load. He went nine for nine against us last year in one game."

"I want us to get some offensive rebound baskets," he continued. "I want you guys to be like linebackers trying to blitz the quarterback in football. Just find a way to get in there. Go get some . . . You guys have really been sharing the ball. Keep moving the ball. Create plays in your mind . . .This is our house. In this league, fellas, you better lace it up right now. They're coming in thinking that they're gonna get you. Buckle up in your mind right now and say 'I'm gonna play tough for forty minutes.'"

A paid audience of 9,057 watched the same four-guard starting lineup from the Florida game jog onto the floor. Grizzard was not yet a starter despite a great performance. The Rebels quieted the audience by scoring at will to open the game. Cotton managed to keep Alabama trailing only 10-8 with 15:40 left by scoring the Tide's first eight points. Tough defense combined with Lockhart and Hicks scoring 10 of the Rebels first 22 points helped hold the Ole Miss lead until the 6:52 mark. But Meade, Grizzard, and Cotton combined for 19 points in the remaining 6:51 to drive the Rebels back into the locker room trailing 41-32. Cotton had 15 points at the half while Meade had ten.

The staff meeting focused mainly on how to guard Hicks. Gottfried complimented Moss who played ten minutes in the role of defensive specialist. The injured Walker would be a somewhat ideal choice to guard Hicks. Without him, Cotton was continually asked to guard taller men like Hicks while Dudley guarded a stronger and bigger man almost every night like Lockhart.

The staff entered the locker room.

"Good job. Alfred did the best job of discouraging the post . . . Rip it through, Rod. They want to scratch and claw the ball away from you. Buck up . . . Get tight and strong with the basketball. Firm up and rip it through . . .This is our home. They're gonna come at you with every-thing they've got. I know 'em. Match it. Match their intensity."

Alabama steadily pulled away from the Rebels in the second half. An 11-point lead with 15:16 left ballooned to 16 by the 10:01 mark. The 16-point lead became a 21-point lead with 6:36 left. The final talley had the Tide chasing the Rebels back to Oxford in a 96-67 rout. The dramatic moments of the game unfolded for the Tide when Davis drained back-to-back three-pointers. Gottfried used every active player. Cotton controlled the entire game, shooting seven for ten and 15 for 21 from the free throw line to earn 29 points accompanied by nine rebounds. Meade, Grizzard, and Martin reached double-figures. London had seven assists and only two turnovers with six points. Dudley grabbed 12 rebounds. Moss scored seven points on two for two shooting.

The locker room buzzed about the non-scholarship players—Davis's three-pointers and a pretty pass from Bakken to Moss.

Gottfried offered very little congratulations.

"We've got Auburn coming up over there. They made up a bunch of comments that Jeremy was supposed to have said last year—their fans were all over him. I think that's bush league. If you look around the room at your coaches, you'll see some guys who did nothing but beat Auburn's butt when they played here. You better make a decision about how badly you want to beat Auburn as a player. Don't let the press bait you into saying anything negative about Auburn. Praise them. They're having a good run."

THE TIDE prepared on Monday for a hostile road trip to bitter rival Auburn.

"I'm not real big on getting extra hyped for one game because all of them are important. Every game is important. If you beat Auburn, it counts one win. If you lose to 'em, it's one loss. It ain't five losses. But I'm just going to tell you something, guys. It is different. It's not, but it is. You've got to step up to a big challenge. And I don't give a crap if we've got one hundred guys hurt. I don't give a crap. And nobody really gives a crap. Nobody really cares. The bottom line is that you're going down to play a team that was preseason number one in the country according to *Sports Illustrated*. They've got four senior starters. They've got a great bench. They're gonna talk trash. It will be loud. They'll be right on top of you, calling you names. You've got to go down there with a mind set and a purpose to come out with a win. Some of you might have read the paper today. I'll tell you one thing that just—screw these people [opening a newspaper].

"This is today's *Birmingham News*. [Reading from the paper] 'Fast forward to the week that will be. Did Custer have to return to Little Big Horn? No, but Alabama must go back to Auburn where it has lost the last two seasons by a combined total of 323 points or so it seems. Can a younger, thinner Alabama team compete with the defending SEC champions? Until halftime? Until the first T.V. timeout? Welcome to the Tide's Wednesday nightmare. Top ten helpful hints to Alabama as it prepares to venture into its own personal house of horrors. Suit up that bunch from last summer's Legends Game.' You should take offense to that. 'Wear Tennessee Orange. Sneak Gerald Wallace into uniform. Have Wimp Sanderson conduct the Monday and Tuesday workouts.' I should take offense to that. 'Don't make any inflammatory pre-game comments.' This guy is writing about what Auburn made up out of the blue about us. 'Two words: four corners. Two more words: forfeit. Have Wimp Sanderson give pre-game talk. Have Mark Gottfried wear plaid. Pray for snow.' In sports, sometimes you just have to dig deep, guys. Let's play our game down there. Play smart."

A hard-nosed practice included much work against a full-court press. The Tide had struggled with the Plainsmen's press last year. A few tough rebounding drills attempted to prepare the team for the aggressive Plainsmen rebounders, N'Diaye and Porter, who had a big edge over the wounded Tide front line.

Cotton dropped out of the Tuesday practice early with a large blister on his foot and nagging ankle pain. Morr worked with him diligently.

Kelsey continued with the forwards. He preached about winning four-minute segments of the game—any psychology to make a tremendous challenge seem manageable. Pearson practiced again at the point guard position for the scout team. One could not have convinced Pearson's muscles in the morning that basketball was not a contact sport. He had been quietly hurting all week while asking for more punishment at lunch with the players. Pretending to be Auburn along with Pearson were Bakken, Towns, Davis (as Chris Porter), and Moss.

In a relaxed moment, Gottfried looked at me with a smile and sarcastically said, "This is a pretty good simulation of Auburn's team."

We huddled before ending practice and boarding the bus bound for Auburn.

"Get your mind right. You're going on the road to win. It's a business trip. Believe in each other. Encourage each other. Nobody around here is giving you a chance. Nobody gives you a chance. You've got to go down there determined. Buck up and do it. It's a great, great opportunity."

The shoot-around on Wednesday morning was like the quiet before the storm. Beard-Eaves Memorial Coliseum would be packed with 10,500 excited fans celebrating a break from the many games of past years when Alabama had defeated Auburn, transforming Beard-Eaves into a Tide pep rally late in the game. Pearson scouted the Tigers. He would not have it any other way. A series of pictures hang on his office wall of Keith Askins sacrificing body and mind to grab a critical lose ball in the '90 Alabama win at Auburn.

I looked at a quiet Scott and wonderd if he thought about this being his last trip to Auburn for a game. Was he reminiscing about the shot he hit at the buzzer in Auburn to send the game to overtime? Had the season turned into a farewell tour in his mind? He would never admit to that. He expected to beat cancer. He expected to win.

The staff was concerned about Doc Robinson dribbling around screens on the perimeter to create scoring opportunities. Defensive rebounding, press break, and guarding Porter were also stressed areas.

"You must commit to keeping yourself between Porter and the goal at all times. Make him shoot over you. On the rebound, fight him out of there. If not, he'll be doing chin-ups on the rim like last year. The guys who were here last year can tell you that it wasn't fun."

When we returned that night, the drawing board in the visitor's locker room was worn and stained with permanent markers. The staff complained. Coliseum staff entered with cleaning solution which failed to have an impact. Another board was eventually brought into the room.

Pearson stood before the team.

"We've got to get back. Slow Robinson down. Find their shooters. That will mainly be 10 [Pohlman] and 23 [Daymeon Fishback]. The big guys have to run too. Their big guys do a good job of running out . . . We've got to rebound. We've got to be physical. They've had a lot of success by rebounding to win games."

Gottfried took over. "We've got to guard them, but they've got to guard us too . . . Play like you've been playing. Be unselfish."

The Tide had decreased its turnovers and increased productivity by often turning away from Gottfried's beloved high-post offense. A more simplified approach had been more comfortable for these youngsters. Gottfried indicated that he would probably use very little of the high-post tonight.

"This is not an X's and O's game, fellas. This is an effort and hustle game. All they're talking about right now is their pride in rebounding. They're gonna rebound! So will we! It will be a great environment. Let's play hard and get it done!"

During the warm-up, I pondered exactly how Gottfried visualized a "great environment." Alabama was facing longer odds than Walter Mondale in the '84 election against Ronald Reagan. Hostile fans were yelling insults at Gottfried that would have infuriated a nun. This crowd would be delighted by every bad turn for the Tide. Loud and obnoxious, the Auburn fans would be in the team's ears all game. The environment did not seem so great to me.

After the warm-up, the head coach truly embraced the challenge.

"[Yelling] If you're afraid and timid, stay in here! You better reach down and bring something tonight! Bring your A-game. Get your lunch pale and your hard hat and go out to play. [Screaming] If you're afraid, don't come play! Don't play!" His explosion triggered the wildest clapping of the year from the locker room.

Grizzard entered the starting lineup in place of Martin. The enigmatic potential superstar Grizzard faced his greatest test in a heated rivalry against Auburn's veterans. A stimulated crowd anxious to forget a painful football loss with a basketball win roared the introduction of the home team. After two minutes of nervous shooting and intense defense, Auburn predictably seized control with a 10-3 run to open the game. A Fishback dunk inspired a thunderous cheer which caused the Tide bench players to glance at each other with the fear of a long, long night. Grizzard answered with a drive into the lane followed by a vicious dunk. Minutes later, Grizzard scored nine points in a less than two-minute span to shock the crowd and notify the Plainsmen that the most gifted offensive player on the floor was wearing crimson. Grizzard's surge changed the tone of the rivalry, giving the Tide a 16-14 lead and raising questions about the preconceived notion that the Tigers would sweep the Tide easily. Cotton took over the scoring burden for the remainder of the half and an effective zone defense gave Alabama a glorious segment of basketball. Holding the lead for almost all of the final 11 minutes of the half, the visitors seemed to be playing in a dream. The dream was somewhat interrupted when Porter undercut Moss, sending him crashing to the ground, unable to cushion the impact for his exposed back. Moss hobbled off the floor with Morr.

A surreal sequence unfolded when the walk-on Davis entered this game. "Sollo" Davis had gone from the practice gunner to a needed contributor in this battle! Auburn decided to allow Davis to shoot from the perimeter. Davis stood alone with the ball while the bench agonized because his team wanted him to shoot—he passed the ball instead. "Sollo" showed that he understood the significance of his playing in the game, turning down a shot that he would normally release with his eyes closed. He knew about unselfishness and his limited role on this team. The team wanted him to shoot, but I loved his not shooting. The free spirit from Mobile cared about his team. He took pride in his jersey.

The Tide led 32-28 at the half. Cotton's 12 points combined with Grizzard's 14 to represent a gaudy percentage of the Tide total. Auburn entered the game 17-3 and considering the hype surrounding their club along with the intensity of this rivalry, an Alabama win tonight would have been unimaginably huge for a Tide team desperately seeking a source of pride. After the Birmingham news had bashed him, Gottfried had done a phenomenal job of preparing his wounded, young, and undermanned team to play Auburn.

A Plainsmen win still seemed inevitable. Grizzard had already been whistled for three fouls and both Cotton and Dudley had two fouls.

"We've got no choice but to play zone," Gottfried said to his staff in frustration about the foul trouble.

A zone prevents many situations where an off-balance defender commits an unnecessary foul. Counseling a team about how to deal with early foul trouble is perplexing. A passive team loses, and a disqualified team loses.

"I'm not very interested in stealing the ball at this point," Gottfried said to the team. "It's a tricky situation. We're thin. We have foul trouble. But we have to play aggressive. If you don't play aggressive and try to save yourself by not fouling, we can't win the game anyway. No silly fouls. No pushes in the back . . . The whole key is to move the ball. Have patience. Take great shots. Soloman, if he backs off you again, shoot it . . . This could be one of the special nights in your life. Lay everything you've got on the line."

As the last person to leave the locker room, I offered encouragement to Moss who screamed with back pain after refraining from sounding out during the half-time speech.

A concerned Morr busily attended to the player. Another injury!

Robinson nailed a three-pointer to open the second half. Porter followed with a lay-up, igniting the crowd and blasting a wake-up alarm on Alabama's dream. Cotton scored four straight points to regain the Tide lead and delay the guillotine. N'Diaye answered with a three-point play, sending the Plainsmen to a media timeout with a 38-36 lead. As the teams walked to the bench, the home crowd stood and cheered wildly as if to say 'this is what we came to see.'

After an intense timeout with Gottfried, Meade connected on a three-pointer to give the Tide a lead with 15:19 left. Pohlman answered with a demoralizing three-pointer. Porter followed with a thunderous dunk and the Plainsmen party had begun. Alabama's defense completely collapsed. The Tigers shot 51.5 percent in the second half after only shooting 34.4 percent in the first stanza. Porter finished with 22 points and nine rebounds. N' Diaye had a double-double, 13 rebounds and ten points. Pohlman finished with 17, and Robinson added 11. The Tide earned a measure of respect by battling to the bitter end but never threatened the Tigers again. London warred for 40 minutes, having the game of a lifetime with 11 points on five for nine shooting and four assists with no turnovers. Grizzard finished with 21, and Cotton added 18. Young Dudley collapsed against the 7-foot-1 N'Diaye with zero for four shooting and three rebounds. Meade also flopped, shooting two for 11. Auburn won, 77-63.

The bench suffered through a volcano of noise throughout the second half. Team chaplain Overstreet was constantly heckled—the chaplain was jeered more than Gottfried. Mal Moore, who joined the team on the trip, left the bench after Auburn fans repeatedly insulted him for his loyalty to Tide football coach Mike Dubose during the coach's recent off-the-field controversy. The only drama in the final stages for the Tide was how quickly the bus driver could get out of Auburn.

Hanging heads and bitter frustration filled the visitor's locker room.

"Get your heads up. I'm proud of you. I love you. You played hard. You didn't necessarily play well in the second half, but you had enough open shots to win. We got away from some of the things we were doing in the first half. Containing the dribble. Guards rebounding. [Long pause] They're a good team. Give them credit . . .You got rattled, fellas. We can't get rattled. [Long pause] I know one thing, fellas. I can't wait for them to come into our gym. Give them credit when you talk to the media. The odds were against you, and you went out there and fought your hearts out."

Hays followed with a somber team prayer.

The coach did not shy away from referring to the second Auburn game. It was no secret that Alabama supporters had identified the Auburn game late in the season as the only important event in that year of growing pains.

PREPARATION for a Saturday game against LSU began on Thursday. The head coach's analysis of the second half against Auburn on tape left him in a foul mood.

"We had a total defensive breakdown. We laid a turd. When the game was on the line, we let them do anything that they wanted to do . . . Erwin, I don't know how you only came out of there with three rebounds. They just took you [Dudley] out of the game. We must have mental toughness to play for forty minutes and finish the deal."

I encountered an aching Moss in the hall before practice. He suffered from back spasms and a hip-pointer. A running joke through the season that former student trainer Rasco truly enjoyed was the imitation of Moss when he described his pain. Grimacing with pain, Moss often urgently began with "My sh— is." "[Pointing to a body part] My sh— is stinging." A good-natured Moss had laughed at himself along with everybody else when Rasco and Morr imitated him. Far removed from the initial pain of last night, Moss poked fun at himself today.

"My sh— is hurting all over," he said.

Walker actually returned to practice briefly today in two non-contact drills. He felt intense pain and pulled out quickly. A healthy Walker would make a big difference on Saturday.

The great LSU forwards would only be faced with poor Dudley. It was bad timing for Walker to be struggling with the adjustment of a rod in his leg and Moss to feel like gremlins were attacking the back of his body with spears. Because of the overwhelming match-up problems, Alabama appeared to be totally hopeless going into a home game for the first time in the short Gottfried era. If the Tide had been anything while this staff struggled to rebuild the talent pool, they had been a scrappy home team. But the remaining home games appeared ominous. LSU, Auburn, Tennessee, and surprising Vanderbilt were all ranked in the top 25 at this time. The head coach addressed that topic on Friday.

"LSU is 16-4. They're ranked in the top 25 in the country. The rest of the teams coming in this building are ranked. I can't tell you how to get every rebound. You've got to put your body on somebody and find a way to get one."

Haginas was practicing again but his status was questionable. With only Dudley remaining inside, how would the Tide grab a rebound against a team like LSU? Young Dudley would be physically man-handled by either of their older studs.

At the Saturday shoot-around, Cotton complained to Morr about the wrap on his blister. The blister seemed to be bothering his game. Meanwhile, an excited Scott scolded Haginas for not getting a defensive rebound. Scott knew that rebounding was the top priority.

Before the warm-up, Kelsey summarized.

"The key thing that we've talked about the last two days is when the possession is finished, we've got to come out with a rebound and not them. If we don't do that, nothing else matters."

Gottfried reinforced Kelsey's rebounding thoughts. He also wanted to use the high-post more often. A zone defense would be tried. The zone was almost a necessity against the much bigger team, but the risk was that pushing people away from the goal in the rebounding action can be neglected when the players do not have assignments.

After the warm-up, the head coach made his motivational plea.

"They've got you on size. You've got to have them on heart. Re-bounding is the name of this game. From start to finish, you have to compete."

Cotton, Grizzard, Dudley, London, and Meade formed the starting lineup. LSU demolished the Tide from the beginning whistle. Offensive rebound after offensive rebound and spectacular dunk after spectacular dunk—the Tide watched passively while an aggressive Tiger team ate them alive. LSU shot an amazing 58.8 percent from the field in the first half. Swift marveled the crowd with his athleticism, flying high over the intimidated Tide players. LSU led 46-24 at the half in a game that was over before it started.

The head coach spent little time with his staff.

"That was the worst freaking half of basketball that I've ever seen," Gottfried said before charging into the locker room.

"[Yelling] That's the worst half of basketball that I've ever seen! Defensively. It's effort! Effort! Effort! It's embarrassing not to come out and play hard! You didn't play hard, Schea! You wanna go watch the film? You're [Cotton] jogging down the floor while they're dunking! Fifteen minutes and three rebounds! If you're [Cotton] not gonna play, then sit down with me! We'll play somebody else. Terrance Meade, you've got to get down and guard somebody! It's embarrassing! You guys get out there and don't even play hard! They shot fifty-eight percent from the field! They're all lay-ups and dunks! They beat us down the floor and get a lay-up while we've got guys jogging! Then we go down there and they steal it from you, Rod! They steal it from you! You're the guy they took it from! The guy comes down and misses a lay-up! But you're jogging and another guy flies by you and tips it in! [Long pause] You wanna lay down? Is that what you want to do? You want to lay down? We've got some guys hurt. Do you care? We've got a lot of excuses. Does that mean we can't play hard? Just concede it? Eight, nine games left— just phone it in? [Long pause] [Screaming] Is that what you want to do? You came out for twenty minutes and didn't play! You did not play! Fifty-eight percent they shot on you for a half . . . Dig deep or quit. It's your choice."

On the walk back to the bench, Pearson observed the injured Moss and Walker exchange smiles. He motioned them to the side.

"There ain't a damn thing funny about what's going on here."

The second half was more of the same. A slightly better Tide effort paid few dividends. Swift and Smith led the Tigers as LSU out-re-bounded the Tide 45-25. The Tigers waltzed in and smashed the Tide in their facility, 93-60. A jubilant John Brady led the cheers of the many traveling Tiger fans who were loving their new experience with winning. Dudley added 16 points and nine rebounds for the losing cause.

A devastated locker room remained perfectly silent for several min-utes. Finally, Gottfried wrote 3:00 on the board.

"The first thing you better understand is that tomorrow at three o'clock you better be down there and ready to practice. The second thing you need to understand is that if you don't practice, you ain't playing.

The whole team walked in here at about one minute before two o'clock.

A long pause interrupting the screaming. "I don't care if we have four players! You had enough players! [Pause] We're gonna tighten everything up, fellas. These bullcrap practices that I've been letting you go through. You better come ready to practice! If you can't handle my practices, then quit! Quit! You've got nine or ten games left to play, fellas! And you're gonna play! We're gonna pick out those guys in this group that can handle it! All the rest of the sissies—you guys can go on home. They run down the floor and dunk on you. It's embarrassing! It was an absolute whipping in your own building! You can't guard anybody! You can't keep guys from dribbling to the basket! All of the sudden at the end of the game, Erwin, you want to start playing and working on somebody on offense. Where were you? Some of you guys don't know what it means to play hard. Who's gonna get a rebound? Who will dive in there and fight for one—put an elbow in someone's throat? You should be embarrassed. All of us should be embarrassed. I'm embarrassed. We could try and find a good excuse. Seven [scholarship players active excluding Haginas]? They've only got seven. They came right into our house and kicked our butt . . . We've got a bunch of games left, fellas. I'll promise you that none of them are easy . . . You lost your mental toughness. We just had a weak-minded group of guys. [Long pause] Go praise your opponent to the media and tell them how great they played. Three o' clock tomorrow."

13

Surviving a Night in Fayetteville

After Gottfried's harsh warning about needing to practice to play on Wednesday, Haginas and Cotton decided that they were not ready to work. Cotton was angry because he was embarrassed defensively against LSU due to his blister. He accepted a pain-killing shot for the blister before the Auburn game, but he regretted that decision because the size of the blister increased by playing on the Plains. He now seemed bound and determined to allow the blister to heal. Morr was surprised by the inability of both players to play.

"I don't know why they're not going. Only they can determine their pain threshold," Morr said.

Cotton's position was clear.

"It pisses me off when I go out there and can't move. These punks thought they were doing me up yesterday, and I couldn't move. So I will wait and get my sh— right. I've got to take care of my body. I'm in a fortress, baby [flexing his giant bicep]."

Scott aggressively coached the post players. (He had been resting all day for this very thing. He had saved his energy for practice hoping to make an impact. He wanted to help the team so badly.)

"Erwin! Son, you've got to find a way to keep it off him. Push him. Battle. Do whatever. I know you're just a freshman, but you've got to be the leader of the post players now."

He was to begin another round of chemotherapy on the following day. This round would be intense like the first one that knocked him for a loop. I considered whether he feared never being able to coach with enthusiasm again after another round of chemicals attacked his body.

Practice was closed. Gottfried's introduction seemed like a continuation of yesterday which was unusual for a guy who usually projected a glowing outlook after a bad day.

"What we did yesterday was a joke. An absolute joke. Schea showed no heart. He showed no heart. A guy comes barreling down the lane, and Schea won't take a charge. Rod jogs back after having the ball stolen and allows a guy to fly by him for a tip-dunk. It was a joke. You're lucky we have good fans, fellas. I've been around programs where they boo you for games like that. That's what they should have done—just booed us off the floor. If anybody wants to quit because we don't have enough guys, that's good. We'll have five guys practicing hard. Schea, when you're not practicing, pal, you better learn our plays. It's February, and you still don't know what we're running."

Cotton rode a stationary bike on the side where he could see the action. Pearson had been lobbying all year to have all the injured guys working hard on the sideline. His attitude is reminiscent of Wimp Sanderson yelling at training legend Sang Lyda to get a bike for an injured player to ride as soon as he dropped out of practice. The psychology is simple. The sideline is less attractive when a bike is waiting there for you to peddle furiously.

A wild loose ball play unfolded early in practice where bodies were diving everywhere. A few guys expressed concern after the play. Pearson took exception.

"What's so horrible about that?" he inquired.

Gottfried turned to the familiar timed sprint of 17 trips from sideline to sideline. He used it before and after practice. Grizzard and Towns claimed to be unable to run when practice ended. The now familiar session of dialogue began between the vocal leaders of the team and the guys who were struggling with the decision to run. Pearson had grown tired of this scenario.

"Hey guys, we can't have a prayer meeting before every 17."

Finally, Grizzard and Towns agreed to an attempt. They both failed. They would stay late to finish.

ON THE Monday before a road trip to Arkansas, Gottfried displayed a radical change of tone and mood. His first comment of the day pertained to the 1983 national champion North Carolina State team that carved its place in sports history with a March rampage that will never be forgotten under the late, great Jimmy Valvano.

He smiled as he spoke. "Everybody remembers the North Carolina State team with Jim Valvano that won the national championship. You've seen him looking for somebody to hug. Guys, they needed the conference tournament to get that done. They were a bubble team if they don't go in and win the ACC tournament. It can be done, fellas. It all starts in March, guys. That's the name of this game."

Upbeat, laughing, smiling, and clapping, Gottfried sent the players out to the first drill with a bucket of hope that he must have discovered somewhere deep within. Morr was gone for a week to care for his ailing grandmother. He left behind many problems. An X-ray revealed a broken bone in Moss's back. Haginas's shoulder was swollen so he, also, was unable to play. Cotton, who went outside of the team medical staff for the treatment of his blister, was unhappy with the performance of the podiatrist that he had chosen to shave the blister.

"My podiatrist f— ed up my cut. He cut too deep. There's no way I can play."

After Scott missed on Monday for chemotherapy, he rested on a courtside table at the beginning of practice on Tuesday. Cotton's best testimony on his behalf pertaining to the blister came from Scott when he viewed the foot.

"Looks bad," he said.

If Scott had not made that evaluation, almost everybody in the gym would have been seriously questioning the commitment of a guy unwilling to play because of a blister on a team decimated by injuries. Scott's testimony defending Cotton at that point was received by the team like the words of the Pope for a Catholic. He had earned the right to exonerate somebody with two words. Scott was Cotton's greatest defender.

The buzz around the workout pertained to the walk-ons, Bakken and Davis, emerging as key players in the upcoming Arkansas game. With six active scholarship players—including Towns who had not found a role on this team—either Bakken or Davis would likely be placed in the sixth-man role for the Wednesday game. Alabama would be a bigger underdog on the road at Arkansas than Charles Manson in a popularity contest.

Cynthia begged Robert Scott not to board the plane bound for Fayetteville, Arkansas, on Tuesday evening. Scott did not enjoy flying under any circumstances. He nearly tossed his tacos on a stormy return from Fayetteville the season before. Apparently annoyed by my talking and apparent confidence on a flight last season, Scott uncharacteristically taunted me when I was silent for an extended period during later turbulence.

"What's the matter, Shaq? You don't have much to say anymore. Don't tell me this plane is starting to bother you?"

I cannot express how much Scott had to sacrifice when he boarded that little plane bound for Arkansas. Not only did he hate to fly, he was suffering worse than ever at that point. Yet he boarded anyway. The decimated team left with just five guys who had been contributing needed him. Cynthia knew that he was crossing the wrong bridge. But Robert Scott boarded the plane with determination and dignity. His team was wounded and vulnerable like a baby in the woods. So he was going to Arkansas.

Fortunately, the plane ride was fairly smooth. We arrived in Fayetteville to perform the typical road routine. After a short break in the hotel room, the team gathered in a banquet room for a meal and a film session. The typical meal is the so-called burger bar featuring inconsistent hamburgers and several choices for toppings. Scott has never been a fan of the burger bar. He has a tortured pronunciation of burger bar that makes it sound disgusting without any other comment. Since Morr arranges the meals, he received a few complaints from the coach.

"John, don't tell me we're having that old burger bar. Please tell me we're not."

After the burger bar and film session where Pearson told the players how rugged Arkansas would play (and I was thinking that this was not the kind of game this shrinking outfit needed), Scott retired to his room.

Visiting with Boatright and Pearson later, in their room next to Scott, I sat helpless during a long conversation while Scott's moans and groans could be heard clearly through the wall—like a man being slowly killed by a murderer who likes to punish. Into the morning hours, we heard Scott suffering. We wanted so badly to help but him but realized that pain was now just the price of admission for Scott in this world.

I found Scott in the morning.

"Did anybody have to hear me last night? I felt bad because I was making a lot of noise," Scott said.

"Coach, I felt so bad for you. I wanted to do something. It sounded like you were hurting for hours," I responded.

"I'm sorry if I kept you awake."

"Coach. I'm sorry if *our* talking disturbed *you*. Did you ever get any sleep?"

"I was awake when Cynthia called at like three o'clock. After that, I took a pill that helped."

"Cynthia called you at three in the morning?"

"She knows how my nights go."

Scott spread his aching body across the chairs on the end of the bench at the shoot-around. He could not hide his intense pain. He seldom groaned in front of the players, but the new round of chemotherapy seized control of his will.

"Coach, is there anything that I can get for you? How about some water?" I inquired.

"That would be good," he replied, slowly.

I returned with the water.

"Cynthia was right. I shouldn't have come. I don't want these guys to see me like this. [Pause] Cynthia, you know, she just does much for me at home now. She gets me through the night."

"She's a great woman," I said.

"I've been lucky."

Those were easy words for Scott to say. On the first day that he had returned to the office after being diagnosed, I spent precious time alone with him in the Coaches' locker room. His first comment to me about his death sentence was "Shaq, I've been so lucky." He talked about how much he loved his family and friends. He described how his career in athletics had always been a blessing from God. His only comments concerning death focused on the greatness of his life. I will hold that conversation in my heart forever. Remarkably, he still believed that he was a lucky man—a lucky man laying on chairs in excruciating pain after being tortured through the night.

ARKANSAS has an arena built for an NCAA champion. The very modern Bud Walton Arena seats 19,200 and features a gigantic picture of Scotty Thurmond drilling the shot to win the championship in the hall. Walking into the arena, Gottfried grabbed my shoulder.

"Shaq, this arena represents a commitment. You see this place, and you know they have a serious program."

The likely story of tonight's game was a simple one. Alabama was wounded like George Washington's army at Valley Forge. Nolan Richardson's Hogs would probably attempt to fast break, crash for rebounds, and press the Tide to death—a strategy that he likes anyway at home where he prefers to press more often. Pressing on the road tends to lead to foul trouble more frequently. Home games also mean the crowd pressuring the enemy.

Forty minutes before tip-off, Pearson warned his team about the fury of the Hogs.

"They're looking to trap you everywhere . . . They will take a bunch of long shots and just go chase 'em. Long shots mean long rebounds."

Gottfried followed with concern about the Hogs' break.

"I'm not dwelling on the past, but you have to learn from past failures. We didn't get back the other night. I'm not interested in watching a team run down there and dunk on us. Sprint and take away all breaks. Let's get our defense established and guard 'em. Let's get it done."

The team and coaches clapped with all the intensity they could muster.

Before the warm-up, Arkansas football coach Houston Nutt dropped by to offer Gottfried some encouragement. Nutt befriended the Alabama coach when they were coaching at Murray State, but he dismissed Gottfried from his daily lunch basketball games when the basketball staff made a requested appearance and drilled the football coaches. Nutt hated losing in any form. During the warm-up, Gottfried shared that Nutt advised him to coach with the same confidence and enthusiasm that he always had at Murray. Gottfried seemed determined to follow that advice. To this day I don't know where he found the confidence. (I guess with Scott in his company any positive thought or belief was possible.) I had none. The team was too badly wounded in my eyes. They had no chance.

Martin, Grizzard, Dudley, London, and Meade formed a starting lineup of the only healthy people with substantial playing time. After Grizzard scored the Tide's initial 5 points to keep the visitors tied, he was whistled for his second foul with 14:31 left in the half. Faced with another dilemma, Gottfried sent Bakken into the game. Bakken shot the ball well from the perimeter when allowed a substantial opening. Arkansas tended to sacrifice open jumpers to gamble with traps and guarantee a fast-paced game. Bakken punctuated a Tide run with a three-pointer from the left corner just minutes later! Unbelievably, the Tide led, 18-10. Richardson called timeout and appeared to emphatically criticize his club. And to the delight of 17,732 fans, the Hogs responded by taking over the game with steals, transition buckets, and three-pointers. The crowd roared a 35-12 Arkansas run to close the half. Arkansas shot 51.5 percent from the field and a remarkable five for eight on three-pointers attempting to continue the woes of a struggling defensive team. Meade charged out of his slump, shooting three of three on three-pointers and scoring nearly half (14) of the Tide's points. The Hogs led 45-30 at the break.

Gottfried had decided to remain patient tonight. No tirade in the locker room. He knew that his team stood on its last leg. The obvious truth that he would never admit was that the injuries had mounted to a point where he could not expect to win a game in this league. He would not risk shattering the confidence and morale of these youngsters by an endless array of verbal attacks. He did, however, challenge Grizzard who finished with two for eight shooting after the early foul trouble.

"Rod, you've got to step up and start playing some offense. You've got to score some points for this team right now."

Grizzard totaled the first nine points of the second half for the Tide on 3 three-pointers. As we noticed in the Florida game, Grizzard was beginning to utilize his truly special talent. Gottfried and his staff had pushed him, patiently waiting for him to develop into the player Scott had believed in. The time had arrived. For a 6-foot-8 player, he is indelibly smooth. He can dribble so effectively to capitalize on his graceful jump shot. His incredible leaping ability allows him to easily shoot over defenders. When he dribble penetrates toward the basket, he can stop on a dime and launch a jumper falling away from the goal that is reminiscent of Michael Jordan. The most important event of that dreadful season seemed to be developing slowly before our skeptical eyes. Blessed with a treasure chest of advise from some highly concerned coaches and desperately needed playing experience, Grizzard slowly blossomed into a good player on the brink of greatness.

Sparked by the freshman's exploits, Martin and London nailed two three-pointers to cut the Hog lead to 52-45 with 14:51 left. The Hogs responded with a 4-0 run and the visitors never threatened again. Primarily because of 13 second-half turnovers, a considerably better Tide defensive effort did not impact the outcome. Practice drills could not simulate the Hogs when they trap a player in their arena. Arkansas won, 81-66. Joe Johnson spanked the Tide for 25 on eight for 14 shooting. Grizzard finished with 24 while Meade scored 19. Dudley grabbed 16 rebounds. Bakken was incredible in his role, shooting three for three with eight points and playing 21 minutes.

Gottfried was satisfied with the effort.

"You guys played pretty good . . . You play as hard as you played tonight and you're gonna crack some folks . . .You played a lot harder tonight than you did the other day . . . Good job." He clapped for his team with enthusiasm.

The weary Tide rested on Thursday. A 16-4 Vanderbilt squad visited the Tide on Saturday. With amazing wins over Florida, LSU, and on the road at Tennessee, the 22nd ranked Vanderbilt Commodores were a national surprise. Bound for the NBA, Vandy's Dan Langhi had been the man leading Cotton in SEC scoring. A clash of the leading scorers seemed unlikely with Cotton very determined to allow his blister to heel. Averaging around 22 points per game, Langhi was not immediately in jeopardy of being caught by Cotton whose average remained around 19.

Scott could not attend the Friday practice. Cynthia arrived and reported that Scott had been in bed since the Fayetteville trip. We discussed his grueling night in the hotel, and she deeply regretted Robert's decision to go. The ordeal was taking a horrible toll on her.

The team looked no better than they had before Arkansas. Haginas shared that he would probably not play because of shoulder pain. Cotton described his pain level as "still high." At his regular Tuscaloosa tip-off club meeting at Outback Steakhouse, Gottfried announced that Moss would probably miss the rest of the year with the broken bone in his back. A supportive tip-off club sympathized with the injury situation.

Morr returned to the team at the Saturday shoot-around to discover frustrating situations with Haginas and Cotton. He revealed to me his doubts.

"The blister on Schea's foot is tiny, Shaq . . . and Sam should be able to play through his injury. Come on, Moss wants to play with a broken back . . . The sort of pain experienced by Sam and Schea should be overcome."

Kelsey conducted the scouting report for his home state Commodores. He described how many countless ways that Vandy used to free Dan Langhi. Vandy coach Kevin Stallings would be a strong candidate for SEC coach of the year at this point if Brady was not such a prominent figure. Credit Stallings for using Langhi wisely.

Scott rested in bed his during the shoot-around and had not arrived when Kelsey began the final scouting report forty minutes before the 4:00 tip-off. Kelsey focused on how the Tide defenders should help each other when Vandy screens for Langhi.

Gottfried emphasized the offensive advantages of a decimated front court versus bigger, stronger, and more physical Vandy.

"They have to guard us too. They're gonna have bigger guys trying to guard smaller guys. Make sure the floor is spread at all times. Spread wide. Let's break when we can. Play to your strengths. We're quicker and you guys know how to expose that."

Moving toward his brief motivational comments to conclude, a long pause revealed his thoughts without a word. There was an empty chair where Scott would normally be sitting. With watering eyes and a heavy heart, he finally linked Scott's suffering to basketball. Scott had left him no choice by continually sacrificing for this basketball team.

"I don't know if Coach Scott is gonna make it here today. [Pause while he fights back tears] He's not feeling real well. If he doesn't, it will be the first game that he's missed. And I know he doesn't want to do that. [Pause] Let's dedicate this one to him. This one is for Coach Scott." The small room ignited into a volcano of noise.

Using the same depleted roster, an inspired Tide team smashed Vandy. Defensive intensity throughout the half and a 14-2 run in less than six minutes helped the Tide open a 38-23 lead by halftime. The crowd witnessed a vastly different effort from the Tide of last Saturday against LSU. Langhi was held to two of eight shooting in the half. A hustling home team surprisingly out-rebounded the bigger visitors. As a team, Vandy was held to 23.3 percent shooting.

During the first half, Gottfried continued to look around for Scott. He was nowhere to be found.

Boatright called Scott during the staff meeting. He was dressed for the game and would attempt to arrive by the end. Watching on television, Scott felt that Vandy was being allowed too many open shots.

When Gottfried addressed the team, he worried about a Commodore comeback.

"They're ranked in the top twenty-five, fellas. They've beaten some good people. They've got pride. They'll come out and give you some great, great shots . . . This is a golden opportunity." Gottfried seeemed distracted as he spoke. He was worried about Robert. He knew that if Robert was absent, he had to be really hurting. Scott never missed a game. It was a bad sign.

Martin nailed 3 three-pointers before the 13-minute mark of the second half, helping to resolve any remaining mystery. Vandy never cut the second half lead below 14 and lost by that margin, 77-63.

Scott joined the team late in the game to enjoy the victory he inspired. Kelsey, who enjoyed a precious win over the school where his spouse had been a cheerleader, led the cheers of an appreciative crowd as the clock expired.

(Coach Gottfried did not see Scott however. After frantically looking for him all game, Gottfried left to do a television interview with JP Sports' Barry Booker and Dave Neil. Gottfried was reduced to tears on camera when he thought about Scott watching the game from his house.)

Alabama simply exerted much more energy than the visitors—the complete opposite of the previous Saturday. The Tide won the rebounding war, 38-27. Langhi finished with only five for 14 shooting. Martin shot five for eight from the three-point line on his way to 19 points. The entire remainder of the starting lineup was outstanding while each logging at least 35 minutes of playing time (Dudley: 18 points on six for six shooting, Grizzard: 13 points and 11 rebounds, London: ten assists and seven points, Meade: 17 points on six of nine shooting).

An anxiously welcomed celebration reached a fever pitch when Gottfried referred to Scott. The players hugged him in celebration of their win. This had become a ritual. When the team won, the focus was on Coach Scott.

"Coach Scott, this win was for you," he said, triggering thunderous applause.

NOW 11-11 overall and 4-6 in the SEC, Alabama prepared on Monday for a Wednesday game at legendary Rupp Arena against the Kentucky

Wildcats. Famous basketball commentator Dick Vitale snubbed UCLA's 11 NCAA titles to choose Kentucky as his mythical team of the century even though the Wildcats were second best with seven titles. He included an intangible criteria that somehow factored Kentucky's hysterical love for their basketball team. I do not agree with his vague analysis, but the power of hoops in the blue grass state is overwhelming—still overshadowing the rest of the SEC while the league has managed gigantic leaps toward national prominence in the '90s. Even when the Wildcats were struggling mightily in Eddie Sutton's final years and Rick Pitino's first season, beating Kentucky was still prioritized. Sanderson pumped fists at the world when the Tide swept the Wildcats in '89. Even the eighteen years without a Kentucky title did not tarnish their reputation. So preparing for Kentucky is special. The Tide players see a large picture of last season's team celebrating the win over Kentucky in the basketball office. They know.

A single match-up problem made an always unlikely win at Rupp Arena seem impossible. Among the league leaders in shooting percentage, the 6-foot-10 Wildcat center Jamaal Magloire was far bigger and stronger than anybody wearing crimson. The Tide would double-team Magloire from different angles.

"Just so you understand about Magloire—he's shooting 58% and the rest of the team is struggling," Gottfried said to his huddled team.

Cotton rode the stationary bike in lieu of practicing. Again. Hays and Moss discussed his status on the sideline.

"Have you seen how small Schea's blister is?" Hays asked.

"What," Moss responded jokingly. "He's just taking some time off, dog."

"I know it was pretty bad at one time, but he's got to suck it up and play. We've got so many guys down," Hays said.

"I know. If he doesn't play in Rupp Arena, he's sick in the head or something."

Cotton, Haginas, and Walker rejoined practice on Tuesday in non-contact drills.

"Holy cow! We've got some bodies out here," Gottfried exclaimed at the beginning of practice.

Scott missed another practice, and I asked whether he was expected.

"I'm afraid he won't make it. He's having a tough day," the head coach replied.

Gottfried commented on the Wildcats in the huddle.

"All they're talking about is running more and turning it up. They're talking about how we shouldn't have beaten them last year . . . They're ranked number two in the R.P.I. rankings."

After strength coach Steve Martin, Morr, and Pearson had a meeting about increasing the intensity of the workout for the injured players during practice, Steve Martin seemed to be very excited about the new policy.

"I brought a medicine ball for all the guys who don't want to practice today," Martin said with his trademark grin—a grin that embraced pain.

Cotton managed to endure all the drills and scrimmages.

Scott arrived before practice ended to the delight of everybody. He announced in the coaches' locker room after practice that he would not be making the trip to Kentucky. The conversation was surprisingly upbeat after that news. We all knew that he would be better off in bed. Scott and I were excited about the high school coaching exploits of last year's administrative assistant Howard Pride—who coached his Decatur High School team to a critical area tournament game over defending state champion Grissom to end their season abruptly.

MR. KEIGHTLEY, a favorite son of Kentucky because of his 38-year career as a trainer, greeted us at 11 A.M. on game day in Rupp Arena where a banner hangs in his honor. His nickname, Mr. Wildcat, summed up his status. Keightley immediately apologized for the "damn cold" in the facility caused by the local minor league hockey team's ice. I was shocked to hear him say that Kentucky only practices in Rupp Arena three to four times a year. Lucky for them because they should hang beef in there instead. I'm glad Scott was not forced to endure that place. Boatright loved it. He loves the cold weather in his beloved blue grass state.

PEARSON's comments before the evening warm-up mirrored his shoot-around concerns about transition defense. If the Kentucky players tell the media that they are planning to fast break often against an 11-11 team, then they are planning to fast break often—no tricks against a struggling team. Gottfried summarized.

"Biggest key is to get back. Sprint and get back. They've got no respect for you. They think they're playing a crappy team. All they're saying is 'we're gonna run it right at 'em. We're gonna shove it down their throat.' We'll see."

The head coach introduced his offense with a predictable message.

"We want to run too. Push it down the floor hard. If you don't have anything, pull it back and set up your offense."

Gottfried engaged me in a rare conversation during the warm-up. I told him about the Kentucky players fielding questions from the media at 5:30 A.M. because they had been practicing twice a day.

"Maybe they'll be tired," he said.

I missed Scott in the locker room. I could imagine him asking Cynthia to find the game on television. Maybe he was listening to the radio.

At the end of the warm-up, Gottfried was excited enough to play.

"We didn't come up here just to play. We came up here to get it done!" he yelled.

Cotton claimed to be ready to play, but the head coach gladly stripped his starting role. Haginas had also rejoined the active roster, but who knows how far he would be buried on the bench? A routine Kentucky crowd of 22,137 watched the Wildcats gradually take control of a half that was played largely in the half-court due to effective defensive transition by both teams. Turnovers and the shooting of the Kentucky forwards linked to offensive rebound baskets were the difference. After a wonderful stretch of games, London exploded with six turnovers. Five other Tide players added a turnover to total 11 for the team versus only one for Kentucky. A 10-0 Wildcat run in just over three minutes excited the home crowd. A struggling Cotton jump-started the Wildcat run with a turnover that led to a lay-up. The Kentucky forwards Magliore, Stone, and Jules Camara combined to shoot 11 for 17. Kentucky led at the half, 38-26.

The staff called Scott at home, and he knew the keys to the game. He said they needed to firm up with the ball and block out. The staff entered the locker room.

"You're playing like a bunch of soft-minded guys. Tarik, as good as you've been playing, you've got 6 turnovers. You're better than that. Just better. You know you are. We've got 11 turnovers. They've got one. That's the name of the game. Bottom line. You've got to firm up. You've got to cut hard. You're just not playing firm and tough with the basketball . . . When they shoot it, they're just crashing in there. You better turn and find someone to make sure he doesn't get it . . . Rod, you just run down to the other end of the floor while they tip it in! I don't know what you're going to the other end of the floor for! Block out! One shot for them . . . Get down and freaking move . . . We didn't come up here not to win. Play to win!"

The Wildcats pushed the lead to 18 with 16:40 left. The Tide seemed to be knocked out. Meade sparked a remarkable stretch of Tide play with four straight points. The tide turned.

Dominating the Wildcats in every phase of the game for nearly fourteen minutes with the use of zone defense, Grizzard outscored Kentucky 11-9 over the stretch! The Wildcats could not make an outside shot. Grizzard finally canned one of 2 free throws to cut the lead to five with 2:57 left. The crowd awoke from a coma to urge the Wildcats to finish their business. Desmond Allison grabbed a critical offensive rebound, and Prince converted a lay-up. Magliore followed with two free throws, pushing the lead to nine with 1:44 left. No more gas was left in the Tide comeback tank. Kentucky cruised to a 66-54 win. Grizzard finished with 20, but the first half numbers won the day for the Wildcats.

The scene was the all-too familiar devastated road locker room.

"Get your head up, guys. Get your head up. I like how you fought. You kept fighting. Kept fighting. We hurt ourselves in the first half. We got ourselves in a hole. You came out in the second half and did a good job. You've got to play hard for forty minutes. If you're not going to play as hard as you can play and leave everything out on the floor and get down and guard people, then we won't have a chance to beat anybody . . . The first half was the difference. We've got to block out and not leak out. Everybody together! Everybody coming together and caring about how our team plays. That's all that counts right now . . . We're going down there [South Carolina] Saturday to get one done."

The theme of practice on Thursday was that the time for a road win had arrived. South Carolina's ugly 10-14 record provided hope, but the Gamecocks had played the toughest schedule in America according to several experts.

"This team has no more excuses about the road. We've got to be able to play through the crowd. You've been in tough environments. It's time to find a way to get one done." Gottfried turned it over to his staff.

Scott stepped forward.

"We're down five last night, and we don't find anybody to block out. Everybody talks about how you don't have assignments in a zone. But you've got to find somebody to put your body on. [Demonstrating blocking out technique] I'm sorry that I'm feeling weak and moving slow, but I still feel like I could block somebody out. Whatever you do, you've got to make sure that nobody around you gets the ball. Be alert. Find somebody. I also agree with coach about the crowd on the road. I know most of you guys are young but come on—it's time to start playing through all this mess. Hey, we're running out of games. So start doing the things that you need to do to help this team win."

I ATTENDED another staff meeting between the Kentucky and South Carolina games. The morale of the team was so low Gottfried called a meeting to address that very thing.

"What we have to remember in a year like this with all the key injuries and young players is that we're moving forward. I don't want our program to get so caught up in looking at the trees, that we can't see the forest."

He paused for a moment. "We've had to be very tough on these kids. When you throw in Robert's deal, they've suffered through more than a team should ever have to." He stopped again for a few seconds.

"We're headed in the right direction. We all know it. Don't be afraid to tell the players that. You can be negative. Correct 'em. Help 'em. Get 'em tougher. But let's not forget to give 'em loving, guys. This has been a tough deal for everyone."

Pearson spoke next. "I think that I've got a good enough relationship with most of these guys so that they know we believe in them." (And he did. Pearson often had players over for dinner, and daily spoke to them about their problems.) "I've been able to talk a lot about next year. That helps. I think a lot of that gets solved in one-on-one conversations. I see you guys really petting them a lot one-on-one in practice. I know that I've done a ton of that this season."

Gottfried concluded the meeting with renewed commitment to positive reinforcement. "Let's do more of that. Grab a guy one-on-one and just let him know he's special. I'm worried, guys. Don't let our team get demoralized. That's not my deal."

After the meeting, Boatright, Kelsey, and Gottfried visited Cynthia and Scott at their house. Scott was in obvious pain, but the coaches later told me that he also obviously enjoyed their visit. They stayed up late talking and joking. Basketball was not brought up once.

GERALD Wallace and the rest of his Childersburgh High School team came to practice briefly on Friday before their road playoff game in this area of the state. At Tide home games, inspirational scenes from Mel Gibson's *Braveheart* were shown on the Sony JumboTrons during timeouts. Like Scotland turned toward William Wallace for liberation from England, Alabama fans had already turned their attention toward Wallace to end the painful absence (rapidly approaching five years) from the NCAA tournament. Gottfried explained to Wallace how many different ways he would find the player open shots next year. The promise of tomorrow was making the present much more tolerable for the coach.

Scott missed practice and would miss another road trip. After Kelsey explained how effective the Gamecocks' ball screens can be, the head coach emphasized psychology.

"It won't hinge on their sets. It will come down to a mentality that we'll do what it takes to win on the road," Gottfried said.

Excitement filled the air in Columbia, South Carolina—not for a winless football team or a 10-14 hoops team—for the heated Republican primary between John McCain and George W. Bush. I was somewhat embarrassed after expressing my excitement about meeting political analyst Jack Germond in the hotel when Boatright responded that he had seen Peter Jennings.

At the shoot-around in Frank McGuire Arena, Kelsey warned about freshman Chuck Eidson who, if Kelsey was to be believed, seemed to be the next Jordan or maybe Superman.

"He will just start dribbling. He'll go all the way to the basket and finish over you. If you give him room, he will shoot from anywhere. He's looking to post you up. He can get you on his hip and draw a foul. He has a nice pull-up jumper. He's a very good passer. So we've got our hands full with him."

WHEN we returned in the evening, Kelsey predicted what the Game-cocks would do against the Tide zone that has become so convenient with the small active roster.

Gottfried discussed playing some zone defense and playing against the Cocks' zone. Age-old principles apply against a zone defense (flash to the middle, dribble attack the gaps and pitch, look for open men in the short corner, reverse the ball quickly . . .). He moved toward a conclusion.

"If you want to have a chance to play in the post-season, you better start getting something done tonight. We've got five regular season games left and one in Atlanta. You've got to start doing it tonight. Don't let the crowd bother you. You've been in enough places. Whether you're mentally tough enough to jump up and strap it on and get something done, we'll find out. If you want to make a move in the league, make your move right now. It starts tonight! We've got to do it tonight."

Gottfried has been competing in college basketball since the mid-'80s and has never missed the post-season. While he has scooted along from school to school, Duke and Kentucky have suffered through awful seasons when Gottfried's biggest disappointments were two NIT berths. He finally stared directly at a bad season. A medically challenged and excessively young 11-12 team with zero road wins faced three road games and visits from Auburn and Tennessee remaining. The SEC tournament would follow. If the Tide did not win against South Carolina, the odds would be overwhelmingly against a winning season. The odds were already long. Tortured by this reality, Gottfried had refrained from participating in the endless conversations that we usually enjoy about jockeying for post-season position. His comments would be the most charismatic during most seasons. He has repeatedly turned away this year or voiced his agitation.

"I don't even want to listen to Packer or Vitale and those guys this year, Shaq. Everybody's talking about bids. I just can't take not being part of it."

DURING the warm-up, the head coach chose the strangest moment to discuss the Tide's position in SEC tournament seeding. Currently the 4th place team in the division ahead of the Mississippi schools, Alabama would be opening with South Carolina in the tournament if it started today. The Tide would need to win four games in four days to reach the big dance. As the quiet conversation grinded to a halt, he remarked about his true concern—a losing season.

"We should be 14-10 or something. Look at Ole Miss. They've scheduled their way to 15-9. Fifteen and nine. I screwed up the schedule."

After the warm-up, he addressed the familiar size differential.

"It's your heart versus their size. They're bigger than you and taller. How much heart do you have? Who's gonna go rebound the basketball . . . Play with some emotion! I'm not feeling very well. I've got a bad feeling in my gut. It would make me feel real good if we win." He concluded with a smile.

The starting lineup remained the same. The blister episode had apparently ended any hopes of a league scoring title for Cotton who found himself in a bench role. 8,552 devout Gamecocks watched the Tide race to a 14-5 lead on four three-pointers including two by Terrance Meade in the first seven minutes. Fogler switched to a man-to-man defense, triggering a 25-11 Cock run over the next ten minutes. The Tide was damaged again by nine turnovers versus one for the Cocks. Alabama seemed to have a lack-of-valuing-the-ball disease. The Cocks shot 51 percent and led 36-30 at the half.

"They're shooting 51 percent," Boatright said to begin the staff meeting.

Gottfried shook his head from side to side in response. "Ridiculous. Ridiculous. We're just not guarding them. We can't guard anybody."

"They're terrible," Pearson added—similar to the depressing realization Kelsey made at Georgia.

"We've got nobody rebounding," Kelsey remarked.

"It's turnover differential. It's the same story in every game . . . Sam's got to do something. He takes the ball right down to the basket and shoots an air-ball," Gottfried said.

A puzzled staff ended their frustrating meeting.

"Sam, you've got to start doing something. When we get the ball down to you on the block, you can't come up with an air-ball. Take it up there strong and get to the foul line or dunk on somebody . . . [Writes "turnovers" on the board] You've got to make a decision about whether you want to be a good team. [Pointing at "turnovers"] And it's right there. South Carolina is sitting here with one turnover, and you've got nine."

After being jolted by an unexpected announcement from a wall speaker that the half would begin in five minutes, the coach concluded rapidly. London was determined before the team chant.

"We're winning this game," London asserted. "We are winning this game!"

Cotton, who had been terrible since returning, broke out of a shooting slump with a three-point play to cut the lead to 39-36 early in the half. The Cocks responded by lighting the Tide up like a Christmas tree with a 9-0 run, capped by a David Ross three-pointer. Alabama never threatened again in an embarrassing blowout loss to woeful South Carolina. The Cocks converted 12 three-pointers thanks to a poor defensive effort from the visitors. The Tide could not negotiate a screen to contest a jump shot all night. The Tide suffered a two for 15 shooting drought which did not help. Carolina won 82-61 as Cock coach Eddie Fogler played 14 guys and was probably tempted to suit up a manager. Martin shot four for five. Grizzard added 15 points. London shot three for four with six assists. Cotton shot one for seven.

Sensing the disbelief on the Tide bench, a Cock heckler captured the moment.

"That's right. You lost to South Carolina. I know you don't believe it!"

In the locker room, several of the players experienced self-hatred associated with the team's performance. When Gottfried entered, he sat down on a bench in front of the team as if he was finally fatigued by defeat.

"[Slowly and quietly] We couldn't make a shot, guys, in the second half. When the shots aren't falling, we have to be even better on defense. And we weren't better on the defensive end in the second half. They beat us down the floor. We couldn't get through any screens. [Pause] Your defense has to be good all the time. Every guy has to be better than that on Tuesday. We have to be better than that on Tuesday."

Boatright clapped quickly, but no one followed his lead. The head coach sent a message: it was a time for hurting and reflection for this team. The game of the year would be Tuesday against Auburn. Win that game, and all wrongdoings would be forgiven by the fans. Before the players could prepare emotionally for a war, they needed to reflect on losing—to better know the ache of defeat. A winner hates to lose. A truly great competitor can grow that hatred like a gardener grows a plant.

A wounded team limped home that night, pondering their most realistic salvation for a nightmarish season. Through all the injuries and the inevitable growing pains, an inspired victory over Auburn would satisfy the fan base and validate the expectations of future success.

On the plane, I wondered how Scott reacted to the loss at home. I was afraid he was too sick to hear more bad news. Yet I knew that he would be ready for Auburn come hell or high water.

14

Redemption

On Monday Gottfried conducted a film session starting with the South Carolina game. The staff had been reviewing the previous game's film and giving advice accordingly in huddle sessions with the guards and forwards. Perhaps this film was so ugly that they wanted company. The head coach made a series of comments on the film.

"They can't get a bucket every time they set a screen."

He finally stopped the film clips when he couldn't stomach anymore.

"It was a pathetic effort." The words hung in the air over the player's heads.

He inserted film clips from the first Auburn game which featured a string of Tiger transition buckets and offensive rebound baskets late in the game.

"This thing turned into a dunk-fest late in the game. They just took the heart right out of you."

Porter grabbed an offensive rebound.

"Schea, you haven't blocked anybody out all night."

The film session closed with analysis of clips from Auburn's last game. Practice began with Moss and Walker participating. Walker had been obsessing over returning for the Auburn game since his injury. The players were impacted by their fellow students who wanted one thing from their basketball team in this year of Auburn hoopla—to beat the

Plainsmen.

Boatright, Pearson, and I ate lunch on big game day in Bryant Hall. Our conversation was interrupted by a dishwasher who had left his post to ask for a ticket to the big game. Boatright and Pearson brainstormed for a possible ticket source for him while exchanging pleasantries. Tickets were scarce. Suddenly, I heard the stranger utter something that nearly forced me to choke on my food.

"I try to go to the game when my team is playing," he said.

"Your team? You mean Auburn?" Boatright asked.

"Yes sir. I am an Auburn fan through and through," he said with a grin.

An irate Pearson remained silent.

"Well, I think you need to contact Coach Ellis and his staff about free tickets. I can give you the hotel where the Auburn team is staying," Boatright said.

"I think you just cost yourself any shot at tickets from us in the future, my man," Pearson said.

The employee returned to his dishwashing post.

Pearson was not happy. "When I played here, somebody around here might have picked that guy up and thrown him out the door for doing something like that."

"I can't believe the size of that guy's balls. He just solicited the Alabama coaching staff on the day of the Auburn game for a ticket in Paul Bryant Hall, claiming to be an Auburn fan while he is working," I responded.

Boatright and Pearson reported the employee's conduct to his Bryant Hall supervisor.

I was shocked on the following night when Birmingham's ABC station covered a story called "Has the Rivalry Gone Too Far" about this employee who was suspended for a day and transferred across campus for leaving his work station. The bitter employee asserted his rights as an Auburn fan to the television cameras. Pearson, Boatright, and I were shocked (and slightly amused) over the extensive coverage.

WHEN THE Tuesday shoot-around began at 1:30, several students wearing their "Mark's Madness" crimson t-shirts had already found their seats for the 6:00 tip-off. There were bleachers on the floor for the students arriving earliest. All of the student sections are first come, first serve. Gottfried had pizza ordered for the students at the shoot-around.

After the pre-game meal, chaplain Overstreet delivered a devotional about goldfish growing to a size consistent with their environment. He invited the team to hop out of their fish bowl and into the big pond where they would grow to be large. If they were going to the big pond, they would have to get there on ESPN tonight. While a win would give the season meaning and a measure of success, a loss would simply condemn the season as a complete disaster.

Engaged in a visit to his doctor in Birmingham, Scott had not yet arrived from a doctor's appointment when Pearson addressed an intensely focused team before the warm-up.

"The first thing we've got to do is get back. Play hard with intensity. Be ready to get screened and get over it. Contest. Rebound. It's gonna be a war in there. You've got to be ready. They'll push you. They're gonna elbow you. They're gonna do all that type of crap.

"So be ready . . . Schea, look out for the lob play that they caught you napping on over there . . . Meade, you can't give Pohlman any room."

Two hours before the game, I wrote a quote on the board to spark the players' memory about a comment by Auburn guard Scotty Pohlman after an Alabama game: "When we got Alabama down 4, they played like they're down 44."

When Gottfried entered the locker room to make his notes on the board, he did not erase the quote. As the head coach stood before the team, the board was filled with keys to winning and x's and o's with Pohlman's quote circled in the middle of a board filled with notes.

"Screen somebody tonight. [Demonstrating a screen in a great stance] Get down and knock somebody out . . . Erwin, you have to keep N'Diaye out of there . . . You've got a great crowd. You've got a great opportunity. It's all about playing hard. I've told you guys before about rebounding. If we turn the tape on tomorrow, and I'm watching their guys just root us out on missed shots and getting the ball, we're going to be disappointed tonight. But if I see our guys fighting hard and getting 'em out of there and finishing a defensive possession, then we're going to be in good shape. That's the whole team. Everybody's got to rebound. That's really their best offense. Just throw it up and go get it. Go warm-up hard."

In the hall before entering the coliseum, an electrified Tide team jumped together in a frenzy. Tonight was the night. An already substantial crowd roared their approval when the Tide entered to warm-up.

Cotton was forced to start and play much of the game. His impressive physique gave him the best ability to guard Chris Porter. In fact, the match-up of the night was Porter versus Cotton. Porter was like Conan the Barbarian last year as an Auburn pep rally unfolded in Coleman Coliseum to celebrate the end of a 14-year losing streak in Tuscaloosa. Porter had dominated everybody—attacking the glass with reckless abandon and manhandling anybody blocking his way. Cotton claimed to be ready. The proud man from Los Angeles told me weeks ago that he had discovered the importance of the Auburn game.

"When we play Auburn again. It's on. That's all they talk about around here. I've got something for Auburn."

An excited team returned to the locker room.

"Schea, you've got Porter. You have to do a great job on him. Do not let him out-work you . . . Everybody get down in a stance. Get through screens. And fight 'em, fellas! Fight 'em! Fight 'em! Don't back down! I watch the tape of our game down there. They're just pushing you in the back and doing all that crap. Push 'em back. Fight 'em. I don't care. Rebounding! That's the whole key to the game. All this is right now is heart. Do you have any? Then jump up and rebound. If you ain't got no heart, then don't play! Take care of the ball . . . I know you can take care of the ball. You've got to do it for forty minutes. Let me say one more thing.

"This whole year I've never wanted to use Robert's situation to motivate you. We did dedicate the Vandy game to him. But it's not fair to him—to use his situation. It cheapens what he's going through. We love him too much. He's going through a heck of a time. [Long pause as tears swell in his eyes and roll down my cheeks] And I hope he comes through that door because he's going to try to be here. He's been in Birmingham. But I'll be honest with you. Some of you don't really know because you don't talk to him everyday. But I'll share what he's done for me. Everyday I evaluate how hard I work at the things I have to do. I look around and see guys getting down because things aren't going their way. But you know what, fellas, I don't care what you've got going on or what I've got going on. It ain't a tenth, a millionth of what he's got going on. So what he's done to me this year is that I've watched more film. I've coached harder. I've evaluated a little more—studied things more. I'm going to be the best that I can be because I might wake up tomorrow morning and be in the same situation. There's no guarantee that I won't be. Take the film home tonight. If you're not playing hard and not running the floor hard, then ask yourself a question. How sorry is that really? Be honest. We can't do everything that we possibly can? I just want you to play as hard as you can play." What followed was the most frenzied reaction of the season.

As every man in the room came together for the chant, there was only one spirit there—total unity. Hays led a special version.

"One, two, three. Roll Tide!" We all yelled.

A capacity crowd of 15,043 exploded when the Tide entered the coliseum. Auburn was well represented in the crowd again this year—the visitors smelled blood. The old phrase "you can throw out the record books when these teams play" has not applied to the Alabama-Auburn rivalry in basketball or football—not in terms of the outcome. The favored team wins with regularity. In basketball where the home court advantage often supersedes the difference between records anyway, superior Tide teams have managed to win eighteen of the last twenty-eight games at Auburn. Often favored Alabama is 33-6 against Auburn in Tuscaloosa. Alabama was 7-3 in the '90s football rivalry and of those ten games only the '90 Tide win could be labeled a mild upset. But the players and fans do forget about the records during the game. Unlikely as it may be, the opportunity remained to wash away the sins of a disappointing season with one glorious victory. Furious action transports a sports-crazed state away from the grind of daily living.

While Moss and Walker rejoined the active roster, Grizzard, Meade, Dudley, London, and Cotton formed the starting lineup. As was the case in the first half at Auburn, Alabama successfully traded blows with the now 21-4 Tigers. Cotton matched his actions with his words, slashing through the lane to score 11 of the Tide's first 18 points. While Pohlman couldn't help the Tiger cause with Meade draped all over him, Porter answered with line-drive hook shots that banked in off the glass. With 8:31 left in the half, Cotton slashed through the lane and collided with the 7-foot-1 N'Diaye. A blocking foul was called on N'diaye who fell hard to the ground. The Auburn center left the game with a sprained knee ligament. Dudley would no longer be forced to guard a stronger and taller man. All of Gottfried's pleading could not prevent the Tigers from winning the rebounding war. Auburn trailed at halftime only 29-27.

Scott arrived during the half and joined the staff meeting. Rebounding dominated a short conversation. They entered the locker room.

"They're out-rebounding us 26-16, guys. We're down ten in that category and that's the reason they're in the game. If there is a long shot, there's a long rebound. Other than that we've just got to box out and buck up and get the ball! You've got to just dive on it and get it! Come out of the pack with the basketball . . . Offensively, we're not cutting enough or hard enough . . . We've got cement shoes on . . . The name of the game is on the glass!"

A national television audience and an emotional crowd watched a continuation of the tense first half. Every possession was a battle in this game of 23 lead changes. With five points in the first half, Grizzard began to take over the game. The bold and confident freshman drilled critical shot after critical shot. Given his struggles and the tremendous work by the staff, especially Scott who chiefly recruited him, to develop his game without crushing his confidence, Grizzard's blossoming as a player on this stage was emotionally overwhelming. Grizzard had been the target of so much criticism. I realized that the staff had achieved a master stroke with this player. I saw in Rod Grizzard a mature man and a future NBA player wearing number 21.

While the Tide threatened to pull away with two different six-point leads, the proud Tigers would not surrender to the crazed crowd. Porter continued to pound the glass on his way to 12 rebounds and 21 points. When Grizzard finished a nifty post move over Porter to make the Tide lead 54-48 with 6:18 left, the crowd began yelling for a joyous ending. A flurry of Tiger scoring from Doc Robinson, reserve post-player Mack McGadney, Porter, and Pohlman delivered a crushing blow to the Tide faithful. Pohlman finished the run with a lay-up, finally giving the Tigers a precious 64-63 lead with just 1:01 left. The Auburn fans roared as if to say 'we came here for a reason and you just witnessed it.'

Having been so close to a tremendous Tide victory, the will of Auburn's veterans had seemingly prevailed. Alabama pushed the ball up the floor and found Grizzard on the perimeter—percentages must be against any more heroics from the freshman. Grizzard launched without fear. Watching the flight of the ball was purgatory—a moment of anxious terror. Swish! He made it! He made another one! The Tide bench was a zoo, but the Tigers still had a chance with the ball, trailing 66-64. Auburn moved the ball around until Pohlman launched a three-pointer from the corner with deadly intentions. He missed! But the rebound flew out of bounds after touching a Tide player. The Tigers trusted their clutch guard Doc Robinson with their next shot. He fired a heavily contested 12-foot jump shot that missed! Meade grabbed the rebound! He was fouled with 17 seconds left. However, the Tigers had committed only four team fouls and were forced to foul the Tide three more times quickly to put the Tide in the bonus and finally send Meade to the foul line. The courageous Meade sank both free throws to finish the Tigers, 68-64! As the clock expired, the students stormed the floor in the wildest celebration that I have ever witnessed at a Tide basketball game. Jumping, yelling, and congratulating the players, Alabama passionately enjoyed a memorable triumph. I lost my right shoe in the mob.

Coaches hugged players when the team finally reached the locker room. An emotional Scott received hugs from the players who had just delivered a precious gift they desperately wanted to give their coach. Next season may be great. This season may have been grueling. But those precious moments of victory would be remembered forever. Wounded and deflated, a young team achieved a truly memorable win and began the path toward something greater.

An emotional Gottfried addressed his players.

"I looked out there, and nobody cared who scored or who got the credit. You played selfless—not worrying about your points. Just playing. That's what happens when you play unselfish and you play together. A top ten team in America just walked in here, and you took them down. Be complimentary to the media. They're a great team. You win with class. Young team. Injured team. You've hung in there and kept fighting. That's all anybody can ask of you."

Mal Moore followed.

"I want to thank you for a great, great win. Great accomplishments are in your future. Be sure to remember how hard you played."

Hays dismissed the team with a prayer for Scott to conclude an emotionally exhausting evening. A time for reflection revealed that there were more key performances than Grizzard's 25 points and Cotton's vital scoring start that provided early confidence. Martin was very good defensively in his 18 minutes. Dudley served as an inside presence, adding 12 points and six rebounds. Meade added 13 points and six rebounds along with those two final free throws. Moss played ten minutes of solid defense and added a bucket with a broken back. Cotton also added some tough defense. London led the team for 38 minutes and defended with intensity. Finally, Walker entered the game for a minute to give an inspirational boost.

After the game, several members of the staff joined a group to eat a late dinner on the Tuscaloosa strip. When Gottfried entered the restaurant, he received a standing ovation from the patrons. Suddenly, the restaurant's stereo was blasting the Alabama fight song. It was the perfect night. And to top it all off, the Coliseum staff even located my shoe before we left.

After a Wednesday of rest and savoring the big win, all thoughts turned toward Alabama's other long-time rival, the Tennessee Volunteers. Like Auburn, Tennessee had revived its program after a ten long years of bad basketball. Sanderson and Hobbs gave the Tide control of the Tennessee series as Alabama slammed the Vols in 18 of 21 games until the Hobbs era made its final turn toward a sad ending in a pivotal and shocking loss to another bad Tennessee team at the '96 SEC tournament. The Vols were enjoying a third consecutive season that would end in the NCAA tournament. Having beaten Auburn and swept powerful Florida, Tennessee (22-4) was the highest ranked team in the SEC! Tennessee would be favored to pound an Alabama team still enjoying an accomplishment that few thought possible.

Gottfried optimistically contemplated the status of the league at practice on Thursday.

"I start thinking about our league—and we haven't seen Tennessee yet and they're ranked higher than anybody. But Vandy beat them twice. We beat Vandy. I look back at Kentucky. I think they're a very good team, but I'd love to play them on a neutral court. You've proven that you could beat Auburn. If you guys could defend people like you defended Auburn the other night—five guys down in a freaking stance, diving on the floor for balls, coming up with balls late in the game, being unselfish offensively, there's nothing you can't do. There's nobody out there that you can't beat—nobody in our league. If we play together and really get down and guard people. You gotta take some pride in your defense. It's a commitment on your part. If you're not committed to doing it, then we're finished as a team."

After an uneventful Friday, Kelsey briefed the troops at 12:20 before a 1:00 tip-off on a truly special Saturday for him. Being a Tennessean, Kelsey saw something special in those orange jerseys (unlike Alabamians who see a tacky uniform). Like Florida, Tennessee was talented beyond description. Point guard Tony Harris was simply amazing with his quickness. Vincent Yarbrough and Isiah Victor were tremendously athletic forwards. C.J. Black was a powerful low-post player as was the freshman Ron Slay who seemed to have injected energy and intensity into a team that had only been criticized for lacking those very qualities. The story of the game was a familiar one for an undersized and weaker

Tide team playing in the most athletic conference in America. Tennessee would have an incredible rebounding edge.

"Black, Victor, Yarbrough, and Slay believe that they will kill you on the glass. You better make a decision right now to put a body on those guys," Kelsey said.

"The best offense against you will be a missed shot. It's a rebounding game," Gottfried said after Kelsey delivers a meticulous scouting report.

When the team returned from the warm-up, Gottfried made a point to hype a bench player.

"Look for Slay to be coming in early. I think he's really good. He's an impact player. Look out."

The final home game would ordinarily be senior day at Coleman Coliseum, but the Tide had no seniors. Save perhaps Scott. We feared that this might be his last game.

"Don't cheat yourself, fellas. This is the last game that we have in this building, fellas. Make your mark. There are no guarantees in life."

A very grateful crowd of 9,053 greeted the same starting lineup from the Auburn game. The Tide proceeded to offer a lackluster first half effort like a team exhausted from an overwhelming win. Slay entered the game early and scored nine points in just over three minutes, highlighted by an offensive rebound basket followed by a barbaric yell as if he was an ancient warrior ready to torch the town. He is my kind of player. The Vols scored at will.

A stingy lead held by the visitor ballooned at the end of the half with an 11-0 run, resulting in a 41-32 Vol lead at the half. Vol forwards Yarbrough, Black, and Slay combined to shoot 13 for 19, outscoring the Tide with 33 points and helping the Vols to a 20-11 rebounding edge.

The Tide shot 50 percent to remain within shouting distance (London shot three for four, ten points, Cotton went four for six, ten points; Moss went three for five, and new campus hero Grizzard went one for six).

The big win had exhausted the team mentally. In my eyes, they simply were not ready to play another emotionally tough match. Especially not so soon.

"If we're gonna win this game, we've got to get down and get our sneakers squeaking. They're in mud out there," Pearson said to the staff.

"Maybe Sam could guard Slay. Moss can't do anything with him," Scott said.

"But Sam isn't the scoring threat Fred is," Gottfried replied.

"The only way to beat them is to take it right at 'em. Play with no fear," Kelsey said.

An angry Gottfried charged into the locker room with a sense of urgency and frustration.

"It's time to get down and ready. Be aggressive. We've got to lock them up. Schea, you've got to guard Yarbrough. And you've just got to get down and guard him, son. He's got 15 . . . Tarik, Tony Harris will probably shoot every time he gets it. He doesn't have a point yet. You better know where he is . . .The bottom line is that our shoes are not squeaking on defense. We are not down and squeaking our shoes and just working and working and pushing and pushing. Offensively, we've got to move the ball and attack the basket. We've got to create spaces to penetrate by moving the ball . . . [Yelling about defensive rebounding] Move 'em out of there! Just belt 'em! Knock 'em over there in the bleachers! I'm tired of seeing teams tip the ball in on us! You've got to block somebody out and rebound! What else?"

"We've got nobody with more than two rebounds on our team. We've got to get some rebounds," Kelsey said.

"We've got to take a charge," Pearson said.

"Come on, fellas," Gottfried began. "We've got the seventh ranked team in America sitting in your building. If you'll get down and play together and play hard. I don't care who scores—who gets the credit. We are not out of this game."

A different Alabama team took the floor in the second half. The Tide's defensive intensity elevated dramatically. Like the team on Tuesday that was out-rebounded by only one in the second half by Auburn, the Tide scrapped for balls with a sense of urgency. Tide guards Cotton, London, Meade, and Grizzard combined for 16 rebounds in the game. Meanwhile, Meade nailed two three-pointers to cut the Vol lead to 46-

42 with 15:06 left. With 13:25 left, Grizzard ignited the crowd with his now signature silky smooth stroke from behind the three-point line to give the Tide a 50-48 lead. Slay, a big man who can shoot from the perimeter, responded with a three-pointer to restore the Vol lead. As the lead changes mounted, Cotton stepped forward for the Tide with six points in a row, punctuated with a power dunk causing a roar from the crowd and a 62-61 Tide lead with 8:03 left. Cotton was suddenly an Alabama hero. Grizzard followed a media timeout with another three-pointer to make it 65-61. Could this team be on the brink of another wild celebration after shocking a rival school?

Always ready for a fierce challenge, Meade helped protect the lead by scoring all of the Tide's seven points from the 6:29 mark until 1:58 remained. Tennessee won at Florida this year and at Kentucky last year. They did not back down from a wild gathering of Tide fans or a veraciously hungry young team. Team leaders Harris and Black combined for five points, and Slay nearly ripped the goal down on a dunk, yelling like a mad man and cutting the lead to two with 2:46 left. On the following possession, London was fouled by Harris. Not a great foul shooter as a guard but an improving, hard worker at the foul line, London nailed both! The Tide led 75-71. Black answered with two free throws after being fouled by Dudley to make the lead 2 with 1:48 left. Slay tied the game at the foul line 46 seconds later.

With the clock ticking under a minute in a tie game, who would the Tide go to? Grizzard. Attacking Slay into a vulnerable position, the big man fouled Grizzard. It was just his week as he made both with 38 seconds left. But Yarbrough was fouled by Grizzard with 28 seconds left. Staring into a maniacal crowd, he missed the first! He missed the second! Another critical late rebound by Meade, and he was fouled immediately to put him in the exact same situation as Tuesday. Leading by two points and the shot clock turned off with a chance to make it a two-possession lead, Meade drilled them both—the unflappable Mr. Meade! After a Tennessee miss, Moss captured the rebound and added another free throw. The horn sounded on an 80-75 win, and the students stormed the floor. Wild jumping in a hysterical mob allowed the players to celebrate and collide with their fellow students. Gottfried grabbed the microphone and thanked the fans for continuing to support the team. I held onto my shoes this time.

Alabama had played an entire basketball season in one week. After an endless string of stormy days, the rain stopped and a rainbow appeared. The tears flowed freely down Gottfried's cheeks. His team had overcome many obstacles. He realized that Scott now had a tangible reason for optimism if he contemplated on his death bed whether all his work at Alabama had gone to waste. It obviously hadn't.

Pearson recalled gently putting his arm around Scott who he had thought was done with his Coleman career. With his arm, he shielded Scott from the the gregarious mob as they left later in the evening.

"[Struggling with tears] I don't know if I've ever been more proud of a team," Gottfried began, sparking loud applause and yelling. "Man, I'm telling you. You got down and worked. You guarded 'em. You've given this staff a week we will always treasure. Thank you.

"We've got two more on the road. And it's time for us to go on the road and win. It's time for us to win on the road. Good win. What a great win. A top twenty-five team and two top ten teams come back-to-back-to-back in your building, and you got 'em. You can play with anybody in the country, guys—when you play hard. But when you don't play hard, you're just another team putting a jersey on."

Hays presented a plaque to Scott whose tears indicated that he was finally emotionally overwhelmed. After all the misery through the season, his most emotional moment came in a time of joy. He could no longer hide his emotions from his beloved players.

"This is for Coach Scott from all of us as a team," Hays began. "We love you, coach. [Reading from the plaque] 'You are the man we all dream of one day becoming. May God bless you as you have blessed our lives.'"

Love filled the room. The players one by one embraced Scott. If that was his senior day, it was a perfect ending.

Many heroes make great victories. Beyond Grizzard's clutch play, London registered a career-high 14 points and grabbed five rebounds.

Meade drilled three of six three-point attempts on his way to 19 points. Cotton shot 8 for 14, adding 18 points. Moss shot three of five with four rebounds. But credit goes to the entire team. The Vols were held to 29.2 percent shooting in the second half. Even Walker managed to play eight minutes and claimed to be ready for heavy minutes in the remaining games. But the true hero of the day was Scott who had survived to enjoy one incredible week.

The rest of the season would not matter. What did matter was that the depleted and downtrodden Tide had risen above all the obstacles and had proven both to themselves and to the coaches that they were just that: a team. The injuries, the inexperience, even Scott's cancer. None of it mattered as the team relished the bond formed by two back-to-back communal victories. The whole season had been redeemed, the pain and frustration validated.

15

Shooting Stops the Pain

The basketball buzz around the state on Monday centered on the plains. The media coverage of Auburn had turned from a team of great potential to great disappointment as team leader Porter was suspended for accepting money from an agent over the weekend. Cruelly and inappropriately, Porter's final game was a loss to Alabama. The Tigers would never recover, recording a tremendously disappointing ending to two years of high hopes and publicity.

"You probably know what happened down the road over the weekend," Gottfried said to begin practice. "Chris Porter is suspended for dealing with an agent. Do not make the same mistakes, guys. Be careful about who you deal with. So many people want to take advantage of you in this world. Don't let it happen. Be alert. He hurt his team and his coaches . . . We're 0 for 8 on the road, guys. We've got to get one done. We know by now that the crowd will be cheering only when they do something. They will make runs, and it will get very loud. You have to be mentally tough enough to play through it by now."

A determined head coach brought in a technician on Tuesday who rocked Coleman Coliseum with extremely loud and unpleasant crowd noise during practice. I yelled playfully without anybody noticing. Gottfried enjoyed the practice although instruction had to be delivered at close range. Pain in his Achilles tendon prevented Meade from practicing.

Scott, who missed yesterday, arrived early today and would travel with Kobie to Oxford tonight. I attempted to humor him, but he is in no mood to laugh anymore—stupidity on my part. His mid-section hurt when he laughed.

Wednesday, March 1, in Oxford featured gorgeous weather, reminding us that basketball season was nearing its conclusion. The shoot-around at C.M. "Tad" Smith Coliseum provoked thoughts of the home team's senior night. The Rebels' best player, Marcus Hicks, was a senior.

Kelsey studied the Rebels.

"It's senior night for Hicks. He will be looking to score on every trip. We will probably cover down on him, and the help needs to come in a hurry, guys."

The head coach understood that they would face energetic Rebels.

"They play extremely hard all the time fellas, but it's senior night and everything will be a little different. They're gonna guard you like crazy— pushing and clawing. The officials will miss a bunch of calls and allow them to push you around. You've got to be ready to firm up, buck up, and accept the challenge. We've got to have this win. Get your mind ready to play through anything tonight."

At the afternoon pre-game meal, Scott was so tired that he rested his small head on the table. He had no positive thoughts about food. The disease had completely robbed his appetite. When the meal ended, he could not seem to find the strength to leave the room. He remained in the dining area ten minutes after the last person other than myself left. I was relieved when he managed to limp back to his room.

One of Mark's high school friends made the trip to Oxford. A positive and energetic businessman, he seemed offended when I defended the Rebels' favored status according to the betting line. After he expressed his strong belief that Alabama would win the game, I felt the need to prepare him for a blow.

"Buckle up. It's senior night. They're 16-11 and headed for the post-season. They play with great intensity, and they beat Auburn over here. We're winless on the road," I told him.

When we arrived for the game in the evening, Scott remained in his car that was driven by Baker. He could not find the strength to come inside. Gottfried asked the coliseum staff for help before entering the locker room for the pre-warm-up session.

After the scouting report, Gottfried issued another warning.

"In this game over here, you better firm up. You better firm up. We'll try to talk to the refs, but you better understand right now that they're gonna grab you, push you, and do everything over here . . .They've got senior night. They've got all kinds of stuff going on, fellas."

Alabama's mathematical situation was simple. The 13-13 Tide needed to finish the schedule and the league tournament 2-2 to be eligible for the NIT. The final scheduled game was Saturday against a Mississippi State team that could not wait for sweet revenge. An 0-2 run through Mississippi would make a losing season extremely likely. The pride associated with avoiding a losing season made tonight's game huge.

Scott refused to miss the game. As the Alabama players waited in the hall to take the floor for the warm-up, coliseum staff slowly rolled Scott into the coliseum in a special wheelchair. The wheelchair stopped near the Tide players. I will never forget watching the players watch him— looks full of deep concern and affection. That was our hero. As tears swelled in my eyes, my heart felt heavy.

There was no Hollywood ending for this season. Alabama missed its best opportunity for a road win that night in Oxford. Grizzard could not produce his magic, missing a 15-foot jumper that would have tied the score with under a minute to play as the Rebels won, 61-57.

The next game was no better. Mississippi State revenged their earlier dramatic defeat in a 92-70 whipping of Alabama (playing without Meade due to an Achilles tendon) in which Gottfried was ejected after his only healthy big man experienced early foul trouble.

After the horrible trip to Oxford, Scott did not travel for the final scheduled game or the SEC Tournament in Atlanta. The doctors told Cynthia that Robert was in immediate danger from the cancer. It had spread so much that it had all but completely blocked the path to his stomach.

Gottfried, Boatright, and I walked to the hotel after the Wednesday team dinner on the eve of the league tournament instead of making the short bus ride. Gottfried talked about a recent conversation with the opposing Gamecock coach, Eddie Fogler. Fogler, who was also on the verge of ending a losing season, said that the loser of the game could at least be relieved because the season would be over.

"Maybe we could make a run here," I said.

"Maybe," Gottfried began his response. "But if not, we'll be out of our misery. Just put us out of our misery. [Long pause] It's like Coach Scott. I love him so much. You've seen what he's been going through. And I know how much you love him, Shaq. But he's had enough. I want his pain to go away. It's just like our season," Gottfried said quietly as a cool breeze blew in the Atlanta night.

Gottfried concluded a passionate plea for the players to seize the opportunity of March basketball before the tournament opener when he paused in apparent reflection on Scott's condition and the season at the end of his speech. Tears began to trickle down his face.

"We've been through a lot this season," he continued before another pause. "Just like when your teammates miss games for injuries, you've got to come together. And you've got one down in the hospital." He didn't say anything else. He looked emotionally spent.

It was all too much. For me. For the team. For the coaches. We huddled together before the game with heavy hearts. An air of finality hung about the players.

The team came together as they had done so many times. Along with the coaching staff, I watched the team during the final warm-up. So much had happened to them. The depleted roster. The injuries. If this had been a movie, they would have won that first game and played all the way to the NCAA finals. A work of fiction would have had them overcome all of the obstacles and achieve victory, with a healthy, healed Robert Scott holding up the trophy.

The world, of course, doesn't work that way. Fairy tale endings are few and far between. South Carolina beat Alabama 69-59. The specifics of the game are unimportant. Alabama had lost. The season was over.

Gottfried addressed a despondent team after the game.

"It's over. The season is over. We're out of our misery, now. [Pause] It wasn't our day today.

"We're gonna work hard," he began his thoughts on the future. "We'll work hard. Weightlifting, conditioning, skill work. Between now and next year, there's going to be a lot of improvement. We're not going to be like this year. We're gonna be a better defensive team. I don't care if we score twenty points a game. We will guard people. I don't want to ever forget this season—13-16. I will never forget. We had a lot going on. A lot of new players. Injuries. But we're going to make a decision. We're going to get after it hard! Real hard. Real hard. Real hard. There's no doubt in my mind that we can be a good basketball team next year. But if you just assume that will happen, we're in big trouble. We're gonna run down the floor and guard people- shut people out. We'll stay together. Be positive with each other. Encourage each other and make yourself a great team. There's a lot of time between now and next year.

"[Long pause and complete silence] I want you right now in your minds as individuals and as a team to commit yourself to each other and commit yourself to being a great team. To have a great team, you've got to be a great defensive player. A great defensive team. If you've got a weakness, then you need to improve that weakness. Our inside guys have to get bigger and stronger. Everybody that we played against this year were bigger and stronger than us. We need to be better ball-handlers, passers, and catchers. [Pause] If you start to assume that we're going to be better, then it won't happen. It's all about work. Work. Work."

After Hays asked for God to help the team make a commitment to working in his prayer, Gottfried made the final comment of the season.

"Win or lose. We're together."

16

The Final Buzzer

On Friday, March 10, I visited Robert in the hospital where he and Cynthia had been given better news about his short-term situation. He would be going home. Earlier in the week, a doctor who had never spoken with the couple before entered their room and abruptly forecasted Scott's immediate danger and certain death in the near future. They were anguished by the doctor's poor bedside manner. They were clinging to hope based largely on Robert's strong will to live—his tremendous desire to help a family and a team. An SEC tournament game was on the television in the hospital room, but basketball was a distant concern at the moment. We sat in a Birmingham hospital focusing on Robert's need for a miracle.

Gottfried coincidentally entered the hospital room while I was there. The head coach had received a call from Cotton, who was leaving school. His father had been diagnosed with prostate cancer, and the son wanted to return immediately to his close family in California.

By April, Robert and Cynthia seemed to realize the overwhelming improbability of recovery. I saw despair in Cynthia's eyes. Robert's body had completely betrayed him. I wondered if Cynthia could grasp the extent of his deterioration. Going days without seeing him, visitors like myself were stunned to see how rapidly his flesh disappeared.

The team banquet proceeded without Robert. He had returned to the hospital in Birmingham. On April 12, Gottfried told Robert in the morning that the team would visit him that afternoon. Because he was so weak by then that uttering a single word was an uphill battle, he began planning in the morning. If he saved his strength and summoned every ounce of his power, he could perhaps impact the team one more time.

I visited Scott in the hospital that afternoon and was there when Gottfried, Walker, and Grizzard entered the room. Players and staff continued to arrive until the room was packed. Haginas, who had earlier decided to leave the team, had changed his mind. Scott, who had continually voiced his belief in Haginas's abilities, told Haginas that he knew he would return. The team began updating the patient on their lives. It was medicine for him. A good coach follows his players' lives closely, and Robert had been slowly stripped of that—his favorite part of the job. He relied on comments from fellow staff members to follow the players' activities. Warm laughter filled the room as the players shared stories. Robert was surrounded by an adoring group whose members had bonded through adversity. But then the laughter stopped. Robert began to speak and his tone was not lighthearted. With death creeping toward his door, Scott reached deep in his soul to give one more lesson to his beloved team. After the hundreds of speeches and conversations that I had recorded during the season, I did not have my recorder for the speech of a lifetime.

But I remember vividly that Scott urged the players to strengthen their commitment to the team. He emphasized the importance of players coaching other players. He shared that he had been elected captain for two years as an Alabama player because the coaches could count on him to coach his teammates—to bring the team together and strengthen their commitment to success. He asked the players to help each other in every aspect of their lives. When a player was not working very hard, he wanted another player to counsel him about working harder. If a player was neglecting his academics, he wanted another player to push him to study. He made a plea for self-discipline.

Robert always believed that a guy should be self-motivated to achieve. He commanded the team to improve their defense with a look of determination. He spoke eloquently despite his suffering.

When Robert finished his message, the team gathered around him to view the highlight film that had been shown at the banquet. Even in his weakened condition, the inspired patient even managed some of his trademark humorous remarks during the film. Watching the scenes of the team celebrating after wins over Auburn and Tennessee, I was aware that it was going be difficult to celebrate future wins without Robert Scott. The film ended with a written dedication to Robert. He was visibly humbled by the gesture. The team left in a flurry of hugs and goodbyes.

SCOTT WAS sent home in late April. His doctors felt he would be more comfortable there waiting for the approaching end. Cynthia was not at ease with this decision. She became understandably uncomfortable with Robert suffering without the benefit of complete medical treatment. She could not give up trying to save him.

On Friday, April 28th (Kobie's birthday), Gottfried received a panicked late afternoon phone call from Cynthia. Robert was having difficulty breathing. Morphine was not adequately controlling his pain. Cynthia wanted him returned to a hospital. Instead of the long trip to Birmingham, she opted for Druid City Hospital in Tuscaloosa. So she called 911 to request an ambulance.

Baker and Gottfried drove to the Scott home to help with his transportation. Describing his body as "incredibly bony—almost nothing but bones," Gottfried told me how he and Baker helped the paramedics carefully lift his body onto a stretcher. Scott was placed into the ambulance. As the doors closed, he appeared to be very frightened. His nervous eyes darted back and forth across the strangers in the ambulance car. Robert was alone.

Gottfried drove in his car with Cynthia and Baker behind the ambulance to the emergency room. That night, Robert was transferred to a room and the entire coaching staff gathered around his bed for about an hour. Robert was shifting in and out of consciousness. Oxygen tubes were inserted into his nostrils. He wore a crimson Alabama hat that he dearly loved, and a pair of glasses that he had been using as if they were keeping him alive. He also wore a simple watch that seemed to be an extension of his skin.

Having appeared to be asleep, he shocked the staff when he suddenly raised his hands and pulled out the tubes. He proceeded to remove his beloved hat and trusted glasses. With the weakest voice imaginable, he called Kobie Baker's first name. Kobie stepped forward. Robert asked Kobie to hold both his hands. Robert squeezed his hands tight. He was ready to die. The loving bystanders were overwhelmed. They breathed a sigh of relief when Scott realized that it was not yet his time. He opened his eyes and orchestrated a reunion with the hat, glasses, and tubes.

ON MAY 8, I returned to Druid City Hospital where Robert had been hospitalized for almost two weeks. I was wearing a Cleveland Browns shirt. Scott was a loyal fan of the Browns, having followed Jim Brown as a youngster. I privately pledged allegiance to the Browns in April as a gesture for Robert, and I wore the same ten dollar Browns t-shirt every time I visited him. Cynthia almost never left his side during this period. The doctors said death was near, but he had outlasted earlier predictions, battling cancer like a proud warrior. His children gathered around him. Robert Jr., 16, Rahshae, nine, and Daniel, 12, are simply the best behaved and kindest children that I have ever encountered.

The *Birmingham News* was filled with stories about Alabama basketball that day.

One article discussed Johnny Jones whom Gottfried recently hired to join the staff. Another article reported Gerald Wallace's announcement that he would forego the NBA draft and attend Alabama. One sportswriter wrote a commentary about how excited Alabama fans were about Wallace. My first reaction was unreasoning anger. It was Robert who discussed Wallace with so much excitement in the car on the way to eat a first meal with Gottfried's staff. When Gottfried had opened discussion about how to rebuild the program, Robert again turned to Wallace. According to Robert, there was a superhuman playing basketball for Childersburg High School. From that day forward, Robert had been obsessed with landing Wallace. He had spent much of his recruiting time battling competing schools for Wallace's attention. Robert's effort was the driving force behind the signing of Gerald Wallace, and the newspaper articles did not even mention his name.

Robert had crossed the finish line with Wallace, but he seemed incapable of understanding the news. An oxygen mask covered his mouth as he drifted in and out of sleep. Daniel passed me the sports page of the *Birmingham News* over his father's body. His father did not acknowledge the paper announcing the final victory—the highest-rated recruit in Alabama basketball history was coming to Rah Rah Scott's school.

In a discussion sparked by the articles, I expressed my thanks to Cynthia for all the work that Robert had done for Alabama basketball. When the children left to get a snack, we discussed them. Our conversation seemed to center on Robert Jr. (Rahmun), who was often overshadowed by Rashae's wonderful personality and million-dollar smile, or by the basketball prodigy, Daniel, with his Magic Johnson-like vivaciousness. Now, Robert Jr., at 16 the oldest child, had been shoved onto center stage because his age burdened him with the best understanding of his father's situation. Robert Jr.'s personality resembled his father's. According to Baker, Robert Jr. had been openly disgusted with his AAU team's lack of commitment to winning. Cynthia told me how Scott had said privately that Robert Jr. would make a great coach someday. Cynthia described Robert's joy when he learned that Robert Jr.'s first ACT score had qualified him for NCAA eligibility. A proud father hugging his son had a deeper meaning under the circumstances.

We discussed the trip to Arkansas when Cynthia had begged Robert not to go. His willingness to endure pain had carried him a long way, from the loud moans and groans in that Arkansas hotel, to suffering in this hospital bed where he continued to beat the latest projections of his death.

In these last days, his determination had captured our imagination. When I prepared to leave the room, Scott suddenly became animated. He wanted to tell me something, but the oxygen mask would not allow him to speak. Cynthia considered taking off the mask but putting it back on would have been troublesome. I wondered what he would have said.

I guessed he wanted to tease me over any doubts that I had about Wallace, but I'll never know.

Later that night I grabbed the *Birmingham News* again, still feeling grief and anger. It was irrational, but I wanted a written validation of Robert and everything he had contributed to me, to Alabama, to the team. The sports columns and the daily scoop seemed so mundane in comparison with the struggle the Scotts were going through. I wanted the articles to celebrate how Robert's sense of urgency had made the difference with signing Wallace. That is what I had told Cynthia earlier in the day. She remembered his insistence that Cynthia send Wallace a postcard from Hawaii during a Christmas tournament. Robert would have followed Wallace to hell and back if the NCAA rules had allowed such a visit. Yet the newspaper didn't even mention him. I threw the paper to the carpet.

Most of all, I wanted to hear Robert's voice. I knew that if he had managed to pull off that oxygen mask, he would have made me laugh one more time.

ON THE following night, Robert's doctor explained to Cynthia the advantages of taking Robert off life support systems, thus sparing him further pain and trauma. Cynthia and Robert had vowed never to surrender, but the battle was now lost. Cynthia had spent so many sleepless nights caring for him. She had given him hope in his darkest hours. It was time for him to rest. Cynthia consented to the doctor's recommendation. Soon afterwards, Robert shared a private moment with each of his three children.

After Cynthia finally surrendered—when she let him go—she and the doctor left to implement the procedures to have Robert taken off life support. When they got back to his room, he was gone. It was as if he had simply been waiting for Cynthia to let him go. The excruciating pain that Robert "Rah Rah" Scott III had endured for so many months was finally over.

Many people who loved Robert were there when it happened, the coaching staff and their wives, Eddie Phillips, John and Cindy Merrill, and the Bosticks—all close friends of the program. They were all crying as the doctors declared Robert deceased.

I was not at the hospital, and neither was Baker, who was running an errand to the basketball office. Gottfried delivered the crushing news over the phone to Baker at the office.

Baker raced to the hospital, sprinted from his car up the stairs toward Robert's room, and fixed his eyes on Cynthia in the hallway outside. Her face confirmed what Baker had been unable to accept. He collapsed in the hall and only remembers Cynthia and Gottfried helping him up off the floor.

Robert's body remained in the acute intensive care unit for a while. Baker could not bring himself to go inside. But Elizabeth Gottfried, Mark, Ashley and Philip Pearson, and John Morr stood around Robert's bed for a time. Mark was stunned by a perception that Scott seemed to be breathing, as if he wanted him to be alive so desperately, that his mind was moving Robert's chest. Astonishingly, later that night, Elizabeth shared that she had experienced the same illusion, an on the next day, Pearson and Morr shared that they also had the same experience.

I drove to the Scotts' house just before midnight. Several other friends and family members had gathered. Cynthia was planning the funeral with chaplain Overstreet. Cynthia comforted me; in her grief, her customary kindness was magnified. She beckoned me to sit beside her quietly while she discussed the funeral plans.

When the mourners started to leave for the night, the children were on the couch watching ESPN Sports Center. They had watched Sports Center thousands of times with their father. He would provide a running commentary that would have everyone in the room laughing. If a player was being dominated by an opposing rebounder, he would say something mockingly understated, like "Can't he block out and get just one rebound?" If a NASCAR driver ran out of fuel, he might say, "Daniel, couldn't you give this man some gas?" But the children had lost their entertainer—never to return. They sat and watched Sports Center anyway. Could they feel his presence in the room? What would he be saying? I felt him that night. I feel him now. I feel his beauty and grace everywhere. I felt him when 12-year-old Daniel approached me, a sobbing adult entering their home, and politely offered me something to drink.

Cynthia planned a Saturday funeral service in Birmingham and a Sunday memorial service in Coleman Coliseum. She labored through her despair to design two excellent services. Reverend Harold W. Bass, who was Robert's former preacher and the father of a former player at West End High School and UAB, conducted an uplifting funeral in Birmingham's Fair Park Arena.

Robert's tangible body was joined in the casket by that Alabama hat that he loved so much. The design of the A on the hat was the same design worn by a young "Bear" Bryant. It always reminded me of the pride that Robert had for having played at Alabama—the great people and teams that he knew. The casket also held a basketball. His body was at peace.

The reverend's son, Lee Andrew, struggled to find words to express his feelings about his former coach. Eddie Philips, a former Alabama teammate and New Jersey Net, described a great friend. Wimp Sanderson, who had tirelessly recruited Scott to play for the Tide, dutifully attended. Robert had often joked about Sanderson bringing the basketball team to watch him play baseball for Parker High School. Recruiting rules were more relaxed then, and Scott liked to joke that Sanderson could have been employed by Parker High because he was around the school so frequently to recruit him. Rod Asberry, a talented singer, performed the first of two beautiful solos in two days. Many people from UAB and West End High also attended. Murray and Gene Bartow showed their support. Asked to speak, Gottfried described his deceased friend as a man who treated people of all socioeconomic and ethnic backgrounds with the same warm respect and attention.

ON SUNDAY, May 14, the Alabama basketball team gathered at 2 p.m. in the locker room. They prepared to enter Coleman Coliseum as if a basketball game was about to be played. The only distinction between this day and a pre-game routine were the coats and ties worn by the players.

Gerald Wallace joined the group. By coincidence, it was the last day he could have declared for the NBA draft. The players formed a semi-circle of chairs around Gottfried with the chalkboard behind him, but there was no chair behind the players waiting for Scott. Gottfried spoke gently about their deceased coach, describing him as a special person. Repeating his comments from the day before, he spoke about a man who treated all people fairly and with equal fondness. He emphasized how much Scott had cared about the players, inquiring about them even while he suffering extreme pain.

"Make sure you understand what Robert Scott was all about. I felt bad for you freshman because you did not get the benefit of a healthy Coach Scott. I want you to remember how he lived and coached—not how he died. He was so pure. Remember his full body, full tough love, full voice. He was so genuine, fellas . . . I won a national championship as an assistant, fellas. When you do something like that, it automatically bonds people together forever. It's so rare. It's so special. But this experience is similar. I want you to look around the room. We're bonded together forever—everybody. We've all learned and grown. Coach Scott gave us so much. We will always benefit from his legacy. We've been given a gift. It's up to you people to use what he taught you."

He told the players how Scott's final long conversation was a phone call from Schea Cotton. Scott had cared so much about Cotton that he expended a substantial portion of his fleeting energy for him. No one but Cotton knows what was said.

Gottfried opened up the floor for comments about their deceased coach. He jump-started the memories by mentioning how Robert would "get on" guys. He laughed about the coach finding the energy to coach with such great intensity on his birthday those months before.

Martin relayed a conversation with Cedric Patton who transferred before the year began. Patton had a small frame and poor defensive instincts. Patton told Martin that he would never forget Scott coaching him. I can vividly remember restraining laughter when Scott continually jumped all over Patton.

Walker followed with the memories of being rapidly charged with eight sprints for being out of position on Scott's birthday.

Gottfried turned the floor over to Baker. Through those final months, Baker had been an angel on Scott's shoulder. He had worked tirelessly to help the Scott family—investing himself physically and emotionally. Through the experience, Baker had found a phenomenal friend in Scott. From his death bed, Robert had managed to give Baker career advice. Baker shared that story with the team, emphasizing Scott's total selflessness.

Concluding, Kelsey shared in a prayer that he would be forever grateful for what he learned about fathering from Scott. Gottfried concluded with the unquestionable assertion that Robert Scott had defined bravery for the players through the season. They could do no less than honor him with their future actions. Scott left behind a legacy of courage.

Gottfried asked the players to begin thinking about a gesture dedicated to Scott for next season. Martin suggested a jersey patch. A period of silence followed as individuals found personal space in the locker room or the players' lounge. Howard Pride, who had a great relationship with Scott, arrived to show his support.

Five months earlier, several of these players had no idea about the work ethic, intensity, or maturity required to compete at the major-college level. On this day, those boys finished their progression to men. They had experienced so much over the past half-year: massive injuries that had doomed the season, confusion, helplessness, young players attempting to lead young players, and the toughest conference in America. They had also experienced determined coaching, positive role models, lasting friendships, and the strength that comes through adversity. And they had experienced the unforgettable courage of Robert Scott. They would carry that with them forever.

Gottfried watched young players who had been attempting to play the role of tough men through the season. Dudley, Grizzard, and Walker had suppressed their emotions for roughly half-a-year. The walls came down in that locker room. They sobbed with each other and their coaches. They had grown so much.

As we grieved, I was thankful to Gottfried for having this formal meeting in the locker room. I could imagine Robert there so clearly. I saw him on the couch. I saw him carefully sharing a profound thought in a halftime staff meeting. I saw him in the eyes of an emotionally overwhelmed Dudley—a man whose character was so adored by Scott.

Gottfried roamed the rooms, comforting his distraught team— gravitating toward the players who seemed to need the most attention. For a man who never wanted to attend a funeral, the head coach was a tower of strength on this day.

We arrived at the appropriate place for this memorial when we entered Coleman Coliseum. Robert had always viewed the university as a family. While almost every person associated with Alabama basketball over the years has been negative to some degree about the national prominence and passionate following enjoyed by the football program, I never met a better Tide football fan than Scott. He would say "I sure hope they win this one" every week with absolute sincerity and concern—this from a man who played on a very good hoops team that was restricted by a small NCAA playoff and was overshadowed while the football team accomplished very rare back-to-back national titles.

Rah Rah's crimson number 10 jersey was framed beside the casket. He was home.

Chaplain Overstreet conducted the memorial. He spoke of Scott as a man who impacted people positively as a priority rather than prioritizing individual goals. Gottfried spoke next. He told the public about how Scott had defined courage with his battling cancer through the season and how his dedication had inspired the rest of the staff. John Bostick, who spent countless hours along with his wife comforting Cynthia, had coached Scott as an assistant at Alabama. He spoke next. Bostick explained that he would remember Robert for how much he loved his children, citing a few examples like Robert's managing to buy and hide an Easter basket this spring for Rahshae.

For the team, the most moving of the memorial speakers may have been Grizzard, who initially seemed unable to approach the elevated stage. Finally, carrying a heavy heart to the podium, he expressed his appreciation for Scott having influenced Gottfried's attitude when he was struggling on and off the floor. He stood in front of the audience and spoke quietly. He ended with a short sentence, "Coach Scott took care of everything for me."

T. R. Dunn, a college teammate who went on to an impressive NBA career, followed Grizzard. He spoke of his evolving relationship with Robert and how it often revolved around discussing sports. Even in the last few months, the two men discussed sports together. A month before his death, Scott detected T. R.'s concern about him during one of their usual conversations. Scott interrupted the sports talk saying, "I know you're thinking about me, T. R." An emotional Dunn concluded his comments quickly: "I'm still thinking about you, and I love you, Rah Rah."

The memorial finished up with a JumboTron highlight film created by Tide radio color commentator Tom Roberts, who does a great job with the banquet video every year. I had anticipated that Roberts's video would be the climax of an emotional weekend. To the music of Whitney Houston's "Hero," Scott sank a jumper against Auburn in Tuscaloosa. He coached intensely at West End. We heard his voice. I wanted to remember him as this man of great strength. The power of the pictures and the beauty of the music released another river of emotion in me. We saw him celebrating with the current staff in their great wins over Kentucky, Tennessee, and Auburn. We remembered Robert's vitality.

The weekend concluded with a long processional from Tuscaloosa to Birmingham, where Robert "Rah Rah" Scott's body was placed in the Elmwood Mausoleum. Wallace, Davis, Martin, Grizzard, and Walker bent their strong young bodies to the honor of carrying the casket from the hearse to its final resting place. We gave our final condolences to the family, and it was done.

Afterword

Although drawn together by the tragedy of Robert Scott's death, the Alabama players and coaches did not all stay together. We had experienced a bond of togetherness forged by the fires of despair. But life moves on, and, after a few months, things geared up for a new season.

Schea Cotton chose not to return to Alabama. He became eligible for the NBA draft two years early but was not drafted. He is presently jockeying to be acquired as a free agent in the NBA. If the NBA does not want his services, he certainly has many opportunities in European professional basketball. Perhaps he will make it. I know that he is good enough.

Rod Grizzard, Terrence Meade, Tarik London, Sam Haginas, Martin Davis, Jim Bakken, Erwin Dudley, Terrence "Doc" Martin, and Kenny Walker are all returning to Alabama for the 2000–2001 season. Alfred Moss graduated in the required time and will return to play as a graduate student.

D. J. Townes decided to transfer.

Soloman Davis reluctantly quit the team to maintain his 3.5 G.P.A. and focus more on his hectic class schedule. He confided in me his determination to stay a fan.

Travis Stinnett's surgery worked. He also will play for Alabama in the coming season, his freshman year in the world of SEC basketball.

Jeremy Hays recovered from his injury through extensive rehabilitation and will repeat his senior year. He has high hopes, as does the more mature team that will surround him.

The team is being joined by the already legendary Gerald Wallace.

At this writing, all the players are healthy and feeling good about the season. The future looks good. Robert Scott believed in these players, these coaches, and this team. Hence, I believe. This year's team has the potential to be one of Alabama's best ever. Four of the seniors recently approached Gottfried about putting Scott's number 10 on all the jerseys. He agreed, and thus the 2000-2001 campaign will be dedicated to Robert Scott. It is a fitting tribute.

John Morr continues to be the trainer for Alabama. I'm sure he is hoping that this season will be nothing like the previous one, for his peace of mind if nothing else.

And Gottfried, Kelsey, and Pearson have stayed with Alabama. They are joined by coach Johnny Jones who has been hired to fill Scott's position. Boatright continues to solve problems for Gottfried. Despite the rough season and the tremendous pressure of their lives, life has continued for the Alabama basketball staff. The late night staff meetings, the video sessions, the constant recruiting all continue. The schedule remains as ever hectic. I'm both glad and sad that I am no longer a part of it.

And then there's me. I graduated from law school. Wrote a book. Got it published.

We all were affected by Scott's death. With the passage of time the pain of the loss has decreased. I stop in on Cynthia and her children from time to time. They are doing well. His sons continue to be excellent competitors destined to follow in their father's footsteps. I can pay no higher compliment.

Robert Scott meant a lot to people of all ages and races. He was a man who devoted his life to young people. He invested his life hoping our youth would do remarkable things with their lives. Because of this devotion to young people I felt strongly that a scholarship fund in his name could and should be created. This educational scholarship fund would benefit young people who find themselves in similar situations like Robert's. So it has been done. The Robert Scott Scholarship Foundation has been created to benefit those young people who have faced a financial hardship resulting from some type of medical care. To make a donation to this foundation please contact:

The Robert Scott Foundation
100 Grandview Place
Suite 110
Birmingham, Alabama 35243.

Acknowledgments

Thanks to Robert Scott and his family for sharing some of their heartaches with the team in their darkest days. I am grateful to the University of Alabama basketball players and staff for allowing me to record their every thought with a microcassette recorder during an entire season. Thanks to Mark Gottfried for gambling on the initial project and selflessly helping to promote Robert Scott's legacy when tragedy struck his team.

My editor Ben Beard was brilliant. I am tremendously grateful for his tireless work. Thanks to everybody at New South Books including Mildred Wakefield for her devoted promotional energy, and to Faithe Hurst, Wendy Mann, and Vanessa Teacher. Special thanks go to Randall Williams and Suzanne La Rosa, two people bold enough to champion noble causes in a world that too often revolves around profit. We share a vision of the new South that is certainly furthered by a picture of Robert Scott, an African-American who was born into a society that wanted him separated from white boys and girls, proudly coaching for the University of Alabama in his dying days.

Passionate thanks to my mother who facilitated my discovery of the magic in writing. She truly deserves to be called a writer because she has given her heart to the pursuit. Thanks to my father who has given me an ocean of support. Thanks to my wife, Tracy, who has endured so many reactions to the opponent finishing with more points.

Index